FROM CONTACT TO ASCENSION

VOLUME 1

Timely Information from members of the Intergalactic Board of Council

FROM CONTACT TO ASCENSION

VOLUME 1

Timely Information from members of the Intergalactic Board of Council

Gesanna

From Contact to Ascension: Volume 1 Timely Information from members of the Intergalactic Board of Council.

Copyright © 2014 by Gesanna

All Rights Reserved. No part of this book may be reproduced or translated into any language or utilized in any form or by any means, electronic or mechanical, including photocopying, recording or by any information storage and retrieval system, without written permission by the author.

Published by Createspace

ISBN-13: 978-1494888732
ISBN-10: 1494888734

Author's Website: www.contact2ascension.com

Table of Contents

Table of Contents
ACKNOWLEDGEMENTS ix

Foreword: From Contact to Ascension - extraterrestrial contact as a prelude to universal ascension xi

FROM CONTACT TO ASCENSION: CLEARING THE WAY THERE 1

A PERSONAL WELCOME FROM MEMBERS OF THE INTERGALACTIC BOARD OF COUNCIL 3

    Figure 1. Intergalactic Board of Council 6

Intergalactic Board of Council's Explanation of Their Title 7

A NOTE FROM GESANNA REGARDING THESE COMMUNIQUES 11

INTRODUCTION TO THE INTERGALACTIC BOARD OF COUNCIL COMMUNIQUÉS 13

By An T'na, MEMBER OF THE COUNCIL AND VOLUNTEER TEAM COORDINATOR 13

    Figure 2. An T'na 19

IBOC COMMUNIQUÉ 21

Session 001 21

    Ascension as a Real Event 21

    SESSION 1 – ADDENDUM: PART A 45

    The Soft Spot of Newly Ascended Beings 45

    SESSION 1 – ADDENDUM: PART B 49

        The Job of Volunteers and the Risks Involved 49

    SESSION 1 – ADDENDUM: PART C 55

        The 3 Waves of Volunteers & Returning Home 55

    SESSION 1 – ADDENDUM: PART D 65

        Ascension of the Planet, Its "Vibrational Skin", ... 65

        & the "Splitting" of the Planet 65

    SESSION 1 – ADDENDUM: PART E 79

From Contact to Ascension

The Ascended Planet— 79
IBOC COMMUNIQUÉ 85
Session 002 85
    Some Clarification on the Matter of Homosexuality 85
    Session 002 – Addendum A 115
        The Increase of Do-Gooders in an Increasingly Materialistic World 115
IBOC COMMUNIQUÉ 121
Session 003 121
    Why Our Volunteers Are On Terra, ... 121
    An T'na answers some reader's questions 169
    Disclosure and Contact for Volunteers – Who They Are ... 180
    Volunteers as Ascended Beings - The Two Levels of Volunteers ... 184
IBOC COMMUNIQUÉ 191
Session 004 191
    Shifting From Stage 1 to Stage 2, Then Stage 3 and 4 191
IBOC COMMUNIQUÉ 215
Session 005 215
    Being and Living an Integrated Life 215
IBOC COMMUNIQUÉ 223
Session 006 223
    Take a Benign Approach 223
IBOC COMMUNIQUÉ 225
Session 007 225
    Ascended Beings 225
IBOC COMMUNIQUÉ 239
Session 008 239

Table of Contents

    The Grays Futile Attempts to Ascend, And Your New Cousins 239
IBOC COMMUNIQUÉ 247
Session 009 247
    The Difference Between Disclosure and Contact 247
IBOC COMMUNIQUÉ 261
Session 10 261
    Understanding Truth-Controllers - Why They Do It, ... 261
POSTSCRIPT FROM GESANNA 277
Index 281
ABOUT GESANNA - ORACLE FOR THE INTERGALACTIC BOARD OF COUNCIL 289
    F I R S T C O N T A C T 291
A Note From An T'na Regarding the Following Information 297
    Links and Resources 301
        Articles 301
        Websites 302

From Contact to Ascension

ACKNOWLEDGEMENTS

I have intuitively known since 1987 that I was to "*write a book*". I made several failed attempts to do that. Other people along the way suggested that I "*write a book*" about my unusual life experiences. But my response always was, "*I'm not finished living it yet*". A psychic told me that I would "*write a book about what you know, and it will be very successful*". Little did I know that she had psychically seen the reality of this book you hold in your hand. At the time she conveyed this message to me (1987), I had no idea that "*what I know*" that I would be writing about, would be the *remembrances* of a higher order of knowledge, truth, understandings that has resided within for 60 years me as *soul memory* of my existence as an Ascended Being and that, in my current life experience, I would be serving as an *oracle* to a group of Ascended Beings who are freely presenting Their knowledge, wisdom and foresight to you in the form of "*a book*".

As this book reaches its final stage and goes to print, its creation has required the help of some skilled and experienced people unto whom I express much gratitude:

To Michael Salla, for his enthusiasm and broad-based knowledge of *how-tos* that has helped me bring together the material and publishing of the book; and for his generous assistance in other areas of this fascinating work that he has so graciously offered. Mahalo nui, Michael!

To my dear friend Mahuleia, for her amazing graphic artist talent that generated the cover of this book and other pieces of art that has added a wondrous touch of beauty to this work. It is amazing to sit and watch her use a keyboard to *paint a picture* just as skillfully as my art professor son uses his paintbrush. Mahalo nui, Mahuleia!

From Contact to Ascension

To my family and friends who have loved, encouraged and supported me along the way. Mahalo nui, Ohana!

And, of course, Mahalo nui to all the members of the Intergalactic Board of Council who provided the enormous amount of material that composes this uplifting book, with more waiting in the wings.

I express a huge debt of gratitude to my friends An T'na, Caer and Dee, who were so patient with me as a "*reluctant oracle*" for the Council, as I struggled within myself to finally "*get the ball rolling*" with this work, and to keep it rolling forward. Mahalo nui, Ladies!

This book has been *in the works* for a lifetime, waiting the right moment for presenting to the world the Intergalactic Board of Council's important messages. That moment has finally arrived, for They have said herein that *the time for contact is not merely on our doorstep but it is about to knock down our doors*.

So, for your edifice, here is the *long-anticipated book*, from me, the Intergalactic Board of Council, An T'na, and all who helped make it possible, to you.

May you enjoy the journey of each page.
Aloha! -Gesanna-

Foreword: From Contact to Ascension - extraterrestrial contact as a prelude to universal ascension

The main idea in *From Contact to Ascension* is that not only the Earth, but the universe is undergoing an ascension process whereby life as we know it is about to change dramatically. We are told that the physical universe is evolving whereby lower energy frequencies are about to end. Incarnated souls will be facing a choice between moving into an ascended state of being described as the "upper triad" comprising the 5th, 6th, and 7th dimensions, or remaining in their present state described as the lower triad of 1st, 2nd and 3rd dimensions. While the upper triad is characterized by an all pervasive unity or "singularity consciousness" where all life is interconnected and unfolds in divine harmony, the lower triad is comprised of "duality consciousness" where individuals live by values based on right/wrong, good/bad, etc. Those choosing to remain in the "lower triad" will "migrate" into worlds in a new physical universe where they will incarnate in new bodies and become the creators of new dualistic value systems for the worlds they inhabit.

Those choosing to ascend, along with other souls, planets, and suns of this physical universe, will remain on the Earth as it also ascends into the upper triad. Ascending souls will do so by remaining in their physical bodies which will return to an original blueprint of perfect health and vitality. In the new Earth, ascended souls will be able to instantly manifest their personal will, leading quickly to a complete overhaul of all technology and physical structures very similar to what Arthur C. Clark described in *Childhood's End*.

"Volunteer souls" that have ascended in a previous life time, but incarnated on Earth to assist it in its ascension process will be given the choice of keeping their present physical body, or regaining their ascended body that is being held in stasis in the upper triad. The ascension process involves not just sentient life, but also planets and suns.

While there have been a number of channeled books that have spoken about a coming harvest of souls to different destinations, *From Contact to Ascension* is the first to offer such a framework for the universe as a whole. In other words, the universe as we know it, the myriad of star systems and highly evolved civilizations, is about to change dramatically. Individual souls, planets and suns will be choosing whether or not they will ascend in this universe, or migrate to an entirely new physical universe. A kind of universal graduation day, where all options are honored as choices are made by the myriad forms of life making up our universe.

The source of the information for *From Contact to Ascension* claim to be a council of Ascended Beings calling itself the Intergalactic Board of Council (IBOC), speaking through a human spokesperson. The IBOC allegedly are a universe wide association of beings that have evolved from different worlds and galaxies, based on a universal state of mind they call "singularity consciousness." I have previously described such beings as "celestials" that can be categorized as Type IV extraterrestrials according to modified typology based on the work of Nikoli Kardashev (1964).[i] Based on my research into the available literature on Ascended Beings, they have been helping humanity for millennia in raising our consciousness in order to deal with advanced extraterrestrial technologies that have become available in various eras. Now, the IBOC is here to help humanity deal with the challenges posed by the universe wide ascension process.

The IBOC spokesperson, An T'na speaks through one of their selected channels or "oracles", Gesanna, who currently resides on the Big Island of Hawaii in the Pahoa region. I have personally known Gesanna for eight years after she volunteered to assist the work of the Exopolitics Institute which I had founded in 2005. She has also volunteered with various public information programs of observatories situated at Mauna Kea, Big Island of Hawaii. My personal opinion of Gesanna is

Foreword

that she is a well-grounded person not given to flights of fancy. She describes her own personal journey to becoming an oracle for the IBOC as beginning with her initial resistance to the information. Gesanna eventually accepted the authenticity of the telepathic information she was receiving and began verbally channeling the IBOC to a small group in Roswell, New Mexico in early 2013. Her initial four IBOC Communiqués were taped and then transcribed. The six subsequent Communiqués, to date, have been psychographically received and released.

When I first read the information in the IBOC communications, it immediately resonated as something worth taking seriously. I have been familiar with the work of many channelers, and I consider the communiqués received by Gesanna to be on par with the best. Here I'm thinking primarily about the RA Material, which is widely respected as among the best, if not the best ET/UFO related channeled material. The RA material also describes an evolutionary process of Ascension and how this impacts on different worlds and societies. What Gesanna has transmitted from An T'na/IBOC takes us to a new level of understanding what Ascension means for us personally, and also what it means for the universe as a whole. Can the universe itself ascend in a way that ends physical live as we know it? This is the most dramatic piece of information contained in the communiqués and it's worth considering whether such a process is possible.

Recently, there has been much scientific interest in the discovery of the Higgs Boson particle that was first theorized in 1964. The building of the Large Hadron Collider in Switzerland from 1998 to 2008 was largely undertaken to confirm whether or not something called the "Higgs Field" existed, and this could be done by discovering an associated particle called the Higgs Boson. The discovery of the Higgs Boson in 2012 simultaneously confirmed the existence of the Higgs Field. The importance of the Higgs Field is that it is what gives the fundamental particles of the physical universe their mass. Without the Higgs Field, electrons, protons, etc., would have no mass which would mean that the universe, as we know it, could not exist.

What scientists have found with the confirmation of the Higgs Field is that it is inherently unstable. Due to the size of the Higgs Boson particle, the universe wide Higgs Field can change at any time which would mean that the mass of fundamental particles would also change. A change in the Higgs Field where mass increased, would lead to particles having a stronger gravitational force of attraction. This would lead to the physical universe imploding in the manner described as the "Big Crunch", which is the reverse of the Big Bang. Rather than the Big Crunch being a remote possibility billions of years in our future, it is going to happen in the near future according to the IBOC. Such an alarming possibility has recently been the subject of a number of scientific studies speculating about what is known so far about the Higgs Field. *Scientific American* published an article on March 26, 2013 titled, "How the Higgs Boson Might Spell Doom for the Universe," and announced:

> Under the simplest assumptions, the measured mass of the Higgs could mean the universe is unstable and destined to fall apart." But don't worry—it won't happen for billions of eons.[ii]

Scientists from the University of Southern Denmark were not as confident that the universe would fall apart billions of years in the future. In a December 12, 2013, Press Release titled: "Collapse of the universe is closer than ever before," the University of Southern Denmark announced:

> Maybe it happens tomorrow. Maybe in a billion years. Physicists have long predicted that the universe may one day collapse, and that everything in it will be compressed to a small hard ball. New calculations from physicists at the University of Southern Denmark now confirm this prediction – and they also conclude that the risk of a collapse is even greater than previously thought.[iii]

Foreword

The IBOC claims that this universe wide ascension process involving a dissolution of the "physical universe" is known on many worlds. The leaders on some worlds inform their citizenry, who then make the choice to ascend with the current universe, or migrate to a new universe. No judgment is held as to which choice is made as it is implicitly understood that the choice is what the indwelling soul of an individual, planet or sun, desires. On Earth, the ruling elite have chosen not to inform their citizenry, with the purpose of creating as much chaos and confusion as possible to minimize the number of individual souls that will choose the ascension path. The IBOC tells us that the Earth itself, as a planetary embodied soul, has chosen to Ascend, and indeed has begun doing so.

From Contact to Ascension tells about frequency jamming technologies that have been developed to cut off the connection between the brain and soul. Cell phone technologies in particular achieve this subtle goal which results in increased materiality. Generally speaking, the communication technologies that have become a mainstay of our post-industrial society have the effect of cutting off the connection between soul and brain, thereby making humanity easier to manipulate. The solution according to IBOC is to spend more time attuning to nature since the Earth herself has chosen to ascend. Spending time in nature, whether it is by the ocean, in forests, in gardens, etc., all help to reestablish the vital connection between the soul and brain that is vital for the ascension process that is envisaged to take between 20-25 years to complete for the Earth.

In addition to the ascension process, the IBOC tells us about an upcoming "Contact Event" that involves extraterrestrials openly appearing and interacting with humanity. This will be relatively soon according to the IBOC. The upcoming Contact Event comprises two broad groupings of extraterrestrials. There will be ascending extraterrestrials, those who like ascending human souls, will evolve with the Earth and other planets to the upper triad. There will also be non-ascending or migrating extraterrestrials, who will be traveling to a new universe. The choice of which extraterrestrial group to work with will be up to each individual based on their stance on the ascension process.

A vitally important distinction is made between "public disclosure" and "official disclosure" by the IBOC. Public disclosure refers to efforts by private citizens that have established contact with extraterrestrials to share this information with the public in an unrestricted uncensored way. It is through public disclosure that the world will learn the truth about the different groups of extraterrestrials interacting with our planet. Public disclosure will also reveal the existence of the benevolent extraterrestrials and ascended beings that are helping humanity deal with its many problems, and prepare interested individuals for the upcoming Ascension.

Official disclosure is a contingency plan devised by government and corporate entities involved in the decades-long extraterrestrial cover up to reveal some aspects of the existence of extraterrestrial life. This would be done deceptively in order to maintain the agendas and power bases of secret government/corporate entities. Official disclosure would focus on fearful scenarios that mislead the public about "evil aliens" in a way that results in political representatives giving carte blanche to the national security apparatus to deal with extraterrestrials as they see fit.

The IBOC thereby strongly recommends that public disclosure efforts are accelerated so that it preempts the official disclosure plan that is waiting in the wings to be released. The IBOC recommends a worldwide program of citizen initiatives to educate the public about extraterrestrial life. Benevolent extraterrestrials and Ascended Beings would assist the public disclosure initiatives wherever necessary. The main benefit of the upcoming Contact Event is that individuals that are ready for it will receive the information they need in order to deal with the ascension process.

From Contact to Ascension gives the reader much material to seriously consider. A universe-wide ascension process, Ascended Beings silently

Foreword

assisting us, extraterrestrial contact, dissolution of the physical universe as we know it, etc. How much of the material is accurate and true? In my opinion, there is much in the IBOC that is consistent with what science is now telling us about the stability of the universe, and what other respected channeled sources such as the RA material have been telling us about Ascension. As far as extraterrestrial contact is concerned, I agree with the IBOC that it is imminent. This is reflected in the ongoing public disclosure events happening around the planet, and the saturation media coverage of the possibility of extraterrestrial life emerging from the ongoing scientific confirmation of habitable exoplanets.

The IBOC Communiqués are available for free online, or in book form. Ultimately, it's up to each reader to decide the relevance of the IBOC Communiqués for their lives. Whatever your personal choice, there is little doubt that in the next 20-25 years, life as we know it is going to change in ways that will seem fantastic to us in our present circumstances. I highly recommend being open to the possibility that the insights in the IBOC Communiqués are navigation beacons for a fantastic journey that lies ahead.

Michael E. Salla, M.A., Ph.D.
Founder, Exopolitics Institute
January 3, 2014

From Contact to Ascension

Endnotes

[i] http://www.exopoliticsjournal.com/vol-4/vol-4-1-Salla.htm
[ii] http://tinyurl.com/c78q4l9
[iii] http://tinyurl.com/p4sty4p

FROM CONTACT TO ASCENSION: CLEARING THE WAY THERE

Welcome to these most important Communiqués, presented by members of the Intergalactic Board of Council and beyond. We have been in communication with an Ascended Master, a member of this Council, and this is what has been delivered to us for your information. This insightful knowledge is brought to you to inform you, and keep you informed, about Extraterrestrial Disclosure and the Ascension Process and how it is affecting you, about what you may expect, and to prepare you for what is coming.

Thank You,
- Channeling Session Facilitators -

From Contact to Ascension

A PERSONAL WELCOME FROM MEMBERS OF THE INTERGALACTIC BOARD OF COUNCIL

WELCOME ONE AND ALL. We greet you with the honor and respect you so deserve. Through our communiqués, we inform you that we are a large group of Ascended Beings who reside in dimensions above and beyond what you refer to as the 3rd dimension (a term that you are familiar with, but it is actually more complex than is implied).

We are benevolent, caring Beings who have volunteered to assist your planet, Terra, with her ascension to the realm of life where we exist. Our great and far-reaching Work with the Divine Destiny of this Universe is elaborated upon in our own words - words that you can understand even if the cosmic processes that are actually transpiring are otherwise very complicated. But you need not the complexities of science or physics or astronomy or mathematics in order to grasp the essence of what is transpiring. You know it in your souls - you can feel it.

We share insight regarding how this cosmic-generated destiny is directly affecting us all, including ourselves, and we give advice on how each of you can consciously cooperate with it in a manner that makes your personal experience that of a deliberate Participator with us throughout this wondrous journey.

Imparting knowledge about the nature of the universe as a living "entity", why it was created, and who it is that creates everything in it, we shed light into the dark where certain groups we refer to as negative factions have kept matters of truth from you.

Along with all of this enlightening information, we are assisting our "ground crew" with the physical creation of public education outlets, with the specific goal of disclosing not only ourselves but other non-terrestrial groups who are here to assist you as well.

From Contact to Ascension

You will learn that public disclosure is different from official disclosure regarding all-things-non-terrestrial, and why we do not agree with nor sanction official disclosure.

You will be informed of the developments of public initiatives for public-generated disclosure and the ensuing educational networks, which will result around the world, designed as a cooperative venture toward the acceptance of this planet as a new member of the Galactic Society. You will also learn that other inhabited planets are also currently being accepted into this higher state of existence.

The information imparted herein is just the start of so much more to come, for you are just now on the verge of making this great leap into the divine heritage which your species was originally created to become.

Conversely, we acknowledge that there are many people - Terrans and other species - who are not moving forward into this cosmic-generated destiny of ascension, and of those who are not, we recognize that their souls have chosen to "migrate sideways" which, we emphasize emphatically, is not a sin, nor a wrong or bad choice of the soul, but is a necessary direction for specific purposes which we elaborate upon in our communiqués. We honor these souls as equally as we honor the souls who are ascending with this universe. We do not think and live in terms of right/wrong or good/bad and so on, because we are evolved beyond the 3rd dimensional consciousness and energy of duality. Ours is the consciousness and energy of Singularity.

We invite you to join us on this grand adventure into a destiny that is directly affecting us all. And whether your soul is ascending forward or migrating sideways it matters not for the information herein will help you understand the destiny your soul has chosen to take you into as your next step of personal evolution.

A Personal Welcome

Either way, it is all good and it is all the grandest adventure ever that awaits us even now as this adventure unfolds at an exponentially increasing rate of speed, as we also explain.

As members of the Intergalactic Board of Council, we know who each of you are, and we love each one of you more than you realize is possible to be loved.

Let us begin this grand journey together.

Members of the Intergalactic Board of Council

Figure 1. Intergalactic Board of Council: An T,na and members materializing into physical form

Intergalactic Board of Council's Explanation of Their Title

We have been asked to clarify our use of our title, the Intergalactic Board of Council. Perhaps the following will do that for you all.

Precisely how to describe the manner by which this group of members functions is fairly complex, meaning it is not as straight-forward as would be perceived by concepts common to Lower Triad thinking. You might call it a multi-layered effect, however the intricacies of it are greatly interwoven.

Let us begin by saying that we are a group of Ascended Beings within the Upper Triad who have come together for the purpose of assisting the universal ascension processes now under way. Each of us *stands in for* various home galaxies within the Lower Triad portion of this universe; and by this we are referring to the time prior to our ascension out of the Lower Triad. Each *ascended member* presides over his or her former home galactic council of Beings.

These Lower Triad councils are composed of members who currently exist within the Lower Triad but who are ascending themselves beyond the Lower Triad to the Upper Triad. These *advanced ascending souls* serve as teachers and guides for the purpose of *personal* ascension. Their soul, and sole, mission in life is to assist other souls who are on the path of *personal* ascension. They do so through psychic and personal interactions. They are your brothers and sisters who are close to having their own personal ascension into the Upper Triad. They are assisting you who are not as far along on the path as are they themselves. They are what you would refer to as Upper Triad *ascension Wayshowers*, your *Vanguards of ascension*.

They compose the Lower Triad councils that the members of our Upper Triad "*board*" represents or *speaks for* during our meetings, regarding the affairs of ascension.

From Contact to Ascension

We could go into greater detail about the composition and function of our *board of council* but such information is irrelevant to the clarification of this matter.

We understand that you have different terminologies for a single word so that communicating with you in words can sometimes misconstrue messages thereby causing confusion regarding the specific meaning that is intended to be conveyed.

So let us clarify a couple of words for you.

In our first session we clarified our meaning for our use of the word "*intergalactic*" with regard to the title we have chosen to be known by. Please refer back to that session if necessary.

We use the word "*board*", per your older use of it meaning a "*committee*". So, we are what you would more commonly refer to as a committee.

We use the word "*council*" with reference to what we as a committee **do**, which is to "*deliberate*" the ascension affairs of this Intergalactic, or universal *Mission*.

Because your word *council* also means a *committee*, and your word *council* can also mean a *deliberation*, there is a double word use here so that when you refer to us as a group, when not using our full title you may use either the shortened term of "IBOC", or "*the Board*" or "*Board member(s)*", or you may use the term "*the Council*" or "*Council member(s)*". Either of these terms is appropriate and acceptable since, according to your language terminology, we are an Upper Triad council or committee representing, during *deliberation* or *council*, Lower Triad councils or committees.

Now perhaps you see what we mean by your language easily misconstruing intended meanings.

Intergalactic Board of Council's Explanation of Their Title

So, for clarity sake, let use interpret our title for you as saying:

"We are a *Committee*, or *Council*, of Ascended Beings presiding over many Lower Triad *Intergalactic* councils or committees; whose purpose it is to *Deliberate*, or *council* the affairs of the ascension of planets, intergalactically, and all souls who are ready to ascend with their home planet into the Upper Triad."

Per your terminologies of these words, we felt that the title *Intergalactic Committee of Deliberation* would not be as appealing to you as the *Intergalactic Board of Council*.

We know that this is a new perspective to digest mentally, but we do hope that it clarifies the meaning and *intentional* use of our title, *the Intergalactic Board of Council*.

Thank you for your attention and consideration of this clarification.

Be well and stay happy.

Our deepest love to each of you from all Members of the Intergalactic Board of Council.

From Contact to Ascension

A NOTE FROM GESANNA REGARDING THESE COMMUNIQUES

These are the messages from the Ascended Beings who comprise the Intergalactic Board of Council (IBOC), conveyed respectfully for the benefit and upliftment of all who stand in open receivership of it.

The communiqués are posted in the order in which they were given through Gesanna - i.e., from past/first to present/most recent postings. Due to the knowledge-building manner by which the information has been imparted, you are strongly urged to begin your journey by reading the first message and then progress chronologically from there. Beginning anywhere else or skipping around will result in a lack of comprehension of the terminologies used by the Ascended Beings as they endeavor to help clarify many issues, concepts, topics, etc., that have been misunderstood by the people of this planet.

The first four communiqué sessions were done in the mode of verbal channeling, which were facilitated by my good friends experienced in such activities. As an experienced transcriber, the sessions were transcribed by me, (which was a very strange experience to listen to my own voice doing the channelings!).

After the fourth session, my Higher-Ups shifted me from the mode of verbal channeling to that of "psychography" (a modern term for what was once called "automatic-writing"). This was done due to the fact that They were in the process of relocating me from my post at Roswell, NM, to my former post in Hawaii.

What follows is Volume One of a series of more volumes yet to come. It is the outcome of these channeled and psychographied communiqués as relayed directly from the Intergalactic Board of Council to Their assistant, An T'na who then imparted it to me. It is my job to make it openly available to the world.

From Contact to Ascension

Enjoy all that follows and more that is yet to come.
Let us begin...from the beginning....

Mahalo nui!
-Gesanna-

INTRODUCTION TO THE INTERGALACTIC BOARD OF COUNCIL COMMUNIQUÉS

By An T'na, MEMBER OF THE COUNCIL AND VOLUNTEER TEAM COORDINATOR

Greetings to you all. My name is An T'na. I am what you would refer to as an "Ascended Being". As with all Ascended Beings, we reside in the higher dimensions composing what is termed the "Upper Triad" of dimensions 5, 6, and 7.

You to whom we are addressing this communication, you reside in what is termed the "Lower Triad", composed of dimensions 1, 2, and 3.

I, An T'na, speak in terms of "we" because I am one of many Ascended Beings who are imparting this communiqué to you. I am the deliverer of it. I convey this information to our Terran incarnated Volunteer and oracle, Gesanna, who receives and passes it on to you.

We compose one of many units of Ascended Beings who have responded to The Call to assist with the universal ascension of planets from their current Lower Triad state to their new Homes in the Upper Triad. This matter will be discussed throughout this ongoing communiqué.

The group of Ascended Beings with whom I am a colleague is termed the Intergalactic Board of Council – "intergalactic" only because long, long ago the members of this Council ascended biologically into the Upper Triad from their respective Lower Triad home worlds which resided in various galaxies. Therefore, we originated from various races, within many different civilizations, cultures, and ethos, which numerously exist throughout the Lower Triad of worlds. Yet, as Ascended Beings these differences bear no burden of class, status, hierarchy, or rank which divides or castes one from another. We are

From Contact to Ascension

distinguished by our assorted physical appearances. This communiqué will, in part, elaborate upon this matter.

This communiqué and many others yet to come are addressed to a specific group of people on your planet, which we call *Terra*; hence, throughout these communiqués your species is referred to by us as *Terrans*.

The group of Terrans for whom this message is directed is, for one, those souls who are ascending from the Lower Triad into the Upper Triad of existence. We refer to you as "Ascending Souls".

Knowledge of this updated information regarding your ascension processes will be expounded upon herein. This information is offered to you to assist your next step in the ongoing education of your ascension experiences that are a side effect of the universe's ascension. This communiqué differs from previous information regarding the ascension event in that this is not a solicitation to everyone on the planet intending to bring you into the flow of ascension, but is designed to reveal what you can expect now that you are in the flow that is taking you out of the Lower Triad and pressing you into the Upper Triad where life is very different from life as you have known it in the Lower Triad.

This communiqué is designed to bring forth clarity from a great deal of misunderstandings that in-turn generated much confusion which gave rise to a host of inappropriate assumptions about ascension, of which has come to you over time, from various sources. It matters not the sources of it. It matters only that you are presented with a clarity of understanding of the ascension event and your days to come within its flow. The information herein is encompassing this topic because everything is being affected in one way or another by the ascension of the universe.

For those Terran souls who resonate with this information, you will be enthusiastically drawn to being educated in your next step toward a new life in a Higher Realm of existence, which you have duly earned.

Introduction To The IBOC Communiqués

For you, this information will clarify The Way There, and in the process relieve you of a lifetime of information that no longer pertains to you, no longer applies to the life you are transitioning into being.

To you Ascending Souls we say, read on. This overall communiqué consists of information that is (1) of a personal nature, which applies to self, and (2) of an impersonal or general nature that applies to all Ascending Souls as a whole.

The information which is of a personal nature, with regard to certain life circumstances, must be clarified for a greater understanding relative to the ascension event which in-turn renders those circumstances incorrect or obsolete with regard to where you are going with yourselves now. Since we are addressing a wide variety of personal life circumstances, we advise you to take what applies to you personally and disregard what does not, for even though you are ascending, there is far more information herein which applies generally to all Ascending Souls.

Now, that is one group of souls unto whom we are addressing this information.

The other group of souls is those who are Ascended Being Volunteers affiliated with this mission calling. Ascended Being Volunteers are distinguished from Ascending Souls by the fact that they have already ascended from the Lower Triad to the Upper Triad. They have, more recently, responded to a particular function of The Call, which requires a specialized activity engaged only by ascended souls who are already capable of harnessing and holding into this planet, enormous amounts of light-energy of a very higher frequency from the Upper Triad. This matter will be elucidated herein.

It is important that you, as our Volunteers, understand, firstly, that you have already ascended, long ago, from the Lower Triad to the Upper Triad. You are not on Terra to ascend again, although there is one exception that will be made clear later. You are on the planet to assist the ascension event in a manner, which only you could fill, which will be clarified.

As Ascended Being Volunteers, we are reminding you that your souls hold all the memories of your existence as Ascended Beings, and of the higher manner of life you were living in the Upper Triad prior to your incarnation into wearing Terran genes, as our oracle likes to say. It is up to you to allow those memories to come forward into conscious awareness by calling forth the memories.

As Ascended Being Volunteers, you are each associated with various groups of Councils deriving from the Upper Triad. They are here to engage this Ascension Mission, not just on your planet, but also on other planets in this and other galaxies as well. Your souls have the memories of which Council and peoples you are most closely associated with. But regardless of which it is, it is important that you understand that the overall mission objective is the same for all Councils; therefore it is the same for each and all of you as Ascended Being Volunteers of these Councils. You are, each and all, on Terra engaging the same "mission duty", if you will, which will be discussed throughout this communiqué. This discussion will in-turn serve as a triggering mechanism of soul memories toward releasing "the specifics" for each of you personally, not just regarding your mission duties, but you will also remember some of the Ascended Beings of the Councils with whom you are associated in this mission.

We refer to you as "our Volunteers", and we say "our" as a means to distinguish you, as Ascended Being Volunteers of the Upper Triad, from another group of volunteers on Terra who are directly associated with what we refer to as Lower Triad extraterrestrials. We refer to this group of volunteers as "extraterrestrial volunteers". It is important that you clearly recall the difference between these 2 groups of volunteers and their objectives, hence this will be made clear herein.

To reiterate and clarify: with many of these communiqués the Council is explicitly addressing a specific audience, so to speak, of people on Terra

Introduction To The IBOC Communiqués

– (1) Ascending Souls, and (2) our Volunteers The information imparted is for your clarification so that you all can more clearly "see" your way Home – to your new Home for you Ascending Souls, and to return Home for you Volunteers.

All Ascending Souls are being educated in this grand adventure that you chose to embark upon for your personal evolution.

All Ascended Being Volunteers are remembering the grand adventure that you agreed to participate in as volunteers of this mission.

In due time, the Council will also address matters specific to non-ascending souls on Terra.

To our Volunteers and all Ascending Souls, it is helpful for you to understand that this communiqué is not addressing the overall population, for there are many, many Terran souls who are not ascending – who are either not ready to ascend, or who simply have no desire to do so this time around. And either way, it is OK. It is all-good. It is not that this information is forbidden knowledge to them, for they are free to read it if they so choose, but rather it is that these souls, who we refer to as "non-ascending souls", simply will not resonate with this information so as to understand and relate to it because it is exclusively focused upon a manner of life which they have no desire to embrace and engage for themselves at this time because their soul's path lies in a different direction. Yet there is a new manner of life of which they are choosing to embrace and engage which is wonderful as well, and which, for your clarity of understanding, will be discussed herein.

We wish you to consider this communiqué as twofold in that it is addressing 2 groups of Terrans, yet the clarifications presented for the divine destination hence outcome of both groups is the same – that of "going Home", of "seeing clearly" your Way There as you enter into the Ascended Realm in Upper Triad.

From Contact to Ascension

This communiqué shall be presented through a few different outlets, the first one of which is online, on your computers, and will be presented in sections. More information will regularly be added as time goes by. These online presentations will allow for your questions to be answered, within reasonable time and manner.

The other outlets for this work will eventually be ebooks and printed books. We desire to "cover the bases", as you would say, because there are some Ascending Souls and Ascended Being Volunteers who do not have access to computer-sourced outlets.

Any questions or comments intended to demean or slander this information will be blocked, recognized as coming from non-ascending souls who do not resonate with this knowledge.

So, calling all Ascending Souls and Ascended Being Volunteers, we welcome you to a refresher course, a sort of "prep school" for all-things-ascension, extraterrestrial and extradimensional. Do open your hearts and minds; be courteous and respectful, as the divine light that you are to others around you.

We invite you now to journey with us on this ongoing adventure of updated information about the universal ascension event and your personal experience of it.

                              That is all.
I am An T'na, of the Intergalactic Board of Council.

Figure 2. An T'na

From Contact to Ascension

IBOC COMMUNIQUÉ

Session 001
(Received on January 10 2013)

Ascension as a Real Event
3 Waves of Volunteers and Their Chosen Missions
Ascension – Why Now?
Lower Triad, Upper Triad, and their Respective Dimensions
Ascension of This Universe and the Creation of a New Universe
Appearances of Their "Ships" and Contact

('C' and 'D' = session facilitators   A = An T'na)

A: Good morning. On behalf of the Intergalactic Board of Council, we greet you. We are ready to impart to you knowledge that will bring forth clarity of the things that are transpiring at this time, of things that have occurred, of things to come, and we shall expand upon that which is brought forth.

I am An T'na. I speak through our oracle on behalf of all those who are of our group, who work together on this mission. Our oracle has worked for us many times in this capacity before she incarnated on your planet, but this particular process is different than how she did it before. We are happy she is willing to do this for us again.

We have information that pertains more to a couple of groups of people on your planet than to the rest of the population. This information is for clarification sake, for those who are ascending, and for our Volunteers, for there is much that has been of a limited understanding, and has been greatly distorted in-general. It is not that one who is ascending must have absolute understanding of ascension, or that our Volunteers must fully remember who they are as volunteers of our mission, but that having an understanding in its clarity and purity contributes to the acceleration of the ascension process overall. It contributes to the awareness of what can be expected without the confusion of getting something different than what was expected, you see.

It is at this time that we bring this information forth because the ascension event overall is going forward more quickly than ever before. You can feel that, and witness it by means of the acceleration of time, as you've known it. That is an obvious 'sign' that things are accelerating, and you can count on that as evidence of the fact. It is reliable proof.

You have been told that there are other signs of ascension which some call "symptoms" of the body. While some of these symptoms have been put out for you to assume as proof of ascension, for most people most of them are ascension side effects of 'ascension resistance', so to speak. It is important for you to understand which so-called symptoms are signs that are supporting you in the ascension process, and which are signs that are a resistance to it. In-short, the symptoms that are resistance to ascension cause pain in the body stemming from a rejection of the ascending frequencies, and this pertains mostly to the souls who are not ascending. It is important for you to understand where any pain is coming from so you can resolve it and release it.

It is just as important for those of you who are ascending to acknowledge where the signs of support and upliftment are coming from, and acknowledge them as contributing to your ascension process. Those signs do not cause pain, but they do cause a noticeable difference in the way that you are feeling and behaving. But there is another type of discomfort that some of our Volunteers and ascending souls may experience from time to time that is connected to the planet, and we shall discuss this later although this type of discomfort is not necessarily signs of ascension.

Some of you are experiencing the ascension process in stops and starts as your body makes adjustments to a given level of frequency before it makes an ascension to the next level.

But now this, we will call it a 'pulse' of ascension, these 'pulsing moments' are, we shall say, beating more evenly, the pulses are drawing together in such a way that there are not quite the long lapses in between. So, as you ascend it becomes a more smooth process, a more unbroken pattern. Now is the time when you have entered that phase of the ascension event. So, it is important that you go with the flow of it. The end of what you call your Mayan Calendar and others, were markers of when the "pulsing of time", as it was known, evens out into a uniform flow, as well as other indicators of change as the universe ascends.

There is much to confer, so now we would like to shift our discussion to the matter of our Volunteers who began coming here in what we call "The 3 Waves of Ascension".

These 3 Waves of Volunteers have all originated, or come to your planet from higher dimensions. The purpose for that has been that they would bring to the planet exceedingly developed souls who are capable of harnessing higher dimensional energy, with which they are already familiar, then anchoring that greater energy directly into the planet.

Now, there has been much confusion as to what the purpose of these Volunteers is. As Beings who have already ascended, which we term Ascended Beings, their purpose on this planet is not to assist the ascension of the Terran species itself, for every soul is wholly responsible for its own ascension process and, due to the Prime Directive, we cannot interfere with that. That is actually what the Prime Directive is all about – not interfering with the ascension of a soul's process and the way they choose to do so. We can inspire, and we can offer vibrations of love, but we cannot interfere with a soul's process in how they choose to experience the creation of their own ascension process. It must be done uniquely unto each soul, because if it is not, if it is intervened, interfered, interwoven, with another's thoughts and dictates of how to experience it, then that soul does not recognize that the experience is their own creation.

So, our Volunteers are not here to "save souls", as is popularly believed. That is a concept that originates with another group of entities, which shall be discussed at a later time. Our Volunteers are not here to save anybody. They are here to help this planet ascend, and by so doing, they are, vicariously, contributing the capacity of ascension of all souls who are ready who are ready to do so. Our Volunteers anchor the necessary energy into the planet that, in-turn, makes it available to any soul who is ready to partake of it. So, it is through an indirect manner that the ascension of Terran souls is being aided, but that is not the primary purpose for which our Volunteers are here. They are here to assist the planet into its own ascension.

The planet is a living, evolving entity and it is ready to ascend. While there are many souls on the planet who are ready to ascend as well, they are enabled, of their own choosing to partake of the ascension process that the planet is undergoing.

Our word for your planet is 'Terra' and we call her inhabitants 'Terrans'. For the most part, most people who are here are what we refer to as "native Terrans" because they've been here for so long, so many lifetimes, and so we refer to them as the natives of this planet. This is their home because they have been here for so long.

Our Volunteers have come here to help the planet ascend and in so doing you are vicariously helping some, but not all, Terran souls ascend along with it.

This is a joint process, between souls and the planet. We refer to it as an experiment of sorts because the ascension of a planet along with its occupants has never occurred before. Over eons of time throughout this universe, there have been many planets that have been ascended, and many of our Volunteers have assisted in the ascension of some of these planets and all of nature that is on them. Some Volunteers who assist in the ascension of planets have done so many times before. Not all Volunteers who are here on this planet have done so before, but many of you have.

There is a reason why Ascended Beings assist the ascension of planets. It is because planets, moons, stars and so on, have no 'higher will' of their own beyond their naturally impulsed genetic blueprint that you refer to as "instinct". The instinct to evolve occurs through encoded processes. Eventually their genetic encodings are fulfilled, so that the next step for them is the point of ascension. Due to having no higher will to engage their own ascension, we discovered that it is necessary for sentient Ascended Beings, who have, themselves, already ascended, to unite or unify themselves with the object or the creatures that are ready to ascend thereby bringing the planet or the creature to their new Home in the Higher Dimensional Realms. This unification is adds a component of the Ascended Beings' consciousness to the non-sentient state of the planet which in-turn directs the planet, or creature, in the pathway to its new Home. It is a vibrational pathway. It is this additional aspect of consciousness, of Ascended Beings, which brings it forth into the vibrational pathway and to its new Home.

So, some of our Volunteers have done this before, so they already know how to do it. They know that this is, simply, the way it is done. They themselves have ascended and this is part of the work, which we call "activity", of Ascended Beings – to assist nature – planets, creatures, even suns to ascend when they reach that point.

It has been assumed that the Higher Dimensional Realms are just a void. With nothing there? No. There is plenty there. It has been assumed that because it is a Higher Dimensional Realm, it is all non-physical, just light. Well, it is light. It is light here on your dimension. It is light everywhere. It's just in various densities.

The Higher Dimensional Realms have density. You call it "physicality". All realms have physicality. Some are denser than others.

From Contact to Ascension

So, to clarify, ascension does not mean going into a Higher Dimensional Realm of nothing but wisps and spheres of light. It does not mean that that is all that you will be either. It means going to a realm, with your bodies, of absolute beauty of all the things that exist there, which are beyond your wildest dreams because your vision of what is possible, of what can exist, is limited to your planet. Not only are there objects in the Higher Dimensional Realms – the creatures, the plants – but the way that you can interact with them, even stone, is so vastly different from the way you interact with such things on your planet. It's all a great, grand, and glorious adventure that those who are ascending will be embarking upon, and which our Volunteers will be returning to.

So, to clarify again, our Volunteers are here to assist the planet in its ascension to its new Home, which includes all of its nature of plants and creatures. All souls who are ready to ascend are being conveyed along with the planet's ascension to its new Home. And that is the experimental part of this whole endeavor – that it is done all together. For it has always been before that when planets ascend, the sentient occupants of a planet would ascend prior to their planet, and if the planet was ready to ascend, then the occupants would, in-turn, ascend their planet as well. That has been the case when there have been mass ascensions on other planets.

And, of course, there has always been individual ascensions occurring, here and there throughout the universe, by those who had evolved themselves to the point where they would move on to higher dimensions, but in this case their home-world was left behind.

But, now we have a whole new and different situation going on here, yet your planet is not the only one where ascension is happening. While the ascension of your occupied planet is an experiment, there are other planets that are also ascending with their occupants who are ready, right at this time.

Why at this time?

IBOC Communiqué Session 001

There is a major universal shifting that is occurring. It is not just occurring only on this planet. It is not occurring only in your solar system. Not just in your galaxy. This is a universal shift.

What is occurring is that the universe itself is very much alive and evolving because the universe is that which the Source is. The Source of the universe itself is evolving. The universe is the Source. As the Source evolves, it releases its lower energies because those lower energies no longer provide the Source with ongoing expansion of itself because those lower energies have been outmoded and no longer provide the necessary stimulation for further expansion. When that occurs, those lower energies become less and less engaged for expansion so that the lower energies lose their vibrational strength and integrity.

Consequently, now, the universe has reached a point in its evolution where the lower frequencies of vibration within the Source field are diminishing and shall soon cease to exist. Your secret science has evidence of this, which baffles them, but it is information, which they do not allow you to know about.

We could say that these lower frequencies, which you call the 1st, 2nd, and 3rd dimensions, are collapsing in on themselves, they are folding up, much like when you pull the string to draw your window's blinds up. The area between each slat on the blind represents a given dimension, so when you pull the string so that the lower 3 slats fold up together, the spaces between the slats do not exist anymore. This is a highly simplified analogy of what is occurring.

We call the lower 3 dimensions the "Lower Triad". Each dimension exists as a triad of dimensions. They do not exist alone in and of themselves, but in triads. Now you know why the triad has always been so revered in your cultures and religions and other fields of philosophy and practice.

From Contact to Ascension

Between each triad is what we call a Way-Station Portal that acts as a barrier or a forcefield that protects the energies of one triad from mixing together with the one above or below it. So, the forcefield barriers are like a shield keeping the energies contained within each triad thereby flowing in an orderly manner amongst each of its 3 dimensions. This area is what you refer to as the 4th dimension, of which you refer to as the dimension of time. There is a degree of truth to this but it is far more than just that. We will discuss this more in-depth at a later time.

Each of the dimensions of 1, 2, and 3 composes a "triad". That triad, which we call the Lower Triad remember, is diminishing in strength and is folding up even now.

As the energies of the lower dimensions diminish there is less and less of the lower, slower energies that are, we would say, contaminating the higher energies. Yet, you must be attuned to the higher energies in order to notice the difference. Many are not, so they do not experience what you are experiencing.

Now, as the lower 3 dimensions diminish in strength and integrity they move close and closer towards the forcefield barrier. Eventually, once the universe had completed the folding up of its Lower Triad, then the forcefield barrier, which once existed between the Lower Triad and Upper Triad, is added to the protective layering or membrane surrounding the universe which in-turn shields this universe from the exterior energies flowing around the universe.

You see, there are more universes out there. Each universe has a barrier or skin around it, like a cell membrane, that protects it from exterior energies thereby keeping its unique creation confined and intact within the order and organization of that universe as it has come to evolve itself to be.

As the lower dimension energies dissipate and the Lower Triad folds up, you are being pressed more and more towards the barrier of time, and it is that compression towards this barrier of time that causes you to experience the speeding up of time itself. This is the reason why time seems to be speeding up – because it is. It is a compression of the vibrational beat of energy. It compresses closer and closer together – remember that earlier we said that the impulse gaps in the beat of ascension are narrowing – eventually compressing all things through the 4th dimension of time and into the 5th dimension of the Ascended Realm.

But we must make it clear that there are souls who are resisting this universally occurring process. They are resisting it not out of defiance but out of a choice, by the soul, to continue their experience in the Lower Triad. Because this universe is folding up its Lower Triad, these souls who choose to continue their experience in the format of a Lower Triad are being pressed into another direction, what we refer to as "sideways" towards that which is a new universe that is being created as a side-effect of the universe's ascension. This new universe will contain the residual lower energies of the Lower Triad, and all non-ascending souls migrate to it in order to continue their experience of the evolutionary process.

So, it is that every soul gets what they want. Those who are ready to ascend will ascend. Those who are not ready will migrate to a new universe. Yet those who are not ascending are no worse off, they are not any more wrong or bad than those who are ascending. It's all a matter of personal preference. We wish for you to "get" this fact because it is important in your ability to unconditionally allow them to make that choice.

C: So this ascension that we're doing, is this in our consciousness, or consciousness and physicality?

A: Both. All things. Everything. The universe itself is all things. It is all aspects. It is consciousness. It is energy. It is matter. The ascension of the universe brings forth that which is a dynamics of processes that are very, we would say, scientifically complex where there is an interconnection, to keep it simple, between consciousness, energy and matter, and what affects one affects the other. And the universe is no different. The Source is no different.

C: So, for the Volunteers here helping with this ascension process, how long do we have left to volunteer here?

A: It varies. There is what we would call a phasing of a few older Volunteers, of when they are ready to leave their loved ones who are not ascending. As far as a timeline, the ascension process itself can occur at any moment from one planet to another. The folding up of the Lower Triad, or what your scientists would call a major change to the universe, is a process that most people assume takes millions upon millions of years to occur, but most people forget that millions upon millions of years has already occurred! And we are now at the point where the ascension of the universe to its next stage of evolution is occurring, thus the folding up is occurring.

Were it not occurring now, our Volunteers would not need to be here. Why put them here if it's not going to occur for hundreds, or thousands, or millions of years to come? They are here now because it is occurring now. And as one Ascended Being has said, you best have your act together because the plug on this experiment is about to be pulled by the universe itself. The universe is, so to speak, demanding it of us all because the universe itself is ascending.

Now, whatever energy is left in the Lower Triad upon the ascension of the universe and the folding up of its Lower Triad gets pressed into the womb of the new universe. That energy becomes the new constituents and particles of energy which the non-ascending souls, who are migrating to that new universe to become the residents thereof, they will use that energy to produce all that they desire to create in that new universe.

Again, this ascension event that we all are involved in at this moment is occurring in this lifetime. Why put our Volunteers here if it's not going to occur now? Why put all the information here that has been coming forth through many people, current and past, now at this time, if this is not the time?

We are not saying that it's going to happen tomorrow – that the Lower Triad is going to cease to exist tomorrow, for you've still got more than enough time. The folding up process occurs at an exponentially increasing rate but you haven't reached critical point yet, so don't panic. But it is occurring in what we would call the lifetime of those on your planet. We cannot pinpoint an exact time on it because the universe is the one that is in control, so to speak. For us to deliberately hasten or stall it, which we could do, but it would be a disastrous outcome. So, it must play itself out organically. So, we're all going along for the ride one way or the other, into the higher dimension or into the new universe, and it doesn't make any difference which one we choose because we all will continue to exist and continue our evolution. So, it's all OK. It doesn't matter! Those souls who choose to go into the new universe are still going to evolve. They're not going to disappear, cease to exist. They're going to go do what they want to do which is great!

It's how it should be. It is the universe, the Source, honoring free will and so should you.

All of you knew before you came here what your job would be. You knew that your job was going to be to ascend the planet, and you knew that you would do that simply by having your presence here on the planet, your soul being able to hold the higher dimensional energy in your body then anchoring it into the planet. It is that energy that is magnetizing the planet to the Higher Dimension, you see. That energy is coming down into this dimension then it's going back. You're already doing it. You have been doing it since the moment you arrived here. So there is nothing special you need to do besides be here.

But, we might add, the better you take care of your body, the better the Higher Dimensional energy comes into you and into the planet because the body is the vehicle that allows you to be here so as to anchor that energy into the physical planet.

So, in-short, you're here in-totality with the planet that's here in-totality, you're bringing in that Higher Dimensional energy, and that Higher Dimensional energy anchors into the planet and brings it to its new Home.

Now, what you choose to do with your personal life, while you're here doing your volunteer job, is totally up to you. It's up to each Volunteer to do whatever they choose to do in their personal life while they're here doing the greater job they came here to do. So there's nothing special that you need to do as a Volunteer – nothing out of the ordinary other than to be good and loving to your body because it is the very thing that is allowing you to be here to do your job.

So, if you feel a desire in your personal life to do one thing or another, you are free to do that.

Now, we will be discussing more information, and we will bring it forth in ways that will be of a subject unto themselves, yet interconnected; to bring forth clarity and to bring forth information of what is yet to come so that our Volunteers can be prepared within themselves for what they will be experiencing in the days to come, for there is coming a great event that is connected to the ascension of the planet. And that event is the appearance of our ships, and our people.

The reason that this will happen is because the "veil" as you would say, between the 3rd and barrier of 4th dimension is thinning, so we and our ships will be increasingly visible. As this occurs, contact by us, Ascended Beings, will be made, but not to all on your planet.

This contact will be specifically for the souls who are ascending and our Volunteers. Our Volunteers are already familiar with the Beings and our ships. This contact will prepare ascending souls to become familiar with us and our ships as a means of accustoming them to the new kind of life which they are entering into as they journey to their new Home. They have never been There before – not as Ascended Beings. They've never done this before. This is their first ascension, and they are in need of firsthand information to help them understand, or get a clearer picture of what they can expect to experience in their days to come, to prepare them for it.

Our Volunteers have been preparing for it ever since they left us and incarnated onto Terra, and they are ready to rejoin their people. The life they will be returning to is nothing new for them. But for the ascending souls, it is very new to them. So, we bring forth this information to help them in their journey to their new Home.

The non-ascending souls will find the contact events of interest, if they are around to experience it. But they will not feel very connected to what they are witnessing. Many will fear it. Others will have no opinion, won't care to be concerned or involved finding it too difficult to believe, so for them ignorance is bliss, as you would say. It will vary from person to person how they experience it. But for the non-ascending souls who do pay attention, their core interests will be more in the nuts-and-bolts, so to speak, of the ships – what makes them drive, what makes them go. They are interested in the mechanics and how they can use it to their own advantages.

Yet, there will be other groups of entities who will make contact as well, and some of them are the ones that the non-ascending souls will be vibrationally attracted to. We will address this matter at greater length later.

D: So, are you talking about, when the ascension event happens, that we will be leaving the physical body, or is it more of a soul, spirit that is leaving?

A: If you're ascending then the body is going with you. It is a spiritually induced biological ascension.

From Contact to Ascension

D: And that is true for the people remaining in the Lower Triad?

A: No.

D: They will go in spirit?

A: Yes, but there is more to it. They are making their transition to the new universe – those who are choosing that destiny for themselves – while the planet itself is ascending, its body is going with it. It is physical. It is just like your body is going with you.

The non-ascending souls have, for a very long time, been in a position where they must make a choice to ascend or go into the new universe. Those who are still living when the Lower Triad finally folds up do not have to die to go there. As they migrate to the new universe they will take with them some level of their body, which we refer to as the "phantom body", which becomes part of the energy to play with, in the new universe. Upon their vibrational migration toward the new universe, what's left of the physical matter of the body will be dispersed. At the very end, they will find themselves, if still in the body, going into sleep-like trance state, so to speak, as the soul migrates closer toward the entrance of this new universe. All physical matter gets dispersed along the way, you see.

The new universe has an entrance. There is a black hole, as you would call it, where-into this new universe is being formed. It is much like a womb where this existing universe is giving birth to a new universe. It's done all the time by universes – universes giving rise or birth to new universes. All non-ascended matter disperses into its energy constituents and flows into womb the new universe wherein it becomes the energy of the new universe's Lower Triad.

C: Is it possible that our universe is ascending because on our particular planet we've outgrown the space, with more and more people being born here?

A: No. That has nothing to do with the reason why the universe is ascending. This planet is capable of handling a very large population, as it is. It is just being extremely mismanaged, or perhaps a more appropriate term is, deliberately mismanaged, by those in control of your planet. That is the problem.

D: Then perhaps it is because we're destroying the planet?

A: No. The planet is ascending because it is evolutionarily ready to ascend within itself. It has reached a certain degree of instinctual evolution, as I said before, and this is where by Ascended Beings comes in — to connect with the planet vibrationally, and draw it Home vibrationally, to the new place where it will be dwelling henceforth. But the planet is being assisted in its ascension by Ascended Beings in direct response to the universe ascending which is folding up its Lower Triad, which is where this and all other planets in the Lower Triad have resided...till now.

Once you ascend, whether you are a Volunteer or a new souls ascending for the first time, your body will be restored to its natural impeccable blueprint. Your body will be transformed to its original blueprint that has never changed since you created it when you came into the body.

Once you ascend you can restructure your form however you so choose. You can make yourself taller if you so choose. You can make yourself however you choose to have your appearance or, let's say your physical functioning apparatus.

C: And will our pets go with us?

A: Absolutely. All creatures are ascending. All of nature is going. Those creatures that have become extinct have ascended. You didn't know that but that's what happened.

From Contact to Ascension

As the planet ascends, all of nature on it is connected to it. The planet is nature and nature is the planet, so it ascends as an integrated unit.

The Ascended Realm has no limitations. It is a place of exquisite creation – creation by imagination, so there is no limit to what you can create, and what you can do when you are in the Ascended Realms.

Ascending planets there, from their dwelling places in the Lower Triad, provides the Ascended Realms with a basis, or fundamental objects with which to expand upon and to enhance the creation that's already there in ways that will dazzle your minds.

Regarding business, for instance, there is no need for business There. You have been told, in your ancient scripts, that in the end times there will be not one building left standing. Do you know why?

Because all of your buildings are created by the consciousness of duality and that state of consciousness exists only in the Lower Triad. They were created out of specific needs for which there will be no need for in the Higher Dimensions. You see?

There will be no need for these buildings that are here because there is no need for businesses. There is no commerce, no economy, and no such things that you have here because everything is very different there. There is no need for houses either for there is no need for shelter from the elements because our bodies are in-tune with the elements, but also we simply create whatever environment we so desire in the moment. We are never at-odds with our environment.

For example, the knowledge about herbs that many of you have, you will have no need for such medicinal therapies There because there is no sickness, nor accidents, hence, no need for what you refer to as "healing". There are plants existing There because they are part of nature that is this planet, remember.

The Higher Dimensional Realm, it exists in another state of consciousness which we call the "Singularity". You have duality consciousness, we have Singularity Consciousness. And by that we mean that there is no opposition, there is no reversal to life. There is only a continual forward-flowing movement of what has been created, and an ongoing refinement of and enhancement upon itself. It never goes back. It doesn't reverse. It doesn't decay. It doesn't become diseased or ill. Those are all states of being that belong to the consciousness and energy of duality that exists only in the Lower Triad. When you get into the Upper Triad, which we would call for you the 5th, 6th and 7th dimensions as the Upper Triad, there is no duality. This is something that many do not understand and which needs to be clarified.

Existence in the Upper Triad is why life There is considered "heaven", "paradise", "Nirvana", "Shambala", "Shangri-La", and so on. There is nothing There that goes contrary to the forward motion of life creating itself ever-anew.

C: Once you're in that dimension, or those 3 dimensions, can you meet up with family that has passed on, or is that in a different dimension?

A: That all depends on whether they have chosen to ascend, or whether they have chosen to go into the new universe. For those who are deceased the same choice applies. Some souls choose to ascend and others choose to go into the new universe and continue their existence there.

Now those who choose to ascend, who are already deceased, they have a different, shall we say, kind of physicality than those souls who ascend with their embodiment.

Now, there is a reason for ascending with the embodiment. It adds another level, aspect, component, and dimension to yourself as a biologically Ascended Being. You become biologically multi-dimensional in nature, meaning you can come and go at will into any dimension you so choose to interact upon.

The souls who have already deceased and ascended in spirit have a type of form that is more vaporous, shall we say, than the bodies that you will have. Your ascended bodies will not be the same density that they have in the Lower Triad. They will be the same density as our bodies that we have, which are not as dense as yours, yet we do have physicality.

As far as the 3rd density goes, you are all the same; your bodies are all equal in density. They may be different in shape, weight, and size, but they are all the same vibrational density.

Now, the idea that being quite heavy in physical weight means that you are holding larger amounts of light energy into your planet is an incorrect perception. Physical weight has nothing to do with your ability to hold the higher vibrational energy into the planet. Holding the energy here has everything to do with you, your soul being capable of holding Higher Dimensional frequencies which the souls who are native to the planet, who are not ascending, do not have the capability to hold within themselves. Their souls have evolved to hold only Lower Triad energies, and their weight has nothing to do with that either.

So, for our Volunteers, as ascended souls, it is the soul that is capable of holding the energy in the body then anchoring it into the planet, it is not the body that is doing it. It is the soul doing it. The body is the vehicle for the soul that is holding the light, or energy if you will. This is why this experiment requires the presence, on the planet itself, of embodied souls that are evolved enough to access, hold, and then anchor that Higher Dimension energy into the planet. You see?

Now, if the body is putting on weight, this excess energy is more to do with biological stress stemming from emotional stress than anything else. It has nothing to do with how much energy you're capable of holding on the planet. That is the function of the soul. As long as the ascended soul is in the body, then the Higher Dimensional frequencies are able to anchor into the body by means of the soul holding it there, but that doesn't mean that the body becomes heavier or bigger or denser. It means that the ascended soul is capable of handling Higher Dimensional frequencies, not in quantity but in quality; that these higher vibrational frequencies are anchored into the soul, and the soul, through the body, anchors it into the planet.

Because our Volunteers are anchored to the planet, you are able to feel what is going on in other places, so any discomforts that you feel are sometimes related to what is going on within the planet. When an event occurs anywhere on your planet and you tune into it, that information is coming to you psychically.

Now as an Ascended Being you have, let's say, a greater attunement to other people on the planet because the part of your brain, the pineal gland's psychic center, is more open to what is being created by others on the planet, whether it is something good or something not good. So you can have days when you're flying high because you may be tuned in to something good that's happening somewhere else, or you could have days where you're in deep, deep sorrow, or fatigue.

That is part of what our Volunteers experience from time to time. They have come here and were not prepared, really, for the tremendous amount of anguish that can go on upon this planet. And it is very disturbing to them because they are not used to that, shall we call it, "psychic pain". But remember that when it happens, you are merely tuning in to something that is going on with someone else, somewhere else. And the best thing you can do is bless them and cease focusing on it.

Recently there were 20 children who were killed in a tragic manner. Their souls had made no so-called contracts to be there at that time in order to make the changes needed on this earth, or within your government or within your states.

From Contact to Ascension

They are souls who chose to go to the new universe. There are souls who are choosing to go there together in groups. So, they vibrationally attract one another to each other, and an event is created, by each participating soul, even the perpetrator, by which they can then make their migration to the new universe together because those souls understood the value of making a group transition to their new destiny. They underwent this seemingly tragic event with great courage and awareness of the manner by which they chose to migrate to the new universe.

Understand, though, that souls who are ascending do not put themselves into such conditions or situations because ascension is an uplifting event unto the soul. It is not an event that causes disruption in the soul's progress toward ascension.

So, this event had nothing to do with these souls coming together as a group to generate changes within your governments or whatever. The countries on your planet will not exist much longer because the planet is ascending, remember. All of that has to be kept in perspective of the greater event that is occurring this moment.

Many of the souls who are in, let's say, major positions of control on your planet, at the soul level they are aware of what's going on. They know. The embodiments that they inhabit, and the altered egos that they have created, are subconsciously aware that something is going on so that many of them don't want to move on. They do not want the planet to ascend. They do not want to have to make a choice. They only want things to continue as they are so that their agendas can continue to unfold. Why do you think you keep hearing them say, "Stay the course"? It has a much deeper message than you have been aware of, yet they understand it.

Your president, for example, is a soul who is ascending. He is not a Volunteer, but he is ascending. Although it doesn't look like it superficially, on the deeper levels he is keeping a balance on the planet so that the souls who are ascending can make the transition as quickly and easily and smoothly as possible, because there is the opposite force at work, by those who are trying to prevent all of that from happening by creating as much chaos and fear as possible in everyone, especially within ascending souls.

Now they know they cannot prevent the ascension event itself from happening, but they do know that through various means of influence they can still manipulate the souls who are ascending. They haven't ascended yet. They're not there yet. They're on their way there but they're still vulnerable-by-influence, so to speak, by the opposing forces. They can still be swayed to the other side. And this is the war that's going on, so to speak. It is a battle over souls, and it plays out physically as your embattlements on ground and whatnot, but the real battle is over souls — between the souls who are ascending and the souls who are not.

Now, one of the things that we have noticed here is that some Terrans feel that there is not a, let's say, negative presence or force trying to influence or prevent this ascension of souls from happening. But there is.

There is an alternative ... let's call them a "faction", a negative faction, an opposing faction, who is and has been trying to prevent not only souls from ascending, but also trying to prevent our Volunteers from succeeding at their job.

They have succeeded with a few Volunteers who have been influenced and distracted away through the negative energy stimulus of these opposing forces. These Volunteers who have, shall we say, been led astray from their jobs, they may still return Home, but their souls are barely still anchoring energy into the planet because they have allowed themselves to be immersed in other activities or other negative focuses in consciousness. But that has not completely interfered with their ability to anchor some degree of energy into the planet.

From Contact to Ascension

It does not require that a Volunteer fully remember who they are and why they are here. It is their presence, as a Higher Dimensional soul incarnated into the physical body, which makes them capable of anchoring the Higher Dimensional energy into their soul and into the planet. That's their job. So, if they are, in their personal life, focused on saving the animals or the rainforests, or whatever it is, that is their personal choice and they can do that. But it is not interfering with their main objective of why they are here, so long as they have not resorted to negative energies of violence and destruction.

Some of our Volunteers have been in contact with them physically and non-physically. We all have. All our Volunteers have. And when I say "we" I am including those of us who here in our ships. We too have come in contact with them, physically and non-physically.

Yet, you are still here because you're doing your job. You are here by so-called divine providence because of your job that you're here to do. They cannot take away the job that we came here to do. They can try to interfere with it. They can distract you but they are not powerful enough to prevent you from doing your job.

They think they are. But do remember this; their adversely focused power is dissipating, as I said, as the Lower Triad folds up. That energy is becoming weakened and it is diffusing.

The planet's ascension is assured. It is ascending. The ascension event has reached a point now where that kind of activity is no longer engaged as it used to be. It is in the process now of shedding its old 'skin', so to speak. That old skin is composed of the consciousness and energy of the non-ascending souls. It is what we refer to as the phantom planet. There is now a completion of that which is the new skin of the planet, which is created by the higher consciousness all ascending souls, our Volunteers, and the Ascended Beings who are assisting.

So, once you ascend, and once those who have chosen to go into the new universe are birthed into it, then what happens to Earth? Is it just going to be a dead star?

No. The planet, Earth, is ascending physically, in-totality. All ascending souls are ascending with the planet, Earth, which we call Terra. Our Volunteers are bringing the physical planet to its new Home. That is the whole point for this experiment, so to speak, of this planet and other planets at this time, coming into the Higher Dimension all together. We are here bring the planet, Earth, Terra, to its Higher Dimensional state of existence, and all ascending souls are ascending with the planet, not vice versa. Understand?

So, at the same time, the ascension of the souls and the ascension of the planet is what you refer to as a feedback-looped system. They are ascending aspects working together synergistically. So, at the soul level there is a coordinated effort that is happening.

To reiterate, because the souls who are ascending have not ascended before, they could not anchor enough Higher Dimensional energy onto the planet to magnetically transform the planet to its Higher Dimensional state. That act required the embodiment of the Higher Dimensional souls to alter the planet vibrationally to its Higher Dimensional state of being.

Now let us address the matter of pain in the body being a resistance.

Some of you have correlated the pain with something going on with the planet; you believe that the planetary events are the cause or the origin of that pain.

A lot of our Volunteers have brought with them their higher abilities which, let's say, vicariously tunes them in psychically and physically to these natural events that are occurring. There is a way for you to lessen the pain by visualizing yourself in the higher vibrational light energy and sending it to where the pain is. And you are also, in the moment that you're doing this, drawing the planet in vibration towards its new Home. That's the job you are here to do, and when you do that consciously then the planet moves more easily and quickly to its new Home.

To be here in the body and not be conscious of what your job is, is one thing, but to be conscious of it and to deliberately focus on bringing the planet with you to its new Home, you have added another layer or, let us say, degree of power to making that happen.

We are ready to end our session now. We thank you for this opportunity to have spoken to you. We do have much more information to impart. We will be with you again soon.

That is all.
I am An T'na of the Intergalactic Board of Council

SESSION 1 – ADDENDUM: PART A

The Soft Spot of Newly Ascended Beings
Volunteers Rarely Come Together as Mates

(Q = Questioner   A = An T'na)

Q: In Session 1 you stated that all your Volunteers are Ascended Beings. Then later on you said that it is rare that Volunteers would find each other as mates. Please clarify this more for us.

We did say it is rare that 2 Volunteers would find each other as mates. We point out now that we did not say that you would not eventually, towards the latter time of the ascension event, find each other as friends, and in other situations.

There are some souls who are participating as volunteers "with a twist", as you would say.

Remember that we said of our Volunteers, with regard to the negative faction who is trying to have its way with you, that you each have a "soft spot", not just biologically or psychologically, but it also resides in the soul.

Let us clarify: Prior to your incarnation on the planet, even though you had already ascended and your former soft spot in the soul had become well closed up, upon immersion back into the energies of the Lower Triad, and upon incarnation back into life on your planet, your mind, body and soul developed another soft spot which is vulnerable to certain stimuli, and when that stimuli is imbibed in enough then you can "lose your way", so to speak. That is free will remember. Even as an Ascended Being you are never locked into anything without having a choice about it.

From Contact to Ascension

Now, in the Upper Triad there are some souls, not many, mind you, who ascended but for personal reasons chose to return to the Lower Triad to teach other family members and friends about ascension. These newly ascended eager-beaver souls, shall we say, would frequently come and go between the Upper Triad and Lower Triad, endeavoring to "show the way Home". Some of them would spend increasingly more time in the Lower Triad, teaching while at the same time becoming subtly more attracted, once again, to some of things that life on the planet has to offer, for there are some pleasantries there as well.

For some newly ascended souls who have so soon endeavored to return to the Lower Triad, their connection began to shift from being dominantly that of the Upper Triad energies to that of the Lower Triad. They became more and more drawn to the life that they once knew in the Lower Triad until finally they fully reoriented their energies to their former dimension of existence. Upon so doing, they lived out their lives in the Lower Triad, died, and then found themselves desiring to ascend, again, with another body. So, they started the process all over again with another incarnation on their respective planets. They did not dread this for their souls knew implicitly that they had much valuable information to offer those people with whom they would interact in the next lifetime.

These formerly Ascended Beings had their personal "fall from their own grace", so to speak, yet having done so was not wrong or bad. They are not condemned or in any other way dishonored. They are recognized as being very compassionate souls who engaged a noble gesture that merely took them off onto a different path, that's all. Free will happened, that's all. And free will is engaged upon personal soul preference, period.

It is well-known by everyone in the Upper Triad that right after ascending There, engaging oneself so soon in this endeavor is a very risky ordeal because until that soft spot in the soul is firmly "closed up", an ascended newbie visiting the Lower Triad is still vulnerable to being

Session 1 – Addendum: Part A

enticed by the stimuli that once fed the soul's soft spot. This is why, when choosing to engage themselves in such an endeavor, it is vital that they limit the length of their stay and the frequency of their subsequent returns. Some did and some didn't. But either way, it is of no adverse consequence to the soul. It is merely a different path, that's all.

So, in the particular case we are referring to herein, one of the Volunteers is a former Ascended Being, who is one of but a very few on your planet who has reincarnated several times since. This compassionate soul, having the memories of a prior ascension, resonated deeply with the needs of the Mission that you are on and volunteered to participate as a support to other Ascended Volunteers and Ascending Souls on the planet.

This is why this soul is a "Volunteer" but not having come here directly from the Upper Triad, as did the other Volunteer we are referring to in this case.

Other previously Ascended Souls here on this planet, and on other planets that are currently being ascended, are also participating in this same manner as "Volunteers" in the Mission. We are grateful for their additional contribution.

We hope that this has clarified the matter for you.

That is all for now.
I am An T'na of the Intergalactic Board of Council

From Contact to Ascension

SESSION 1 – ADDENDUM: PART B
The Job of Volunteers and the Risks Involved

Q = Questioner   A = An T'na

Q: During a previous session it was said that each Volunteer need not be consciously aware of their "job", of holding Higher Dimensional light onto the planet, in order to perform that job; and that we are free to do with our personal lives as we so choose. Is there anything we might do which could prevent us from doing our job and even from returning Home? And if so then has this already happened to some Volunteers?

A: It is true that you need not be fully aware of your Volunteer identity in order for you to anchor the light-energy through your body and into the planet. And it is true that you are free to do as you choose with your personal life, but we did not mean that everything you could choose to do would be to your benefit to performing your job or going Home, for it is true that there are things you can do which will diminish your ability to hold enough Higher Dimensional energy in order to do your job well, and which could jeopardize your ability to return Home.

As Volunteers, even you are susceptible to the Lower Triad energies, as we explained in a previous communiqué. If lower attitudes and behaviors persist strong enough, for long enough, then you literally flip your vibration from its connection to the Upper Triad to that of the Lower Triad, and when this occurs then the level of energy that you are able to access is no more powerful than that which the non-ascending souls access.

What would cause one of our Volunteers to do this? For one thing, being influenced by the wrong crowd, so to speak. While you came to this planet and into the body for the specific purpose of being a light-energy anchorer, your mind is free to focus upon whatever is flowing around you to view, to dwell upon, to engage in. And because you are free to choose your thoughts, if you are not living from the core of your

From Contact to Ascension

Being where your soul memory guides you per your Volunteer work on the planet, then you are more susceptibly influenced into counteractive directions of attitudes and behaviors which can vibrationally interfere with the job you chose to do. In other words, you can sink so low to the level of disempowering yourself from the Higher Dimensional power that you originally brought to the planet with you.

In our last session, we discussed the fact that there is a large negative faction dwelling on this planet who is deliberately endeavoring to sabotage the entire mission by doing whatever is necessary, by them, to influence our Volunteers into counteractive, counterproductive directions. They are doing this through whatever means will work from one Volunteer to another, each of you having your "soft spot", as spoken of previously. Consequently, the less attuned and connected you become to your soul memory as your dominant guidance and source of personal information, so that you remember, even a little bit, who you are which allows you to engage your Volunteer work more effectively, the more possible it is that you could fall prey to their influences instead, becoming more easily caught-up in the trappings of life, sinking into the manner of living in the energies of Lower Triad.

There is a fine line here that is crossed, and while it requires of you a great deal of disregard or ignorance of your soul memory, that line can so subtly sneak up on you that before you know it you've crossed the line and flipped over from your Upper Triad connection to the Lower Triad.

Now, while this can happen to any of you, it has not happened to very many of you at all. A few have completely succumbed to the pitfalls which the negative faction has put in your way, and due to these "fallen Volunteers" vibrations having been lowered from that of their original Higher Dimensional frequencies, they have consequently "lost" their entire connection to the Higher Dimensional Realm itself. They have lowered themselves back down in frequency to the level of the Lower Triad. But that is not to be considered wrong or bad of them, for free

Session 1 – Addendum: Part B

will ruled, and that is a divine intent of this universe. These souls simply chose another path to engage for themselves, so all is well with them.

So, this is one of the great risks that all of our Volunteers knew about and signed-up for when choosing to join this mission. You did not come into this mission without understanding the inherent risks involved.

This is why, while in your Higher Dimensional Life, the people you were closest to felt great concern for you when you chose to join this mission. They did not discourage you from joining; they did not try to dissuade you from participating, for free will is honored There, unconditionally. They were not in fear of what might happen to you, for there is no fear in the Higher Dimensional Realm. But they did know about the risks inherently involved in this mission, which made it a challenge for them to see you go to a place of such extreme chaos and struggle such as occurs on Terra, because they knew how it would make you feel once exposed to it all. That was their concern. Having ascended, they still have the soul memories of what life is like in the Lower Triad, so they knew what you had destined yourselves for again. And so did you! Yet you bravely took on the mission, undaunted by the tremendous challenges that lay ahead of you because you felt that whatever the risks, it was going to be worth it all in the end.

So, there you are on Terra, immersed in all its chaotic swinging to and fro in every aspect of life, trying to maintain a balance within yourselves while endeavoring to consciously do the divine activity that you agreed to do while, conversely, the negative faction endeavors, simultaneously, to undo it all for you.

Our advice to you: Stay out of their way and stay out of their fray. Do not give heed or attention to their influences or concepts of who you are, of what your life is all about, of how you should live it. Instead, embrace the soul memory of who you are as a Volunteer on Terra, and engage your divine activity, your "divine job", consciously, deliberately. Ascending Souls, embrace who you truly are as a Source-Being evolving to a new understanding of yourselves and of a new way of life in a Higher Dimensional reality where your new Home awaits you.

For a few minutes each day, visualize the light-energy that you are anchoring into the planet becoming stronger, brighter, whiter, lighter, because your conscious focus adds another degree of power to that which is already being done through you without your conscious focus. Visualize this light-energy anchoring into the planet's core, and radiating out from there to surround it in a field of Higher Dimensional light that is literally transmuting the entire planet, all of nature included, into its pure pristine state of existence as an ascended planet.

Your conscious focus on this also helps keep strong your personal connection to the Higher Dimensional Realm, your Home.

We suggest this same activity to all Ascending Souls as well. The more, the better. This will help to vibrationally attract you to your new Home in the Higher Dimensional Realm.

Now, when we suggest that you do this to the planet, for assisting the ascension of the planet, we do not mean that you do this for any soul dwelling on it, for "personal salvation", so to speak, is not your business to engage – that's why it is termed "personal".

Like a fish in water, every soul is directly immersed in this light-energy, and every soul is capable of knowing whether or not it is time to embrace that light for its own evolution, or its own ascension, or not at all. Every soul knows exactly what it is doing, what it needs for its own evolution, and when. It is not up to any of us to assess, judge or decide that for another soul; consequently we do not anchor the light into them like we do into the planet. The planet is enfolding every soul in the light-energy and each soul can partake of it or reject it. That is free will. Your job as Volunteers is to be a provider of the Higher Dimensional energy, anchor it into the planet by way of your embodiment which, in-turn vicariously makes that light more available

Session 1 – Addendum: Part B

to all souls who are ready to open up, let it in, and engage it within themselves, for themselves.

That is all for now.
I am An T'na of the Intergalactic Board of Council

From Contact to Ascension

SESSION 1 – ADDENDUM: PART C
The 3 Waves of Volunteers & Returning Home

Q = questioner   A = An T'na

Q: In the previous session, the subject of the "3 Waves of Volunteers" was brought up, but more clarity is needed. Please share with us your definition about it, with regard to what others have said about it, and when the first Wave started incarnating. And correlated with that matter, during our last session it was mentioned that some Volunteers would return Home soon. Please clarify these things for us.

A: Long before the Mission Plan was put into action, when it was in its formulation stage, a major Council was convened in order to coordinate the Mission's plans so that everyone would be "on the same page", as you put it. It was determined and agreed, amongst the many groups participating in this Mission, that the most appropriate course of action to take was "infiltration by incarnation". This meant that all Volunteers were to be sent forth in what would amount to as 3 stages of incarnation. This part of the Mission was then commonly referred to as "The 3 Waves of Volunteers", or in-short, "The 3 Waves". This is why some of our Volunteers use this term – they are receiving it from soul memory.

Each Wave of incarnating Volunteers agreed to become the parents of the 2nd Wave of incarnating Volunteers, who would then be that parents of the 3rd Wave.

It was determined that, by the time the 3rd Wave had matured to adulthood, the Greater Objective of this Mission would be completed, meaning that there were no further plans for another incarnating Wave.

What was the overall Greater Objective of the Mission? To insert a critical number of Higher Dimensional Volunteers amongst the planet's population, whose souls are evolved enough to hold high-capacity intensities of Higher Dimensional energy which in-turn would be anchored into the planet's core.

It was predetermined how many Higher Dimensional souls would be necessary to do this successfully, taking into account that there were always the odds in free will that a few souls would "fall" in vibratory frequency from performing their agreed-upon "job". So, more souls than was necessary were calculated to compose the number required for success.

The Greater Objective of the Volunteer's missions would be to anchor as much Higher Dimensional energy into the planet as possible during what would be the typical life span of the native species on the planet – for remember, this same Mission is occurring on other ascending planets as well whose life spans are different than it is on your planet.

For this planet, it was determined that the total span of 75 years would suffice. The necessary numbers of souls incarnating during the span of each of the 3 Waves were assigned a span of 25 years for each Wave interval. This would allow each Wave of Volunteers the needed time to mature and become stabilized as independent adults capable of parenting their peer Volunteers who would incarnate in the successive Wave.

During the Volunteer briefings regarding the Mission Plan, the first 2 Waves were informed that they would parent the next Wave of Volunteers. The 3rd Wave would not parent more Volunteers but would parent other incarnating souls, some who are on the path of ascension and others who are not.

So, in all eagerness the Volunteers of the first 2 Waves, prior to incarnation, assessed amongst themselves who would be the Volunteer children and who would be their Volunteer parents. Their birth path was predetermined and fully known prior to incarnating.

Session 1 – Addendum: Part C

The first Wave of Volunteers, of course, had no Volunteer parents to incarnate through, as would the 2nd and 3rd Wave Volunteers. To address this matter, the councils agreed that it would be necessary, therefore, to seek out native Terrans who were on evolutionary paths that would suffice the hosting of our Volunteer souls. It was determined that at least one of the two parents was somewhat spiritually evolved. Two would be better, but we have found that that is a rare situation among Terran mates.

At any rate, all of the would-be Terran parents were carefully screened by us for their ability to live up to the task, so to speak. These so-called "chosen ones" were souls who chose to agree to participate in the Mission.

During sleep each night they agreed to be taken out-of-body to a so-called "training center" located in what you call would call a sub-space dimension, where they would receive the necessary "grooming" of how to host and treat the Volunteer souls incarnating into their family life. They understood that their role was to raise and protect their Volunteer children to the best of their ability. They were strongly cautioned against abuse of any sort. Free will being what it is, some lived up to that command, while some didn't do so well.

This 1st Wave of Volunteers began incarnating into their Terran family situations around the year 1944-45. They, the 1st Wave, did so over a span of 25 years, some 1st Wave Volunteers incarnated sooner than did the others but all within that 25-year span of time.

This staggering of incarnations within each Wave served the purpose of keeping the light-energy steadily increasing over time rather than having it increase all at once thereby alarming your planetary controllers and alerting them to our Volunteers presence.

By around 1969-70, the 2nd Wave of Volunteers began incarnating. You must remember that once the older of the 1st Wave of Volunteers were ready to be parents, the successive Wave of Volunteers began to come in, again not all at once but incrementally as each set of parents were ready.

You must also remember, as previously discussed, that it was predetermined by the Councils that due to the rapidly increasing population on this planet, the widespread placement of each Volunteer around the world would result in Volunteers being located so far apart from one another that coming together as mates who would parent Volunteer children, was understood to be near impossible.

Prior to incarnation, at the Volunteer briefings onboard your respective ships or planets of departure, it was well-understood by all Volunteers that they would pair up not with a fellow-Volunteer but with a native Terran whether or not they were ascending, but most likely not ascending, as you will learn further on. You all knew this before you incarnated, and you accepted it as the way it would be for you.

So, prior to incarnating, your mission duty was to seek out Terran mates, who were not yet born, but to find their souls, make contact with them, inform them of the Mission, and invite them to participate. Not every soul approached with this invitation chose to accept it. You each spent much time doing your research until you found a native Terran soul who agreed to do this with you. Your Terran mates were then given the same grooming procedures at the training center, as had the parents of the 1st Wave of Volunteers.

Now you must also understand that you knew that these native Terran souls were unlikely to be souls with whom you had any prior involvement. You are ascended Volunteers who already existed for eons in the Upper Triad, while these Terran souls have been existing for eons in the Lower Triad. This made it highly unlikely that you had any one-on-one involvement in the Lower Triad with these unascended souls. In other words, reuniting with "old friends or flings", so to speak, was not going to happen, and was also not the point of, nor pertinent to, this Mission. Except for the 3rd Wave, your Greater Objective was to

Session 1 – Addendum: Part C

find Terran souls who, as mates, would help you bring onto the planet the Volunteer souls who agreed to be those known as your "children".

So, on Terra, when you were ready, you intuitively hooked up with your native Terran mate, and who perhaps turned out to be a dud, aye! Well, noble-you had great expectations for a good life, but the odds that life as the spouse of a native Terran would be a bowl of cherries went out the door when the honeymoon wore off and Terran reality set in. Didn't it?

But you also knew that the Terrans you would hook-up with would be directly immersed in-your-line-of-firelight, so to speak, so that regardless of whatever else happened, these souls would in some way benefit vicariously by your presence in their lives, and benefiting from it to whatever degree they were ready to evolve in this lifetime or the next. Yet you knew that it was not your job to "save them", although before you remembered who you truly are some of you did try to do that and utterly failed. But in your soul, you knew that you did not come to the planet to "save souls", nor even to directly assist their evolution or ascension, but instead to assist the planet's ascension which in-turn would assist all Terrans to have access to Higher Dimensional light which they could embrace unto themselves for their own evolution, or for their ascension as the case may be, or not at all as they so choose. So, your mates "were in the line of firelight" the most, and they most likely have resisted it the most. Yes? It is OK, as it needs to be for them.

So, remember that you did not come to this planet with the expectations of hooking-up with your fellow Volunteers as mates. You knew the odds of that were slim-to-none. Instead, you came here wholly expecting to be the parent of one or more Volunteers who would be your embodied "children".

Now you know why the Terran mates you have been with have seemed so primitive, backwards, unevolved, thick-headed, and that is because when compared to your point in evolution you are light years ahead of them. But there can be no judgment in that because they are still the same Source that you are, just at a lesser stage of the soul's evolution. Nothing wrong with that, or bad about it. It just is.

So by now, the 3 Waves of Volunteers have all incarnated. This part of the Mission, Infiltration by Incarnation, has been accomplished. You are all anchoring much Higher Dimensional light onto the planet so that its ascension is occurring; its pathway Home is thus assured.

In-lieu of that, many evolving Terrans are souls who are ascending for the first time beyond the Lower Triad. Remember that you are not responsible for causing their ascension to occur. They are their own cause of it. Your presence on the planet merely added to the lesser vibratory frequencies that were already on the planet for them to embrace and engage per their own ascension. Your high-energy presence anchored through the planet has been like a booster shot for them.

Most of the 3rd Wave Volunteers are now mature adults who are becoming the parents of a wide variety of souls evolved to different stages. Remember, this Wave is not giving birth to more Volunteers. All our Volunteers are currently incarnated and in-place on-planet.

Now, there is a misconception, often amongst new age people, that many of the children incarnating now are highly evolved souls, and various labels have been assigned to them. This is simply not the case. There has been an attempt to justify the unruly behavior of many children who are, supposedly, souls more evolved than even you; the claims being made are that while they are highly evolved, they are simply maladjusted to the dysfunctional life on your planet so they rebel against it in often crude, rude, hurtful and destructive ways. Yet, this is simply not what is going on. That is merely more dysfunction compounding the existing dysfunction.

But we shall reserve this matter for a discussion at another time.

Session 1 – Addendum: Part C

For now, your last question was in regard to when Volunteers would return Home.

We are well aware that there is a lot of asking going on, by Volunteers, to return Home. We hear it all, all the time and we empathize with you. We understand why this is occurring. But, remember, you did sign-up for the duration. In other words, you signed-up to remain on the planet, holding your soul's light-energy in-place until the planet is ascended to her new Home in the Upper Triad. This is why your so-called prayers, verbal or silent, have gone unanswered – because you gave yourselves that answer when you signed up for the job. It is not our place to revoke that for you except in the unlikely case of your lives being threatened by the negative faction bent on destroying you along with the planet.

When, in the previous session we said that some Volunteers would return Home sooner, we were referring to those whose health is now failing for one reason or another. Although they will physically die soon and return Home spiritually, the death of their Terran embodiment will prevent them from ascending their Terran body Home with them as their "prize" for a "job-well-done", so to speak. Yet, because all our Volunteers are Beings who have already biologically ascended, upon leaving the Upper Triad to incarnate into their Lower Triad Terran bodies, they do still have their "other bodies" lying in-stasis into which they will return their spirits and be revived, to live their lives in the Upper Triad once again. So, these Volunteers will not be left body-less upon their Terran deaths.

But this is also another topic of discussion for another time.

As much as you would love to hear us say that all of you are returning Home soon, that our Volunteers will be disappearing off the planet in Waves, the truth is that the bulk of our Volunteers will remain on the planet, holding their soul's energy in its core as it ascends. That is what you signed-up for.

Plus, as the planet ascends you are serving to literally create for it a vibrational pathway of transcendence into its new Home, a path it has never taken before, to a place it has never been before. Your souls, anchoring the energy from the Higher Dimension into the planet, acts much like an umbilical cord by which you are, literally, vibrationally transcending the planet into the Upper Triad. You are its lifeline, so to speak, and all of nature upon it, within it, around it. To "cut that cord" prematurely would be devastating to the planet, and would be a disastrous disruption to the entire Mission Plan.

But let this fact cheer you up: as you remain on the planet during its ascension to its new Home, all of natural life gets a total makeover, yourselves included. And this is another topic to be discussed later.

But we want you to feel better about remaining on the planet by knowing that as it is ascending, your personal lives improve even though you may observe the lives of non-ascending souls getting worse as they continue to struggle with their lessons, as the folding-up of the Lower Triad literally "squeezes" them, so to speak, off of the physical planet. We put it this way to explain that their unevolved souls simply cannot withstand the increasing intensity of the incoming higher-frequency-pressure that is being exerted upon the state of their lower-pressurized soul. It's a complex metaphysics thing.

But simply put, these souls are being vibrationally squeezed off the planet as it ascends in frequency. Once deceased, they are in-turn forced by the naturally exerted frequency-pressure to withdraw from the planet and its vicinity, and to seek another place to reside that is vibrationally attuned with their own soul's frequency-pressure. Due to what is transpiring with the ascension of the universe itself and the folding up of its Lower Triad, the only other place where they can reside now are on some primitive planets grouped together near the womb, or black hole, of the new universe. And that is yet another topic to discuss later.

Session 1 – Addendum: Part C

We joyously wish our Volunteers to know that your lives are becoming and will continue to be increasingly more fulfilled, more free, more fun, as will the lives of all Ascending Souls. But, we emphasize, it is up to you to access, embrace and engage that truth as your personal experience of the ascension event. You cannot, on the one hand, be on a path of ascension where the frequencies are continuously becoming more "divine", shall we say, while on the other hand you continue to experience the increasing lower negative events that you are consistently leaving behind. As you ascend, your life and the life of the planet itself becomes better and better, so why would you expect it to do otherwise? That defies the very metaphysics of the nature of reality.

On the other hand, if you expect life for you and the planet to stay bad or get worse, then you have shifted yourself off the path of ascension to the Upper Triad and onto the path of descension, if we may use such a word, into the Lower Triad where your fellow perceivers are the non-ascending souls.

Our message to you is that so long as you expect your life to get better because of the ascension that is occurring, your life will get better, because that is simply how it works.

As you observe the life of non-ascending souls remaining bad or getting worse, there is no need for you to panic, believing that it need in any way affect you. It won't unless you "fall from the grace of your own state" into fear that it will, and so it will. You see? You have free will in this, so which will do you choose?

And it is not your job as a Volunteer to endeavor to jump in and try to save non-ascending souls from their unpleasant lives. It is their soul's path of evolution, and it is your job to allow them to engage it without your input or interference – which is the real Prime Directive – the other Prime Directive you've heard of is fantasy being advocated as fact. Ignore it. But, if these suffering souls consciously ask you for your assistance then give it to them, for if they are ready to ask for

From Contact to Ascension

assistance then they are ready to receive it. Otherwise, leave them alone on the path that they need to be on.

So, in closing to this topic, sadly you will not be returning Home tomorrow, next week, or next year. Happily, though, your lives will become increasingly better and more joyous over the next several increasingly short years, as the beat-of-time continues to speed up. Know that as a fact. Focus on it as a fact. And so it shall be for you. To do otherwise is to crucify yourself, so to speak.

Know that you will return Home, with planet-in-tow and body-intact, and that a great day of celebration awaits you all. You can count on that. The festivity plans are in the works even now.

That is all for now.
I am An T'na of the Intergalactic Board of Council

SESSION 1 – ADDENDUM: PART D
Ascension of the Planet, Its "Vibrational Skin", & the "Splitting" of the Planet

(Q = Questioner A = An T'na)

Q: In the first session it was stated that this planet is ascending, meaning it is making a physical ascension to the Higher Dimensional Triad. It was also stated that as it is ascending it is leaving behind a kind of "skin" that is being retained by the souls who are not ascending. Please clarify what you mean by this; how does this serve those souls when the Lower Triad is folding-up, and when all that which remains in the Lower Triad is being vibrationally attracted to the creation of the new universe. And, does this correlate to some people's ideas that this planet is splitting off into 2 or more versions of itself?

A: It is true that the planet is making a physical ascension, just like your bodies are making a biological ascension. For those who are ready, their embodiments are biologically responding to the planet's physical ascension, and vice-versa. You see? The 2 are interconnected, and this is why the planet is ascending physically, rather than as some have speculated, as merely a spiritual ascension. You do not need a body; you do not need to be physical in order to generate spiritual ascension.

Your embodiments are a direct part of the nature of this planet. Because the body's biology is directly connected to rest of the planet's natural creation, as the planet and all of nature on it ascends, your embodiment naturally endeavors to ascend with it because your bodies know they are of that which the planet is, as is all of nature. The planet is ascending, period. All of nature is ascending, period. All Terran embodiments are naturally attempting to ascend, period. But there is a big 'but' here.

From Contact to Ascension

All Terrans possess a soul, which has soul-consciousness, which through free will allows the soul to resist ascension by process of resisting its own evolution when an ascension event is occurring.

It was previously discussed that the ascension of the planet generates a frequency pressure and this pressure in-turn acts directly upon the soul. As ascension is resisted by the soul, for its own needful purposes, this frequency pressure creates a vibrational tension between the body's natural response to the planet's ascension, and the soul's choice not to ascend. This vibrational tension becomes stressful to the biology of the body, which eventually results in various crippling illnesses, fatal diseases, plus fatal and crippling accidents due to dwindling mental and nerve functions, as well as accelerated aging processes due to the acceleration of the beat of time.

So, while the planet and all of nature is ascending, only the bodies of those souls who are ascension-ready are fully hooked-up with the natural flow of the planet's ascension. The embodiments of non-ascending souls are naturally hooked-in as well, but the resistance of the soul does, over time, gradually disconnect the body's biology from the ascension processes.

By now, by this point in the ascension of the planet and all of nature, all Ascending Souls are shifting into an acceleration of health and wellbeing, while all non-ascending souls are shifting into an acceleration of diseases, illnesses, accidents, and aging.

Keeping all of that in-mind, the ascension of the planet, of all of its natural creations, including your ascending embodiments, are transcending out of the vibrational framework of the Lower Triad, and as that occurs a transformation of matter takes place.

There is that which we call the "scaffold" upon which all matter adheres itself into the density relative to the dimension it is manifesting upon. This scaffold is much like how coral is formed. If you look at the coral, you see that it has tiny holes in it. But if you look it more closely,

Session 1 – Addendum: Part D

you see that these holes are formed by a scaffold structure upon which the mineral substances adhere to. If you look at the densest thickest part of the coral, it appears to be solid but when you put it under your microscopes, you see that the scaffold is there as well. The closer you look, the more scaffolding you see.

All matter has its basis upon this scaffolding. The scaffolding structures itself according to the pattern of the idea, of the image held in consciousness that is to be created into physical form. This process occurs on all dimensions, not just the one you are on, but it occurs relative to the level of density generated by a given dimension.

So, in the Lower Triad the level of density depends upon which dimension you are dwelling upon – the 1st, 2nd or 3rd. Each of these 3 dimensions has their own level of density. The level of density where you are, which you refer to as the 3rd dimension, has a scaffolding custom-tailored to match the vibration of the 3rd density within the 3rd dimension.

Your deceased souls descend back into the 2nd density level, and this occurs because death is a step back from going forward in consciousness to a higher vibration within the Lower Triad, which would be the 4th level of understanding. The 3rd dimension's 4th level of understanding has its own density. But the 3rd dimension's 4th level of consciousness is not the same thing as that which you call the 4th dimension. The 4th dimension is beyond the Lower Triad's vibration of the 3rd dimension wherein there are 7 sub-levels of understanding and density. This matter is another subject of discussion for another time.

Now, the planet and all of nature is ascending by means of a transformation occurring within the scaffolding itself. The scaffolding is patterned after the ideal blueprint of the planet, as are all things created by the planet itself, including your embodiments. The ideal blueprint never degenerates or disintegrates, regardless of how much change or decay occurs within the materialized form. The nature of the ideal blueprint is to be constantly improved upon; the only change it accepts is toward a constant state of enhancement and refinement.

Since before the planet's material formation, there was an ideal blueprint designed, held firm within the consciousness of the Source, which we all are. The entire planet and all of nature has its own ideal blueprint, including your embodiments. Even your soul has an ideal blueprint that it is constantly striving to enhance and refine.

So, the planet's scaffolding is itself being transformed from that of a 3rd density structure to that of a 5th density structure. Now, those of you who are ascending along with the planet will not physically notice much change, not yet, because your body's scaffoldings are transforming in-tandem with the planet's scaffolding transformation.

In other words, as the planet's scaffolding shifts from a 3D state to a 5D state, your bodies are doing the same thing right along with it. This natural entrainment process causes you to not notice any difference in density relative to that of the planet because your body's ascending vibrational rate of speed is the same as that of the ascending planet. Consequently, you can still feel or touch the physicality of the ascending planet and all that is around you. This has to do with metaphysics. Like to like and all of that.

Now, for those who are not ascending, their scaffolding gradually loses vibrational touch with that of the planet as it ascends. While the planet's scaffolding is vibrationally shifting to its new 5D structure, their scaffolding remains as that of a 3D structure. As this gap between the 2 states of scaffolding structure grows greater, a little bit each day, the non-ascenders have no sense that the planet itself is ascending, and the reason is this – something else is simultaneously occurring for them.

As the physical planet ascends, meaning, it is taking its 'body' with it to its new Home in the Upper Triad, its former 3D scaffolding is left behind. Now relate this to our coral analogy; what is left behind by the planet's ascension is, basically, a somewhat 'ethereal skin' composed of

Session 1 – Addendum: Part D

the 3D vibrational scaffolding that is becoming increasingly vacant of all 3rd density matter. Just as old dead coral loses the minerals that once gave it a density of substance, so this is similar to what occurs with all things as they ascend. This is what is occurring with your embodiments as well. The increasing transformation of the vibrational scaffold into the higher 5D state causes an atomic dislodging or shedding of all substance of a 3D nature. This 3D substance which was once held-fast to the scaffolding, loses its integration-capacity to adhere. These dislodged atoms and subatomic substances then become "free-floating building-blocks", if you will, within the field of the Lower Triad.

As you and the planet ascends further into a 5D scaffolding with its relative density and substance, the planet's former 3D scaffold-skin is gradually left behind as the 5D scaffolding increasingly sheds its non-adhereable matter. The vibrational scaffold-skin of the former 3D planet becomes increasingly porous, like that of the porous layer of coral – its 'skin'.

For those souls who are not ascending but have chosen to remain in the Lower Triad for continued evolution, their embodiments are still very much attuned to the 3D vibrational skin – the 3D scaffold which the ascending planet was once composed of.

The embodiments of non-ascending souls are losing their ability to adhere 3D substance upon their 3D scaffolding, which itself is losing its adherence function. In other words, the biological 3D scaffolds are breaking down over time.

As the 3D vibrational skin loses its adherence function, it loses its ability to retain substance unto itself, thus it sheds the remaining substance that it has left and is unable to adhere more substance unto itself, so the scaffolding of non-ascending souls body's increasingly becomes more porous. Eventually the scaffolding disintegrates into its former original idea or image of its former state of existence, having "fallen" back, or descended into the 2nd level of density, which is where your deceased dwell as what you call ghostly images of their former selves.

Those souls who are not ascending are undergoing the same 'loss-of-vibrational-integrity' process as the planet's 3D scaffold-skin is doing. Their embodiments are literally, shall we say, dematerializing backward into the same level of density of your deceased souls – to the level of their image patterning, which you call ghosts. But, since their embodiments are vibrationally attuned and connected to the vibration of the dematerializing skin of the planet, they do not notice anything out of the ordinary occurring either. They are literally experiencing the vibrational opposite of what you who are ascending are experiencing. You see?

Both processes are occurring simultaneously, superimposed upon one another. Each of the planet's states of existence is transpiring simultaneously yet not they are connected together. The 2 states are moving in opposite directions of vibrational resonance from where they were – one moving higher in vibration, the other moving lower in vibration.

Now, in that all dimensions are superimposed one upon another, the ascending and descending aspects of the planet is really not going anywhere directionally in space. The planet remains stationary while each aspect of its transformation shifts into a different flow of vibrational-time relative to where it is going.

Its ascending vibration is releasing itself of its former 3D scaffold, right here and now, where it is. Eventually the ascending planet will no longer be seen or interacted with, except by those in the Upper Triad where the planet is becoming increasingly more visible and interactable in its new 5D state.

At the same time, the 3D skin of the planet is dedensifying into a disintegrated condition of the planet's former 3D state in matter, and this process is also occurring right where you are, right under your feet, so to speak.

Session 1 – Addendum: Part D

So, this dual shifting of the planet, vibrating out of one state and into another, transpires gradually over time, but the planet is moving nowhere in space as it accelerates itself in one direction, while decelerating itself in the reverse direction. To give you another analogy, it is like 2 sides of the same coin having 2 different reality-experiences transpiring at the same time.

We do hope you are getting this because it will help you understand your next question of how the vibrational skin of the planet hosts the non-ascending souls, and their creation of the new universe, which applies to the universe folding up its Lower Triad.

As the physical planet ascends out of the Lower Triad to the Upper Triad, its continued existence in this universe itself is assured.

As the planet's 3D skin or scaffold disintegrates into the 2nd dimension, possessing a 2nd level density, along with the embodiments of all souls who are not ascending, those non-ascending souls will find that things are slightly different from how they used to be.

Ascending souls will have simply vanished from their presence by means that they would consider to be mysteriously unexplainable, while simultaneously the deceased souls who are not ascending will have just as mysteriously seemed to have been "resurrected from the dead" back onto what they perceived as their former planet. But in reality, the planet that they are seeing is actually as much a ghostly image patterning of their former planet, as they themselves are of their own former image.

While the disintegrating scaffold-skin of the planet will have descended back in vibration to a non-matter state of existence, it will seem real to those non-ascending souls who vibrate at the same rate of speed.

The non-ascending souls' collective remembrance of their former planet projects an image-patterning upon the disintegrating scaffolding so that it appears to be real to them, which we refer to as a "phantom planet", and yet in time, even that phantom planet will give-way to the ongoing disintegration processes.

Now, with that in-mind, the Lower Triad of the universe, which consists of dimensions 1, 2, and 3, remember, is no longer providing the Source of this universe with any vibrations that stimulates the expansion and refinement of itself. The evolving Source is outgrowing its use for the vibrations in the Lower Triad.

Its increasing non-use of these lower vibrations is generating a weakening of the vibrations relative to each of the 3 dimensions in the Lower Triad. This vibrational abating generates a collapsing of vibrations within each dimension. In other words, the vibrational scaffolding of each dimension is weakening and, consequently, collapsing in on itself, much like a disintegrating piece of coral will do over time. The overall vibrational function and capacity of each dimension to hold itself together is breaking down.

This is occurring, again, by the increasing non-use of these vibrations by the Source. As the Source's need for those lower vibrations decreases, the vibrations likewise decrease in strength. An analogy of this would be like your muscles of which you have a saying, "Use it or lose it". The non-use generates the loss of strength, whether it is a muscle or a vibration.

Yet there still exists within the Lower Triad the non-ascending souls who retain, in their soul memory, everything they have ever experienced during their numerous journeys throughout the Lower Triad.

Many non-ascending souls will not be aware that they have actually died, meaning that they have descended down in frequency, without having actually gone through a physical death because the body dematerializes into its 2nd density image, which we refer to as the "phantom body", you call it ghosts. As the Lower Triad's vibrations weaken, their phantom body's scaffold continues to disintegrate until

Session 1 – Addendum: Part D

all that is left is the soul itself. They are then souls of pure spirit; no density left whatsoever, yet they are not aware of that change in density. They just know that they still "exist".

Eventually the Lower Triad will have lost all substance so that all that remains is a gradual weakening of vibration. Before the Lower Triad's vibration is totally flatlined, so to speak, some of the vibrations of the Lower Triad are even now being magnetically drawn toward an area of the universe where we-the-Source created a womb for the insertion and holding of the unused vibrations of the Lower Triad.

More and more non-ascending souls feel vibrationally compelled to migrate toward this womb. For them it is a very natural and comfortable experience because it is the desire of the soul, which is directing them there for continued evolution. The soul simply knows where its next path of evolution is, so it innately moves itself there.

As this womb of the new universe gathers unto itself all that remains of the Lower Triad, including all non-ascending souls, a stage is eventually reached when it is 'developed' to the point where this new infant universe can sustain itself on its own, without being symbiotically attached to its mother universe, we shall say. The new universe then separates itself from its mother universe and is free to evolve itself independently of any and all outside influences.

The explosive 'big bang' theory that your scientists have given you is not an accurate description of a much more gentle process of how universes are created. There is a "big separation" that occurs, but it's not in the form of an explosive big bang.

So, all that remains of the Lower Triad will give rise to an entirely new universe, replete with everything necessary to boot-up new life therein, including the intelligent souls who will do it. They are the new Creators of that new universe. They are the new Source from where all creation will come. They are off on a new adventure of being the Creators of their own whole new universe. So, this is where your non-ascended loved ones will go and what they will do there. So, grieve not for those who are not ascending with this universe, for they are ready for their new adventure.

Now in-lieu of that, guess where we, all who are here in this universe, came from? Yes, we were the souls who once existed in another universe, and we all chose not to ascend with that universe, but instead we chose to remain oriented in that universe's Lower Triad. So, we "migrated sideways" into the womb of the newly forming universe that had been created there.

Upon its separation from its mother universe, we all became the Creators of this universe, the Source of all that is in it! How did we become the Source? We took the potential latent energy, which came through with us, and through brilliant ideas, we created the scaffoldings of those ideas upon which the energy would adhere to, in order to become substance, relative to the dimension we were creating upon, and we imbued "life" unto that substance.

You think that life just happened, all on its own, as your scientists want you to believe is the case? No. It took a vast intelligence to make it all happen, and that intelligence is you, I, and all of us together. Ever heard of what you call "intelligent design"? That is us. Every one of us. We are the intelligence and the designers. Is this not the definition of a Creator and the Source of that which it creates?

Are we the energy that came with us into this universe when it was birthed? Of course we are that energy. The soul consists of that energy arranged into the unique scaffolding that composes your soul and my soul and every soul in existence. Everything has a soul and it consists of the energies of the universes that each soul traverses through.

So where did the energy itself first come from? What is its origin? That is the great mystery of all mysteries and no one has the answer to that. It just is. It is the unsolved mystery that shall forever remain unsolved.

Session 1 – Addendum: Part D

Yet, here we are, so solving the mystery would not change the fact that "we exist".

Consequently, since we are the souls who chose not to ascend with our former universe, but instead chose to migrate into this one, how can we justifiably condemn those non-ascending souls here for choosing to do the very same thing now? We cannot. So, cease with any belittling or demeaning of those who are currently migrating toward the womb in order to become the Source-Creators of their new universe. They are not "going to hell" or any such version thereof, for there is no such thing. You can safely toss and can that hogwash, as you would call it. They are becoming Creators of their own new universe. And how cool is that, because look at us – we did it here, and it is marvelous. Many of us are ascending with this universe, while many are becoming residents of a new universe, yet life in each direction goes on just as well. So, it's all OK. OK?

Now, as the Source of this universe ascends, it means that this universe is ascending because we are the Source who is ascending ourselves firstly. The universe is responding in-kind to our own ascension as the Creators of it. It is all interconnected, you see. But we are initiating the ascension event itself. All of life in the universe is going along for the ride, with the exception, of course, of all non-ascending entity-souls who have chosen a different, yet just as wonderful, destiny.

Now, something else is transpiring as well. As we-Creators have less and less need for and use of the vibrations of the Lower Triad, and the Lower Triad collapses in on itself and its energies are vibrationally magnetized to the womb, simultaneously while this is occurring there is a whole new Triad that is coming into this universe, and this new Triad is what some are referring to as the 9th, 10th, and 11th dimensions. The 8th dimension is becoming a new time-portal, the new barrier between the 2 sets of Triads, one upper set and one lower. This is how and why the universe is ascending. This new Triad of higher vibration is being brought in. This is the nature, thus definition of ascension.

From Contact to Ascension

As the Source-Creators of this universe, we are vibrationally attracting this new Triad into this universe because of our increasing desire and need for new vibrations, with which to continue creating diversity, thus expanding, enhancing and refining our universe, which is our playground.

This new Upper Triad of higher vibrations offers us new types of energy that we can combine together in unique never-before seen forms of substance thus matter. An analogy; we are getting new toys to play with in our cosmic playground.

Now, there is scientific-astronomic evidence that confirms that there is new energy coming into this universe. It has been seen by them, if not quantified and understood by them. But this fact is not publicly well known. However, now you know about it.

So, your next question regarding claims of this planet splitting itself off into 2 or more versions of itself: this is a misconception of what we have already said is transpiring. There is a misconception of the process we've already discussed which stems from the uneducated viewers or perceivers of the process who have drawn inaccurate conclusions of what is actually transpiring. Seeing it and understanding what you are seeing are two very different things.

The so-called split-off planets, which are being viewed by some perceivers, through dreams and intuition and so on, they are seeing the phantom image of the planet as it descends into the 2nd dimensional level. It is understandable that the appearance is that of second or twin planet being formed, but that is a misunderstanding of what is actually occurring. What they are actually seeing is the superimposed images of the phantom planet that is descending from the 3rd to the 2nd density state, and the physical planet that is ascending from the 3rd to its 5th density state. This event is not a "splitting off", nor a "cloning of" this planet into 2 separate physical versions of itself. That is a misconception of what they are observing in their visions.

Session 1 – Addendum: Part D

So, the answer to that question is 'no', especially the idea of some Terrans who claim that one version is positive and the other is negative. That is the thinking of uneducated minds that are still thinking in terms of moral duality. What is transpiring is how we have presented it to you herein, and there is no negative-positive about any of it. It is simply the nature of the ascending universe and all souls who exist in it.

Now, one other thing: because we are the Creators of this universe, therefore the Source of all that is in it, the folding up of the Lower Triad is not the first time that this event has occurred.

The folding up of the original Lower Triad occurred after our most basic creation plans for this universe were no longer needed.

Let us give you another analogy: when you want to build a house, you draw up a set of plans according to how you want the house to be arranged and so on. Once the house is built, you no longer have need or use for those plans. The house you've built can now be enhanced and refined upon with new plans added to the already existing house.

This is what happened when we created this universe. We all participated in formulating the original set of plans by which to construct our new universe. Once our universal-house was 'built', so to speak, we no longer had need or use of those architectural cosmic plans.

The vibrations of those plans composed the Lower Triad that existed at that time. Eventually we stopped referring to the plans so that the non-use of the vibrations in that original Lower Triad weakened and diminished. Consequently we folded-up that Lower Triad and sent the residual energy into a black hole pocket which would later become the womb for the new universe.

And, just as we are doing now, so back then we vibrationally brought into this universe a whole new higher Triad to replace the former Lower Triad, with which to continue creating this universe. This set of Triads is the current ones which we have now. But, as then so now, as the current Lower Triad is once again being disused for enhancing and refining the universe, therefore the vibrations in the Lower Triad are weakening and diminishing, we are about to fold it up as well, once again. Simultaneously we are drawing-in a whole new Triad of fresh unexplored vibrations for our ongoing creation.

Those souls who do not want to do this with us have chosen to migrate to the new universe to be the Creators of something entirely new and different there. So on and on it goes, as new universes are born, replete with the Creator-souls who prefer to create something totally new and different. At the soul level, they are already eagerly engaged together, conceiving the creation of their new universe. Why wait when you know where you are going and there are plans to be made!

So, from the Source comes something for everyone. Right?

We do hope this helps clarify the matter for you. We enjoy sharing such information with you so as to help our Volunteers remember these things, and to help Ascending Souls gain your initial understanding of them.

That is all for now.
I am An T'na of the Intergalactic Board of Council

SESSION 1 – ADDENDUM: PART E
The Ascended Planet–
When All things Manmade Shall Cease to Exist,
&, Global Economic and Political Matters

Q = Questioner   A = An T'na

Q: How do you see the money market right now? Can you offer some guidance on this?

Q: In a previous session it was stated that once the planet has ascended to its new Home in the Upper Triad that all things of man will cease to exist; that ancient scripts mention that not one stone shall remain standing upon another, that all things manmade shall become as dust upon the planet. Please clarify what is meant by this perception.

A: I have requested that these 2 questions be addressed together, for the one will help clarify the other.

First of all, we do not give heed to the economic matters of the planet because we know that these things are constantly adjusting themselves to whatever the current needs may be nationally and globally. We do know that all such things are in a constant flux of change, therefore, to pinpoint specific outcomes on any of them is futile and can be misleading to those seeking answers for the current or long-run future.

If you feel you must know what the trends are in these matters, then we suggest that you give attention to what those souls who are not ascending are seeing as the possibilities or the outcomes. We suggest this because they are the ones who creating it, firstly, thus they are the most concerned about such matters, therefore they are the ones most controlling of them. This is true due to the fact that their perceptions in life, concerning their survival and wellbeing, are still rooted in the issues of the Lower Triad thoughts and corresponding energies. In other words, they are non-ascending souls who continue to live their lives around whatever is occurring externally to them. Hence, they can and most often do live in the fear and anxieties that these matters evoke, based upon developing events that they feel is beyond their control. This in-turn generates competition amongst one another for winning the best booty that fulfills their imagined needs and desires.

Our focus here with Terrans on this planet is, as we have stated from the start, to assist all Ascending Souls and our Volunteers with clarity about the events that are occurring above and beyond those of the Lower Triad events of existence. We know that Ascending Souls and our Volunteers are aware that their livelihood and wellbeing is rooted within their own consciousness, hence they also know that it is within their own control, meaning that they do not rely upon the trends or outcomes thereof for their personal existence. Their focus is not upon matters external to themselves, but upon matters internal to themselves. They know that they, as Ascending Souls and Volunteers, are senior to all external matters, which means that the manner in which they live their lives is what determines whether they thrive, or merely subsist and survive, consequently thriving according to their internal environment, not the external environment.

In-lieu of that fact, for us to give advice regarding the political and economic affairs of your world, as having any major significance to you personally, is for us to turn your attention and energy away from your internal environment, which is of major significance to you personally, thereby influencing you to join the non-ascending souls' dependency upon externalized matters and the fears and anxieties that goes along with it.

Instead, if you are indeed an Ascending Soul, we suggest that you "go within" and behold the state and condition of your own internal environment so as to be sure that you are immersed in the higher frequencies that are above and beyond those of the Lower Triad. If you are immersed in the higher frequencies then you will feel confident that regardless of whatever occurs in your external environment, all will nonetheless be well with you personally, and you will feel

Session 1 – Addendum: Part E

encouraged by your confidence to remain in a state of certainty about it. You see?

As Ascending Souls you will find yourselves becoming less and less concerned about what transpires externally to you and more and more concerned with what transpires internally. In so doing, it is not that you are putting yourselves into positions of potential situations of hardship, or that you are being unprepared for whatever political or economic disasters may befall the masses; it is that as Ascending Souls you come to understand that whatever does befall anyone external to you is exactly where their soul needs them to be, and where your soul needs you to be, for the purpose of gaining an understanding about such things.

As Ascending Souls, your increasing internal paradigm shift away from external matters is a natural part of the ascension process. This is when you begin to rely more on your own personal point of power as the Creator-Source that you truly are, and less on the impersonal power of those around you, whose personal agenda it is to make their agendas yours as well.

As Ascending Souls, you will come to realize that the place to where you are ascending has no such matters to be concerned over. The lesson here for you, right now, is to move yourselves beyond these Lower Triad thoughts and energies because nothing like them will exist in the Upper Triad for you to focus upon. In other words, if you insist on clinging to the consciousness and energy that the Lower Triad is composed of, with all its polarized beliefs and ways of existence, then the natural result of that is that you will not vibrationally align and engage the higher consciousness and energy that composes the Upper Triad, hence "you will in no way enter into that kingdom", or dimensional realm, as your scripts state.

What we are teaching you here is the greater understanding of that which you call the laws of relativity, like-to-like and all of that. So, how does this information fit into the next question?

From Contact to Ascension

As this planet continues to ascend, changes are made to the scaffolding that holds all things together in their 3rd dimensional state of being. We have already touched upon this matter to some degree in prior communiqués, so we ask you to read or reread those entries in order to comprehend this teaching.

Once the planet has made its final transcendence into the Upper Triad, there is no 3rd dimensional scaffolding left on the planet for the adherence of anything possessing a 3rd dimensional atomic structure. All your buildings and apparatuses that have been constructed by Terrans for uses beyond that which naturally occurs in nature, have been so constructed by the consciousness of need that in-turn must meet the needs of the social structures that have been conceived of in the minds of Terrans existing within the framework of survival which the Lower Triad offers. It is not that these manmade constructions were at all necessary in order for you to exist in your experience of the Lower Triad, but it is that such are what you as a species chose to do; it is how your lives have been shaped and funneled, if you will, more recently in history by the greed of your planetary controllers determining how life shall be and not be for you. You are thus living in a very artificial construct manner of existence.

In that these artificial constructs originate from within the minds of Lower Triad thoughts and energies, they are held together by 3rd dimensional scaffoldings. As the planet ascends, it is losing its ability to retain this Lower Triad scaffolding, and once it has been secured permanently within the higher frequencies of the Upper Triad, all such manmade constructs simply lose their ability to adhere atomically. As we stated before, the Upper Triad does not have atoms. That which adheres together in the Upper Triad does so by constituents that is not atomic-based.

So you see, we encourage all Ascending Souls to understand that you can expect that once the planet has entered into its new state of existence in the Upper Triad, you will not even find your homes left standing for such constructs will have no use there within a type of environment that requires no separation or isolation between you and it. Your 3rd dimensional homes have been artificially constructed as a means of protecting you from your natural environment because you are not living in harmony with it. In the Upper Triad, there is no such thing. Your attitudes and understanding about this must change here and now in order to accept this as your new reality, thus align yourselves with the new environment you will find yourselves existing in.

All of your buildings of business and politics, and so on; all of your modes of transportation and so on, will also lose their atomic-integrity so that they too will be "returned to the dust from where they came" – in other words, the material from which they are made will literally disintegrate and be returned back into their non-atomic state, for all things of an atomic nature exist in a non-atomic state first.

In the Upper Triad there is no need for politics, or business, or economics, or any of the concepts that Lower Triad Terrans have dreamed-up as so-called "necessary" aspects of existence. The Upper Triad functions upon a very different type of consciousness and its relative energies, which we have touched upon briefly in other communiqués, and more will be said later about that.

In that no such concepts or states of being exist in the Upper Triad to where all Ascending Souls are ascending and to where our Volunteers are returning, we want all of you to know that this is why we do not focus our attention nor yours upon manmade matters and constructs which all non-ascending souls continue to hold near and dear to themselves as their perceived, and we will say more correctly, misperceived means of survival. For us to focus you upon such things would be for us to dishonor your personal power as a Creator-Source and, in-lieu of that, to influence you to remain focused in the same direction and aligned with the same energy in evolution as the non-ascending souls.

From Contact to Ascension

But we reiterate what we have said before, which is that if you choose to focus yourselves in that direction you are indeed free to do so and we consider that choice to be the right one for you, for your soul innately knows where its destiny in evolution lies. And, into whatever direction your soul needs go, it is not a matter of right or wrong, or of good or bad, or of better or worse; it is a matter of necessary personal evolution about which there is nothing right or wrong, good or bad, better or worse. And from that point of understanding we honor, respect, and celebrate your choices, for that is, in-turn, honoring and respecting and celebrating free will itself.

We hope that this has clarified both questions.

That is all for now.
I am An T'na, of the Intergalactic Board of Council

IBOC COMMUNIQUÉ

Session 002

Some Clarification on the Matter of Homosexuality
Nature of the Soul, Oversoul and Soulmates
Walk-ins
Going into Ascension or Going into the New Universe
Knowing and Accepting Your True Identity
More About the Three Waves of Volunteers
Starseeds, Crystal Children

(C& D = session facilitators   A = An T'na)

A: Good Evening. I am An T'na, and I am glad to be here in this capacity again. We are going to speak about a matter on this planet that is quite sensitive to many people, but it is necessary that we clarify this matter for the sake of all Ascending Souls and our Volunteers, regardless of whether this matter concerns anyone personally or impersonally. It is information that will bring forth a greater understanding of yourselves as well as of others so that you stand in a place of unconditional love for yourselves and others equally.

This matter concerns that which Terrans have termed 'homosexuals', and we shall use this time to help everyone understand this subject more clearly, for there is a great misunderstanding on the planet regarding 'souls' and the nature of the soul.

Our observations of Terrans have led us to understand that amongst your genders there are a lot of unpleasant experiences that occur between the opposite sexes. And from our perspective, it is quite understandable why there are a lot of mixed feelings between the opposite sexes, and why some Terrans have switched genders as mates.

From Contact to Ascension

For the most part this act has been done out of a misunderstanding of how to resolve issues concerning past experiences. This misunderstanding has been, shall we say, assisted or aided by a growing current movement in Terra's population to become mated with the same sex. This has created a, shall we say, 'trend' in your planetary situation that has grown very large, very quickly.

It has been believed that all same-sex matings are occurring because of homosexuality, but for the most part, most are not due to anything of that nature, but to a shifting of issues from one gender to another.

We wish that Ascending Souls and our Volunteers understand this clearly so that clarity comes forth to resolve inappropriate beliefs and attitudes about it.

Aside from actual cases of homosexuality, there is much misunderstanding of what the soul is, what its nature is, which forms the basis of this misunderstanding that is generating the growing popular trend which, in-turn, is leading Terrans to believe that what they are doing is the result of being homosexual in the soul. There is no such thing as a soul that is homosexual, and we shall clarify this confusion in session.

First of all, let us speak about the nature of the soul. From where we are in our greater understanding of the soul, in our journey leading us from our Dimension of Origin, in order to arrive where we currently exist, all of us traveled through each dimension as, shall we say, integrated spirits. We eagerly explored each successive dimension into which we had lowered ourselves vibrationally. Upon fully exploring and experiencing one dimension we then stepped down in vibration in order to explore and experience the next one, and the next one, until we came to the 4th dimension, which, as we discussed previously in Session 1, is a barrier between the 5th dimension and the 3rd dimension; that the 4th dimension is the barrier of time, but it is also a major overarching portal consisting of infinite minute portals that lead you to any point in time and space, be it past, present, future, as well as that of alternate realities.

So, while we were in the 5th dimension descending our way down the Realms of Vibration, we came upon this barrier. As integrated spirits, we could not pass through the barrier. We were all quite puzzled over this mystery but the mystery itself compelled us to endeavor to solve it. After eons of exploration, we discovered that in order to go further into the next dimension we had to split ourselves into 2 charges because, as we learned, that is the point in energy where it splits into opposite polarities. The next dimension we wanted to explore and experience consisted of polarity, opposites, which resolves itself into the nature of what you term duality.

Due to this dualized energetic state, and due to the energetic state of our evolving integrated souls, we realized that we could not go there as an entire, integrated spirit. Eventually we came to understand that we would have to split our souls, which is housed by our spirits, into two equally polarized charges.

Before this point in our evolution, there was no such state of being in existence. This was something entirely new to us and, as exploratory Beings by nature, we felt innately compelled to experience this new state of being. Our reasoning was that if we were to continue exploring and becoming all that we could possibly become, then doing whatsoever was necessary in order to engage this so-called "spiritual edict", then so be it. So, we chose to fervently pursue it.

Now, this knowledge was common knowledge in your ancient times. The Terrans of that era understood that the soul became that which they called a "split-apart" wherein one half of the soul held a positive charge, and the other half of the soul held a negative charge, yet the 2 halves forever composed the same soul, which some in your time have termed an oversoul, but of which there is much misunderstanding regarding this subject as well. The term oversoul simply refers to, in truth, the overall knowledge and wisdom held by both parts of the soul as one overarching collective understanding of the single spirit unto which the 2 soul mates belong. The subject of soulmates has also been greatly misunderstood, and this matter shall be clarified as we proceed.

Each polarized soul, each soul mate, traversed through the barrier and entered into the 3rd dimension, which is the upper third part of the Lower Triad. Eventually, biological gender was created into the physical forms that each soul would indwell, and there was a reason for this, as we shall discuss later.

We created 2 biological genders, each one being charged in polarity relative to the charges of the 2 souls. The feminine or female charge of the soul would always indwell a female biological embodiment. The soul that is of masculine or male charge would always indwell a male biological embodiment. It was created this way, and meant to be this way because it was in-keeping with the natural order of the nature of reality in the Lower Triad of duality. The science and physics of this was completely understood and accepted by all of us.

After eons of time perfecting the biological embodiments that we were indwelling, something astonishingly unusual happened – a very disappointed soul broke the natural laws as a way to get around a situation that he found unbearable, rather than complying with those natural laws.

In the ensuing history of your planet, the 3rd dimensional experiences of many of Terrans became agonizing, especially for the female gender. Each gender, in their own way, increasingly suffered at the hands of a few power-hungry souls who were bent on dominating and controlling their brothers and sisters through tyranny and torture. Emulating those above him as a means of gaining his own kind of power and control within his own life, many of the male gender began to engage tyrannical behaviors upon his physically weaker sexed women, as well as upon his physically weak and helpless children.

Terran history is a case replete with, to coin you a new word, incompassion run amuck.

The following story is a well-known one by everyone in the Upper Triad, of how confusing and outlandish things can become in the Lower Triad.

After eons of such unpleasant reincarnations, and after the death of one particular male soul decided he'd suffered enough at the hands of his fellow gender, so he came up with what he thought was a great idea. From his detached point of view, he felt that the female gender had it much better than he did as a male. So, he privately conceived a plan whereby in his forthcoming incarnation he, as a male soul, would insert himself soul into a female body. That would fix everything, or so he erroneously assumed.

It was only after carrying out his plan that he discovered that what he had actually done wasn't so brilliant after all. But now he was stuck in his female body and was suffering more than he'd ever suffered before as a man. It was this *shifting to the other gender*, a rewiring effect of the polarities that subsequently generated tremendous confusion in his soul over who, or what, he truly was. The male soul consisting of a positive charge was indwelling a female body consisting of a negative charge so that the 2 charges, when rewired backwards, are diametrically opposed to the presence of one another in the same space-time scaffolding of the body.

Not only does this rewiring effect generate confusion in the soul, but it also generated confusion in the body itself. While the female-charged body is endeavoring to be what it was designed to be – female – the male-charged soul is giving the body opposing signals that causes the biology of the female body to produce male genital parts, usually not fully developed, therefore secreting unnatural amounts of male hormones. This female body will display itself in a somewhat masculine appearance and corresponding functions.

The fact that the male soul indwells the female body does not change the male souls' innately polarized attraction to female souls, meaning, to other women. The female body is not the one choosing to mate with other females. It is the male soul, misplaced within the female body, who desires to mate with his female soul counterpart; it is not the body that is doing it.

And this same crossing over effect has also happened in the reverse, with the female soul indwelling a male body. She looked upon the male from her detached point of view thought, "Oh, he's got it so good. He's the one in control. I'm tired of being beaten up. I want to be male." So, the female soul crossed over the gender line and entered into a male body, with the same but opposite effects occurring to her.

These are the true homosexuals. It is a matter of polarity and the nature of the soul relative to the nature of the polarity and gender of the embodiment.

It is necessary that they come to terms with their past, that they forgive the opposite gender for the harsh treatments they have received and are attempting to escape from. We understand that much of the male gender on this planet is not all together that together. We understand that they have been put through a lot of hardships themselves, coming down from their own gender upon them, and that has caused them to be, in-turn, difficult people for anyone else to live with, especially their women.

We want homosexuals to know that they are beautiful souls, and there is nothing they lack other than to forgive themselves and their opposite gender. Once they forgive, then they are no longer in need of anyone else in their lives on an intimate basis because they are instead intimate with themselves, with who they truly are. They are so in love with their own true nature that they do not need anyone externally.

We are clarifying this matter so that while what they are doing seems common and perhaps increasingly more acceptable, that does not mean that such a belief is for one's personal greatest wellbeing. In other words, there are many Terrans who believe that they are homosexual but who in fact are not, and it is this erroneous belief which is not to ones greatest benefit.

We may have more to say about this later, but we hope that this has imparted some degree of clarity on the matter.

Now, we shall speak of another matter that is referred to as walk-ins wherein it is believes that when a spirit leaves the body but it's too soon for the body to die, then another spirit comes in, or "walks in", as you put it. Often it is believed that a male spirit can inhabit a female body, and vice versa.

Just as already explained concerning the crossing over of polarities pertaining to homosexuals, so the exact same thing applies in the circumstance that you are describing. For such a circumstance to occur it would produce such polarized tension in the body that great health problems would result, so great that those health issues would result in severe diseases based in duality.

If there are truly any walk-ins, having crossed over in polarity or not, then you must understand they are not of a higher frequency because it is a fact that advanced souls would not insert themselves into a body that someone else did not want, for one thing. An advanced soul would have no need to do such a thing in the first place.

The only type of soul who would do that would be ones who are of a lower 3rd dimensional level of understanding, doing it for their own self-aggrandizing purposes. Much of what you call "possessions" is of this, again, unnatural nature. It would be a selfish act. Rather than the soul incarnating into a body of their own they're taking a shortcut. Consequently, they're sort of 'cheating' life and thus themselves.

From Contact to Ascension

We know it is a popular concept – these walk-ins – and that it has been perceived as something desirable, even "angelic", but this subject has been another greatly misunderstood notion.

We wish you to understand that Beings who still exist within the Lower Triad, yet who have evolved into higher understandings of life would never need to engage in such actions. Such Beings have advanced to the understanding of that which you call immortality. They are what some of you have come to call Ascended Masters, which when applied to them means that they have ascended mentally to greater levels of mastering life, but they have not yet biologically ascended beyond the Lower Triad to become what we recognize as Ascended Beings. These, we shall refer to them as Immortal Masters have learned how to continually regenerate eternal life within the cells of their bodies. Your own science already knows that this can be done, and how it is done, yet they do not allow you to have this knowledge because immortality is not good for their enslavement business.

Likewise, Ascended Beings who are beyond the 3rd dimension, beyond the Lower Triad, have the ability to come into this dimension with their own body.

Our point here is to help you understand that what is being perceived of as walk-ins is not all that it's cracked-up to be, as you would say. True cases of walk-ins are rare because, as we said, the only souls desiring to engage such a situation are ones who are not very evolved, who are what we refer to as non-ascending souls. No Ascending Souls would resort to such acts.

You must understand that there are planetary controllers who have their hands in everything in your lives, especially the spiritual aspect of your lives, and that it is their self-ordained job to create as much confusion as they possibly can about these matters because this in-turn generates much chaos, thus division amongst those whom they control, in the forms of you being intolerant, unallowing and unaccepting of one another. Do not be so quick to assume that the subjects of souls and soul mates, homosexuals, walk-ins, starseeds, indigo and crystal children, possessions, ghosts and so on, have not been tampered with thus greatly distorted by them, for they have. It is our intent with you to help clarify these matters for you, putting the truth back into their original teachings based within fact.

It has been important for you all to understand that the nature of the soul has, in its truth, been buried, so to speak, from your knowledge under thousands of years of the negative faction guiding you away from all truth and into distorted misunderstandings that are intended to keep you from being who you truly are, to keep you from being the empowered soul that you are. And when there is confusion in the soul, you have diminished your power to that degree. It has been this manner of unloving treatment of you that generated the desire within souls to cross over in the first place; that created the desire within souls to possess bodies not their own and who thus cheat themselves out of a life of their own; that created the desire within souls to mistreat one another in order to gain their own level of power and control within their own lives, and so on it goes.

Now, we have something we would like to clarify for someone who has a question regarding the matter of Ascending Souls.

This person has been feeling that her mate is not on the path of ascension and wants to know if this feeling is correct or not. From our higher perspective of her mate, we see that she is correct in that he is not ascending, but he is evolving. But we emphasize that every soul's evolutionary direction is subject to change at any moment so we can only state that for now he is not ascending.

Please understand that there is a difference between evolving, and having evolved to a point where you are ascending. We want her to understand that though he does not display it, though he does not show it, he is evolving, but he is doing it in his own way, on his own time despite how she has, in the past, tried to, shall we say, help him along.

She discovered that doing that didn't work. And it took her many years to discover that it wasn't working!

But we want her to understand that it is OK that he is not ascending. We want her to understand that we understand how difficult it has been for her to live with a mate who is not ascending.

Most Ascending Souls and our Volunteers are in that same situation. And this is one of the matters that we discussed in one of our communiqués.

As we already clarified, our Volunteers hooked up with the native people on this planet, most who are not ascending, and there was a reason for that. And the reason was, as you all knew when you agreed to be Volunteers for us, that in the process of doing your job of anchoring light into the planet you were vicariously affecting the lives of others, which includes the mates who you chose to be with, although you may have tried to influence them, teach them, share truth with them, even though they rejected it; and they may have made fun of it, they have humored and patronized you, they may have taken your truth and turned it back against you in ways that would appease themselves or to get what they wanted, but the seed of truth was still planted.

You were still an influence simply by being in their presence. You did not have to try to influence them in any other way, verbally or in any other manner. That was not part of your job description, so to speak. It was your presence alone, the light that you were anchoring into the planet, which has been radiating from the core of the planet to surround the entire planet, that has immersed everyone in this higher dimensional light thus in-turn allowing them to access that light for their own evolution – if they want it, and for their ascension – if that is what they want to do.

And many souls have been receptive to the light. There are more Terrans who are ascending now because of this added light that has been brought here, than would have otherwise occurred. But directly assisting their evolution or ascension was never your job to do. Your job was and is, simply, to anchor the light and allow whoever chooses to open up to it to do so. That is what it means to be a light unto the world. It, the light, doesn't talk.

So, we wish that all of you come to some clarity within yourselves about this matter, so you will find peace within yourselves about it; and that you will come to rest, shall we say, from thinking that you need to, in any other way, influence your mates or anyone else around you.

Although your mates are not receptive to a lot of your understanding and awareness, they are simply just not ready yet for the way of life that goes along with those understandings and awarenesses.

We see these souls choosing to migrate into the new universe. And we see them very happy about this choice.

We wish you to know that all of those who are choosing to migrate and become part of the new universe are all very excited about it because they know that it is their opportunity to become creators of this new universe and to be the source of all that is in it! They, therefore, get to create something that is wholly different, unique, from this universe that has been their playground for eons of eons.

It's kind of like, tinkering. In the new universe, they will get to tinker and rearrange the ideas and energies so as to create something new and different than what they've created in this universe. And they are all very excited about it. This is their path. It is all OK!

For those who are remaining in this universe, and ascending onward, if we could put it that way, you are all just as excited about doing that as they are about going into a new universe and being the creators of it. So, there is a saying among you, "Something for everyone". No soul is being forced to do something that they do not want to do. They are choosing it, and that is in-keeping with the law of this universe of free will.

Now, some people have claimed that free will exists on this planet and not others, or on some planets and not other planets. But that cannot be. It exists everywhere throughout this universe. This is a free-will-based universe. We all designed it to be that way. It is an experiment to see what we are going to do with free will on a universal scale. Wow! We have been having fun! That's what we have been doing!

D: So, there has been a time, before the free-will universe, there was a time that people didn't have free will?

A: There are other universes based in other principles. Free will is not, shall we say, common amongst all universes. This one became, sort of like what you would call a prototype for free will.

So, free will exists on every planet, where every Being, every soul exists. Everyone is exercising their free will, whether they know it or not, whether they believe it or not. You have free will. You are free will! We are the inventors of it and we are experimenting – where is it going to take us next? What can we do with the new energy that's coming into this universe? How is free will going to affect it?

So, we are having lots of fun. We wish as many souls in the Lower Triad to join us as possible. Back to your presence here on the planet, as anchors of light from the higher dimensions, this is adding to the numbers of people who will be joining us.

But we wish to clarify that it is common among people here throughout the whole planet, to somehow, in some way, distinguish yourself from what you call God, or Source, or Creator, or Higher Power, but we tell you, that is a misconception that we wish you to let go of because it is not true.

The more you distinguish yourself from the truth of who and what you are, your degree of that distinction to that degree diminishes your power to be who and what you are, in the fullness of who and what you are thus the fullness of your power.

When you realize within yourself that you are the Creator, the Source, and you accept it wholly without doubt, without shame, and you know it absolutely, that is when your power returns in-totality. And your life begins to change in wondrous and miraculous ways because now there's nothing separating you from you from having what you want. You see?

Make no distinction. Allow no distinguishment to exist in your consciousness. Your soul knows who it is. You have been resisting it in your consciousness because it's not acceptable! Because you have been tortured and punished for thousands of years, to beat out of you the truth of who and what you are. So, no wonder you deny it! It is cellular. Your body does not want to be beat up any more!

But we say, times are changing. More and more people are coming to know who they truly are and they are coming to accept it. And they are coming to say, "I am indeed God! I am Creator! I am Source! For if I am not, who am I and what am I."

So, it cannot be that you can be anything other than that! That's all there is! How could you be anything else? You can't! So more and more people are coming out of their closets to say the truth of who and what they are – "Behold, I am God!"; but, they are not doing it in a way that makes a big deal out of it! They don't go around advertising it. They don't need to because when you realize your true identity, in totality, then you realize the same thing for everyone else. So then, how could it be a big deal? It's no longer a big deal. You're all equal so you don't go around making a big deal out of it.

When you realize who you truly are – that you are the Source, you are Creator, you are God – and that there is nothing else you can be, then you move out of the denial that has been beat out of you, and you find yourself in a new state of consciousness. You open up a part of your brain that has been resisting greater awareness and greater knowledge and greater power because of that denial. So, once you open up and you accept it fully unto yourself, things begin to change – for you! You won't see a major change in the world around you. It's going to continue doing its thing because it's based upon the closed-mindedness and the fear of those souls who have not yet come to the understanding that you have come to. And for the most part that is what is populating this planet. And those souls are the ones who are, shall we say, moving sideways, migrating into the new universe.

So, we have found that although the planet is going to continue through its turmoil, you, on the other hand, are not going to be affected by it because you are letting in your true identity and your greater power that is connected to it. So, your life changes for the better.

C: That's what we've been seeing. We've been noticing that, all last year. It didn't matter how bad the economy got, our store and our lives just went on as usual.

A: And this is how it's going to be as you continue into the ascension – moving more and more out of the Lower Triad, and into the Upper Triad. And you're going to continue seeing your lives improve.

Now, we shall address a matter to our Gesanna concerning the Volunteers, because she had a question about going Home. As you know, she has wanted to go Home the moment she took her first breath.

We have sent her back into her body many times! We have protected her many times from the negative faction in order to keep her here to do what she agreed to come and do. As a teenager undergoing surgery, she decided that this would be a good opportunity to get out of her life at that time. But her ascended father was in her presence and he stopped her from passing over. He literally seized her in his arms to hold her back, to keep her from going forward with her plans to leave her body. His restraining action greatly upset her. She was so surprised that her father would do that to her that it took her a very long time to come to terms with *why* he did it. At the time, she was unaware of all that she has now consciously remembered about herself and her work as a Volunteer so that the whole incident was very confusing to her. It simply didn't make sense.

Now, there are some Volunteers who will be leaving their tour of duty on Terra early, and these ones are having medical difficulties. They will be allowed to return Home due to their great medical difficulties. And they are returning Home not as pure spirit but returning to re-embody their bodies that they vacated as souls when they incarnated on Terra.

So, you might be wondering why we don't just heal them, and each of you, so you can continue with your jobs of holding the energy into the planet. The answer to that is because were we to go around healing our Volunteers of all their maladies then this would look very suspicious not only to your family and friends but to your negative faction leaders who would eventually be alerted to what would seem to them to be a threat to their agendas of enslavement. Longevity and immortality are not good for the slave business because you would live long enough to figure out what their diabolical game is with keeping you as their slaves.

The other reason we do not step in and heal our Volunteers is because if we do the healing for you then how does this look so far as you being an example to Ascended Souls about what we, and you are teaching them? Correct? You agreed to this when you signed up for the job. You simply forgot that this is what you had agreed to. Now you know.

Now, all of our Volunteers have embodiments of some sort that they left behind upon their incarnation into their Terran bodies. Their original bodies are in-stasis either on the mothership or on a planet that they frequent which exists within the Upper Triad. When our Volunteers return Home, they will have a choice to make – "Do I keep my Terran body that I have inhabited for a lifetime, or do I take up my former original body?"

For our oracle, it was a tough decision. During out-of-body experiences, she has seen her original embodiment where it rests in-stasis in its life-support chamber. She knows what it looks like and it's not quite like her Terran body because it is of another race of entities, which is a combination of Delton and Pleaidian species. Her Terran body is much shorter and more, shall we say, fragile than her originally ascended embodiment. It is of a pale creamy skin color with a faint hint of blue. It is tall, very slender but very robust.

After giving much consideration to this matter, in the final analysis she chose to do something quite spectacular. She decided to donate, if you will, one of her 2 bodies to her Terran mother who is an Ascending Soul but who passed away before she could ascend with her own embodiment. Because her mother is a long-time native of Terra, having had many Terran embodiments, Gesanna reasoned that her Delton-Pleaidian embodiment was, if you will, wired differently than what her mother is used to biologically inhabiting. So, she chose to donate to her mother her Terran body, and return to her own embodiment that she'd ascended with eons ago.

Now, with regard to appearances of Ascended Beings, you must understand that amongst all the Beings who exist in the Upper Triad, who have already ascended, there are a vast variety of shapes and sizes and features.

There are Beings in the Upper Triad who are very different looking. And it's all OK. No one cares. No one in the Upper Triad is concerned about 'tall' or 'short' or 'big' or 'small' or 'normal' or 'weird', and so on. These are perceptual attitudes that we left behind when we ascended. For us, it matters not what you look like for we see and interact only with the Source that everything is. It's all about being creative and exploring what we create. That's the fun of existing in the Upper Triad.

So, with regard to our Volunteers are wanting to go Home, we wish them to understand that we are sorry but it's not going to happen tomorrow, or next week, or next month. You are here for the duration. You signed up to be a light anchorer, anchoring Upper Triad energy into the planet until the planet has been taken to its new Home. You can't just give up and go! If you did then you would pull your light back out of the planet which would nullify what you came here to do. You are here to hold that light in the planet until it has made its final transformation into its 5th dimensional state of being.

Your return Home will occur in your lifetime, either upon the passing of your embodiment whence you will return to your original body, or upon the ascension of the planet, which will occur sooner than you're expecting, but it will not occur as soon as a lot of you would like it to, including our oracle.

She has known that her people would not contact her until she accepted the fact that she is here for the duration, that she has a job to do; and that she has agreed to her agreement to stay! She just didn't know that the job was going to take so long! From her limited perspective, she felt she'd already done her job. She felt that her work had been completed. So, she felt ready to go. And this is the way many Volunteers feel.

Now with regard to that, let us discuss more about The 3 Waves of Volunteers.

What happened is that due the Lower Triad folding up and this universe ascending, prior to any Volunteers going anywhere into the Lower Triad, there was a big council of Councils who got together and parlayed as to how to best go about bringing forth the ascension of as many planets in the Lower Triad as possible into the Upper Triad. By so doing, this effort engaged on their respective planets would vicariously influence as many ascending souls as possible to get on with their chosen destiny of ascension.

From Contact to Ascension

So, our Volunteers were instructed with specific understandings about their job. It was decided in this council that the best way to go about this was "infiltration through incarnation". Volunteers would be assigned to certain planets. It was determined that each planet has a different time cycle, shall we say, and therefore different life spans. On this planet, it was determined that each wave of Volunteers would be assigned 25 years, per wave of incarnation. This is the timing for which each wave of Volunteers would come onto the planet.

The first set of Volunteers came onto the planet in 1945. Now, all Volunteers agreed to parents of the next wave of Volunteers. So, you have the First Wave being the parents of the Second Wave and the Second Wave being the parents of the third wave.

Many of you are part of the first wave. Now, the First Wave did not have Volunteer parents because you had not begun to incarnate when the First Wave came in.

Consequently it was decided that before the First Wave of Volunteers would come through parents who would have to be found for them amongst the native Terran people.

There was a big search for spiritually attuned native Terran parents who would agree, in their souls, to be the parents of these higher dimensional souls. It was determined that at least one of these parents would be that spiritual parent. It was not necessary for both, but it would have been nice for both, but it was not necessary.

So, there was a lot of research that went into this before any incarnations ever occurred. And, you, or we, were all part of that, and I say "we", as I include myself because I am a Volunteer team leader of one group of Volunteers. For instance, I assisted Gesanna in finding parents who would be suitable for her to incarnate through. And, we have to add, her ascended brother incarnated through them as well so he is also her Terran brother.

So, when we found her parents, she went first. We prepared her parents. With their permission we took them, while they slept, to a training center. These training centers were preparing these parents to host these higher dimensional souls that were coming into their lives. They were given precise information about how to host these souls and how to treat them. They were cautioned, very strongly, against any abuse of any kind, but to protect them. That didn't mean that both parents were going to do that.

At least one parent was going to be your protector. And they may have failed to some degree in their job, but here you are nonetheless.

The more unpleasant experiences that you have all had have ended up being knowledge that you can use to help others with. That became a vicarious thing in your lives, meaning that it was not intended that it be an experience that you had to have. It just came with the job, if you will. You knew coming in what the risks were! You signed up knowing that! You said, "OK, let's go for it."

You felt, and you knew that in the end it was all going to be worth it. The end isn't here yet, but when the end arrives, you will know it will have been worth it.

So you came here as Volunteers, but why are your siblings so different than you? Because they are either ascending souls or they are evolving natives of the planet. You will know the difference between an evolving Terran and an ascending Terran by the way they think, the way they speak, and the way they behave. Your scripts say, "By their fruits shall you know them". That is how you know the difference. You know the difference between an evolving Terran because they have absolutely no interest in ascending. They don't get it and they don't want to get it. They have no interest.

C: And because you're so different, they tend to shun you because they don't understand you. They think you're the weird one.

A: It's not that they're deliberately shunning. It's that they have nothing of themselves to relate with you. So, there's a natural resistance. A natural, shall we say, deflection of energy going on. And it's OK.

So, these souls, these siblings who are not ascending souls, they are evolving in their own way, but they are not ascending.

Now Volunteers who became influenced by the negative faction at any age, through drugs – what you call marijuana – alcohol, tobacco – the substances - these substances have the ability to numb you down in the nervous system so that you lose contact with your soul. You cannot draw upon soul memory to remember that you are a Volunteer, and what you came here to do.

Yet, in a small way they are still anchoring light, but they have diminished their ability to do that from what they originally came here as.

Some Volunteers were your ascended siblings before you incarnated into your Terran missions.

So, you see the dynamics that comes into play here with the Three Waves as they came in. The First Wave who came in through Terran parents, this is why you feel that at least one of your parents may be or was a Volunteer. They were Volunteers of the mission directly, but a volunteer indirectly by participating with this program as parents of Volunteers. So, in a sense, they are volunteers through participation but they are not Volunteers from the Upper Triad where you come from.

So, the Second Wave of Volunteers came in through parents who had already incarnated here. They had prepared the way for the Second Wave.

Regarding the souls who are ascending, the ascension event itself is going to be crescendoing from here on out. The pace of awakening for these souls is accelerating with the acceleration of time because time is connected to consciousness. You cannot have the acceleration of the one without the acceleration of the other unless the soul is not ready to partake of that experience. These souls will block it. And they do that for a purpose for themselves. And it's OK. It is OK that your siblings are not evolving to the point of ascending. They may appear to be not evolving at the moment.

It's OK that most of your family members are not ascending. They're not ready. And this has been expected. It was known.

Now, regarding the Council's search for proper parents for the First Wave of Volunteers, sometimes it just didn't work out that the parents that you had chosen to be born to were going to be the ones that were going to end up with you. Sometimes a last minute shift had to be made to another set of parents, because these souls, who are native to this planet, are free to change their mind about participating in this program. At the last minute, some parents changed their minds.

In such cases, which were not all that common, your initial set of parents, who you had expected to incarnate through, you had already imprinted yourself on their energy field. When the plan changed at the last minute you had to shift over to someone else and imprint yourself there, and the imprinting took a while to occur.

So, we want you to understand these 3 Waves so that there's a, shall we say, a consistency of truth that is being shared here. The 3 Waves consisting of the 25-year period was to allow for souls to incarnate incrementally, that you all would not incarnate right here on one day.

Throughout the first 25-year period, the First Wave would incarnate. They would grow up to the point where they were mature enough to be the parents of the Second Wave who would also incarnate incrementally. And the same with the Third Wave.

Now, the Third Wave of Volunteers, at this point in time, are reaching adulthood, if they haven't already gotten there yet. Those who have gotten there are starting to incarnate Terran souls who are mostly native to the planet – souls who want to come in and either experience the ascension of the planet that is going on, or to get together with other souls who are migrating to the new universe.

C: And these are starseeds that are coming in or crystal children?

A: Not too many of them. Not as many as has been claimed. These terms are an attempt by many people to justify the behavior of their children. So, they have produced these categories of definition, to define these children as advanced souls. Most are evolving souls. Some of them are ascending souls, and you will recognize those souls by their behavior that is kind, gentle, loving, and they have talents that will blow your mind. But they don't make a big deal of it. They are sweet children. They are sweet souls. They have no agenda. They are not disruptive in your life or the life of others. They're not disruptive wherever they go. The children who behave that way are the souls of children who are evolving within the field of the Lower Triad, and a lot of them have never before incarnated on this planet and they're finding it very difficult to deal with their new way of life.

There are a lot of them who are incarnating. But you cannot assign to them definitions that are not true because you do them a disservice by doing that – by telling them that they are something that they aren't.

So, this popular trend to justify the behavior of these souls who are coming in is doing a disservice to these children. They are to be understood for who they are and treated no differently.

But now you have a generation of parents who are afraid to discipline. This generation of parents who are resistant to disciplining their children came to be that way because they didn't like being disciplined as children themselves. So, they aren't going to discipline their children.

Consequently, the upper levels of your governments have made disciplinary policies based upon the desires of the parents.

This all came about as more and more children were becoming increasingly immersed in materiality. They had access to more material things than all of the generations before them. The more they were indulged by their parents in such things the more they were becoming the spoiled generation. To throw in discipline upon an already spoiled child results in resentment and a backlash of, "I don't like how you treated me. I'm never going to treat my children that way!" And so, it has come to be that way.

So now we have evolving Terran souls who are coming into these family situations where there's little to no discipline, so the child is having a heyday with it. They're being disruptive because they can.

But you will notice the vast difference of the souls coming in who are ascending. Those souls are the ones who are making a great difference on the planet as well. They are here as ascending souls influencing the Terran species to ascend.

There are ascending souls who are coming in who are, shall we say, highly compassionate. They are doing things that display sincere compassion to others.

And then there are those who you see in your media who, some of them are doing it because their parents are pushing them into it because they want their child to be a public figure.

So, again, you need to discern what is actually going on. And, yes, there are some wonderful ascending souls incarnating right now – they are compassionate. Some of them have exceptional talents, and we do not include in this description your academics. Any child can be born with a brain that can remember facts, figure, places, dates, and can add and subtract, and all of that. That is not the hallmark of an ascending soul.

From Contact to Ascension

An ascending soul will have other signs, and those signs will be actions of purity that touch people in the soul, uplifts and inspires them. These children are doing it naturally. It comes naturally. They're not trained for it. Their parents do not coach them into it. It is coming from their soul that has evolved to the point where it's ready to ascend. It has amassed enough information to know how to do what they are doing. And they are doing it well.

These are the children of the Third Wave who are ascending. We are excited about this. It is wonderful because your job on your planet, of anchoring light into this planet and then have it radiate outward has been a success! It has influenced, vicariously, a large number of souls who otherwise would be progressing along so well had this not occurred by our Volunteers being here.

These souls who are ascending in a large number, yet relatively small percentage-wise compared to your entire population, they are beautiful and they are ready for a new Home in the Upper Triad. And your job is to vicariously help them get there by being here on the planet and anchoring the light. As the planet gets there, these souls get there too. And so do you.

This is how you're going to go Home, from right here; from wherever you are on the planet.

There is one other thing that we would like to include here, that might be of help, and that is that when you incarnated here, there were specific energies that aligned at the time of your incarnation. They aligned in such a way that made it more advantageous, let's say, for you to be at this particular alignment on the planet – I'm not talking about right here but wherever that alignment occurs.

Once you discover where that is, and you set it up once you came here, by the timing of your birth, once you discover where that is, you are free to go there. It will activate your, let's say, portal, your personal portal to be opened a little bit more to receive more light. It's not that you have to be there or that it's going to make a lot of difference in your job here, but it will make a difference in your personal life to some degree.

So, you are free to be wherever you want to be on the planet, but there are specific areas that you might call a personal vortex that would enhance your life on the planet and in-turn enhance the job that you're doing here because you would be in a state of fulfillment and a state of joy because your life would be enriched.

So, if you want to discover where this is for yourself, you have people who are qualified to give you the information. From that information you will know where that point on the planet is, where your vortexes are.

Each vortex has a particular type of energy to it, and that vortex energy would enhance that part of your life. So, if you wanted to enhance a certain part of your life you would look for that vortex provided in this information and you could go there. That depends, too, on the country because there are rules that can make it difficult to be at that particular vortex. So, you would choose another one.

It has to do with what you call astrological energies configured at given points on this planet that relates to where other planets were at the moment that you were born. These points create that particular type of energy for you. These people who generate this information have the charts. They know where the planets were in alignment with this planet when you were born.

So if, let's say for instance, the planet Saturn, when you were born the planet was pointed right at the center of the Atlantic Ocean, you certainly wouldn't want to live there even though it would enhance your life and enrich it in a way that you would like it to.

None of the energies are totally "bad" for they all offer positive energies. It depends upon what you would be wanting more energy for in your life, such as Saturn's energy pushing you forward into your ascension. You can use that energy in positive ways.

So, if you look at your planet and you discover on your map where these points are when you were born, and you chose them to be there prior to your incarnation, then you'll be able to discover where your greatest potential lies that will enhance and enrich your personal life and in-turn your job all at the same time.

So, it would be something advantageous that you can do if you so choose to, but keep in mind that wherever you are on the planet you are still doing your job because you are Volunteers.

It enhances your personal life, what you have chosen to do here with your personal life. It's not crucial to find these personal vortex points on the planet in order to do your Volunteer job, but it will help enrich your personal experiences.

We are thrilled that you are doing what you came here to do, and you're doing it so well that all of our Volunteers who came onto this planet are, except for a few, still alive and doing their job so well. It has turned out to be a major success. It will continue to be so because now the ascension has sped up so that ascension is assured.

C: Is that why time seems to fly so fast?

A: It depends on whether you're ascending or whether you're not, you see. For those who are ascending, yes, time is speeding up because you are accelerating more quickly towards the Upper Triad and in the Upper Triad time has a much quicker vibrational rate of speed. The closer that the planet comes to entering into the Upper Triad the more that you will experience time speeding up. It's not going to quit.

When you get to the 5th dimension time will, as we say, "flip". You will flip into a whole other time-stream. It will be something you will have to get used to again...

D: Will that affect our eating habits, or the type of food we eat?

A: It's affecting everything in your life. You will notice – and these are signs of ascension – you will notice that you will be eating less. You will require eating less. You'll be getting hungry less. You will notice that when you eat too much you really pay for it. You will notice that your choice of foods is going to change. But, you're not forcing yourself to do that.
This is a difference between the evolving soul and the ascending soul. The evolving Terran has to force themselves to change their diet, force themselves to eat less, force themselves to do whatever it is they need to do to take care of themselves.

For those who are ascending, it is coming naturally. There is no forcing. It's an adjustment, yes. You have to adjust yourself to what is going on, and what the body now needs because it doesn't need what it needed before. The body is biologically ascending and as it ascends, its needs change. It's up to you to accommodate the change of the needs of the body. You will find your ability to sense – your 5 physical senses will change as well. Everything is going to get better because your body, biologically is, shall we say, reverting itself back to its ideal blueprint and in so doing it is releasing atoms.

There are no atoms in the Upper Triad. The Upper Triad is held together by a different substance for all bodies, things, planets, and nature. Atoms are particular to the Lower Triad. It is what makes the Lower Triad physical. It's what gives it matter.

The Lower Triad has a scaffolding that is based upon the energy within the Lower Triad. It is this scaffolding upon which the atoms adhere to make these forms and patterns that you recognize as your body and the things in your life.

The Upper Triad has a different scaffolding. Every dimension has scaffolding unique to its consciousness and energy configurations. And the scaffolding in the 5th dimension is a 5th dimensional scaffolding. Its scaffolding is somewhat different. It is not as dense and that which adheres to this scaffolding is a form of light that you would call sub-quantum energy. It adheres to its scaffolding to create the physicality that exists in that dimension. Each succeeding dimension is slightly less dense than the other. But from the 3rd dimension to the 5th dimension, there's a big difference. That is why there is a 4th dimension separating them.

So, as this planet ascends to the 5th dimension everything on this planet is losing density.

You have a concept here of the planet splitting itself into 2 or more versions of itself, and this is a misconception of what is actually going on. What is actually going on is that this physical planet is losing density and ascending in vibrational rate of speed to a higher frequency where it becomes no longer seen by those who are remaining in the 3rd dimension of the Lower Triad.

Now, for those who are remaining in the Lower Triad, what is happening is that as the physical planet is ascending the souls who are remaining in the Lower Triad are having their own experience of the planet. They are experiencing an event in the reverse of what is happening as you are ascending. They are, shall we say, dematerializing but in the opposite way.

What they recognize as the planet becomes de-densified to the point where it matches the vibrational rate of speed of where your deceased are. Your deceased are not in the 4th dimension. No one dwells there. It is 'time' and 'portals'. They go back into the 2nd dimension, which has what you would call a 2nd level density. So the planet, for these non-ascending souls, as the Lower Triad is folding up, the planet for them is losing its scaffolding, but it's not loosing its, shall we say, blueprint. It has this level of blueprint created by the minds of those who are not ascending, but the ideal blueprint is going with the planet as it is ascending. So, the evolving souls who are not ascending have their own concept of the planet and collectively they have a, shall we say, a psychological blueprint of the planet, so that, for them, as their version of the planet is descending into the 2nd density they are meeting up with the souls who are there who have been deceased. All of a sudden, there's a great resurrection going on! And these deceased souls are appearing on their version of the planet. "Oh my goodness! The ancient scriptures must have been right. They are resurrecting!"

This is what your ancient scripts were talking about! It's not that the souls who are dead all of a sudden jump into 3rd density physicality again, it's that this version of the planet is going backwards to meet up with them, while those who are ascending are going forward and disappearing! "Where did they go? Oh my goodness, we lost some and gained some! What's going on?"

We shall bring this session to a close now. We have enjoyed this interlude with you. We look forward to more to come. We shall be with you and return again soon. We will say, that is all for now.

I am An T'na of the Intergalactic Board of Council

Session 002 – Addendum A
The Increase of Do-Gooders in an Increasingly Materialistic World

Q: An T'na, in Session 2 you said you might further clarify why it is that a lot of the children being born now are, as you said, being prompted by their parents to be what we would call "do-gooders". Would you please speak more on this matter?

A: Yes. We wish you to be aware that there is a relatively new trend developing in your more recent generations who have been subtly funneled, by your negative factions, into being more material oriented in your focuses of everyday life. Materiality is gradually replacing spirituality, including religion, as the foundation upon which everyday life is being engaged. This is an agenda for the mind and all-things-material are the external tools being used to funnel you ever deeper into this insidious agenda.

With this comes an increasing focus on the world of fame and glory that is being increasingly promoted by your media. This hyped-up focus is integrated with the material existence because it engages, what you refer to as, the altered ego into directions of thought and desires, thus behaviors, that are rooted in the acquisition of the stimulations of the ego as it attempts to boost itself up in its unnatural world so as to continue its survival through this artificial means.

We are now seeing on your planet, especially in your country, an increase of parents who are nudging their children into certain directions where the child exhibits the least bit of talent or skill, even beauty. The parents then stimulate their children into feeling special, prompting the child to the level of putting him or her onto a public stage that in some way will bring attention to the child, thus to the parents, and if it goes far enough, then the child is conveyed along to fame, then glory, and the parents benefit from that situation.

From Contact to Ascension

In your mainstream populace there is an ever-increasing sense of competition amongst one another, however subconsciously it may be, yet it is very real nonetheless, that is being fed by the increasing desire for materiality in order to obtain personal material stability through fame and glory of one sort or another, at one level or another. It pays very well if you can get into the upper levels of that way of existence and there is a lot of competition for this.

This increasing desire for materiality is originating with those who are controlling your planet, engaging it as a vicarious means to cut you off from your souls. They understand how this entrapment works in the field of psychology so they are using it against all Terrans, and many succumb to the trap.

This negatively orchestrated and carefully controlled instilling of your populace's desires for materiality is gaining strength. It is spreading to other countries around the world, even amongst more primitive cultures who are being unwittingly indoctrinated into desiring materiality as the preferred way of life.

Materiality is quickly becoming the new religion, so to speak, on your planet. The more your controllers can remove spirituality from everyone and replace it with materiality, the less you know who you truly are, and the less you desire to know who you are. Your focus of desire is being deliberately shifted onto being dominantly set on satisfying yourselves with the latest gadgets and things that your money can buy from your controllers who keep producing more and more stuff for you to consume.

Non-ascending souls are being trapped by this insidious effort to have control over their souls, for if the cabal can control them through the shutting-down of their access to their souls, then they have them right where they want them – not merely enslaved unto their controllers, but enslaved as automatons to them.
\What you call your industrial age was the beginning of this materialistic agenda, their objective of which is "control through

circumventing the soul", and the menacing creators of this agenda have honed it to a fine point that can cut through the common sense part of your brain, by-passing common sense with specific psychological processes employed against you, and you never know the difference unless you are evolved to the point of being aware of what they are actually doing. But most Terrans are not that evolved yet, and so they are caught up in the frenzy of feeding off of the dry lifeless bones that the negative factions are connivingly defining for you as 'life'; "This is what life is, it's the way life is. This is who you are. Didn't you know that?"

They are regressing you back to your aggressive fight-or-flight stage of existence, but now it is being engaged in a very sophisticated manner compared to your more primitive ways so long ago. It is the same behavior recycled into another disguise designed to keep you entrapped as slaves. So unless you are an evolving ascending soul, then you are out of the loop of consciously realizing what is actually going on so you can then resist it, walk away from it, so you do not fall prey to its lethal grip as it squeezes more and more real life out of you.

If you understand what is going on with this materialist agenda, then you understand why there is an increasing trend amongst parents, and some children themselves, to promote their children into fame and glory, because for them it means survival.

Now, we are not saying that this is the rule, yet, amongst all parents and all children, but it is a fast growing trend which is well on its way to becoming a pathological plague on your planet.

Yet, it is all OK because this is the path that non-ascending souls are collectively choosing as a means of sustaining themselves on their chosen journey of migrating to the new universe.

We bring this to your attention so that you are not fooled by the media-hyped appearances of children being promoted, either by themselves or by their parents, to positions of fame and glory as a sign that they are all advanced or ascending souls. We wish you to understand that most of them are non-ascending souls who are migrating to the new universe, while a smaller number of these children are ascending with this universe.

You need to discern the difference so you are not amongst those who are being duped into believing that all or most of the children being born now are somehow highly evolved ascending souls when that is simply not the case. A few are. Most aren't.

There is also a growing trend to categorize the unruly children into definitions that place them into concepts of spiritual specialness and exceptionality, of divinity, is all part of the same pathology of this unfolding agenda.

As we briefly mentioned previously, those concepts of indigo, rainbow, crystal, and who-knows-what-else-next, children, these labels are covertly and connivingly being handed to you on silver platters by what you could call "spiritual moles" who are actually members of the negative factions controlling the unfolding of their materialist agenda that is gaining increasing power over the people that it entraps.

Part of this agenda is to convince the populace that these children, who are disruptive, rude and unkind, are somehow special and divine when in-fact they are merely part of the non-ascending masses that is being inculcated into a new form of control. Give them a new divine spiritual definition and you have the attention of the adults around them, coupled with their efforts to promote their children as such, which in-turn merely strengthens the pathology behind it. So, you see the insidiousness of what is transpiring here.

We wish to leave you with the reassurance that there are ascending souls incarnating now who are authentically compassionate souls, who require no training, no promotion, yet who have innate talents which their souls are sharing with other souls around them that inspires and uplifts all souls whom they touch. Their souls are promoting a new and higher way of life that has nothing to do with the academics and intellectuality of what you term as education or religion. Although they have a certain allure to them, their innate disposition is unassuming, unpretentious, and quiet. They are sweet, kind, gentle, loving, considerate souls. You will know who these souls are by the fruits of their lives. In comparison, they are light-years evolved beyond those souls whom your negative factions are promoting, per their agenda, as evolved, special and divine. These cabal-promoted children are being used as the wool being pulled over your eyes, so to speak, so you do not recognize the truly evolved souls who are a genuine light to others because that light is a threat to the negative faction's materialist agenda. It's all part of their strategy to keep you from seeing and realizing who you truly are.

We hope this has brought forth clarity on the matter.
That is all for now. Be well and happy.

I am An T'na of the Intergalactic Board of Council

From Contact to Ascension

IBOC COMMUNIQUÉ

Session 003

Why Our Volunteers Are On Terra, With Regard to Frequency-Jamming Devices, Why Staying Connected to the Planet is Essential

C & D = Session Facilitators   A = An T'na   Q = Question

A: Good evening. On behalf of the Intergalactic Board of Council, we are glad to join you again.

C & D: Good Evening. We're glad to have you with us again. We have a list of questions for you.

A: Yes. You may read the first one on the list and we'll go from there.

C: Clarify what it is to be a Volunteer - what is the nature of the Volunteer, and how does this relate to where they come from?

A: We will begin by reiterating that all our Volunteers originate from what we are calling the Upper Triad. The reason for that is because the souls of these Volunteers have already evolved to a higher vibrational state of being.

Keeping that in mind, it was determined by the Councils who are participating in this mission of ascending planets to the Upper Triad, that what was required in order to help a planet ascend, especially this one, would be vibrational frequencies higher than those that are natural to the Lower Triad and thus to the planet itself. That meant that the needed higher energy would have to come from the Upper Triad. It was determined that ascended souls from the Upper Triad would be capable of holding that higher energy onto the planets while they are dwelling thereon.

From Contact to Ascension

We have previously discussed, in-part, the presence of our Volunteers on this planet, and we will now offer further clarifications on this matter.

Of all the planets that are ascending, this one is particularly difficult. By saying this, we do not mean only to the planet itself, but also those Terrans who are endeavoring to ascend themselves, for the human situation here is unlike the situations of humans on the other ascending planets. While those of other planets have their own issues to deal with in order to accomplish their ascension event on their respective planets, this planet is the one that is most troubled by a large negative group of souls. This planet is where these souls have gathered in greatest numbers, and they have done so because for them there is, as you say, strength in numbers – or so they believe is the key to complete ownership of the souls of this planet unto themselves.

Now, while we have stated that all our Volunteers incarnated upon each planet to which they have been assigned, for the specific purpose of assisting the planet itself to ascend, on your planet in particular there exists a much greater need for bringing in a vaster amount of light-energy to the planet.

In the planning stage of this mission, this critical situation was well understood by all our Volunteers, as well as by all the Councils who had determined that it was necessary to have a much larger number of Volunteers stationed on this planet than on any of the other ascending planets.

We have discussed the fact that your planet and its Terran inhabitants, both, are being plagued by the negative factions who have gathered here in large numbers.

C: Are these negative factions composed strictly of Terrans, or are some of them extraterrestrials?

A: They are a combination of both. There is a large faction of unevolved Terran leaders who have given themselves over to being the appointed and, you might say, "anointed priests", who carry out the bidding and commands of their self-aggrandizing extraterrestrial overlords. Some of these leaders are aware of their extraterrestrial overlords while some of them aren't, but either way, the orders they receive and are expected to carry out remains the same. Much of it is done unconsciously as they are vibrationally attuned to their puppet masters.

You must understand that extraterrestrials of various kinds have been visiting your planet for a very long time. Prior to being merely visitors here, some extraterrestrials resided here, with this planet as but one of their residents throughout this and other galaxies. Of those who were formerly long-term residents, they were benevolent Beings who cared for themselves, one another and the planet.

Regardless of that though, there have always been squabbles over who owns, thus resides, on this planet. Long ago, there was an uprising between native Terrans and their non-Terran neighbors to where the native Terrans drove away the extraterrestrial Beings who then returned to their other homes in other places, galactic and intergalactic.

Long story short, as you would say, prior to a much more recent invasion – and we shall call it that since that is what it is – for a long time the native Terrans dwelt on this planet most often, but not always, amongst themselves. Before the more recent invasion, other visiting non-Terran Beings came and went freely but they didn't reside here. This history has been handed down through many of your own cultures as fact, but in more recent times you have been told to believe it as merely myth, and as the fantasies of primitive minds of yore making up campfire stories, and that view is the lie which they want you to accept as "fact".

From Contact to Ascension

The current invasion that we speak of occurred in a very subtle manner so that it has been easy for your leaders to hide the truth of it from you.

The most recent visitors came to this planet as two more commonly known groups of extraterrestrials.

Non-contact visitations by extraterrestrials were occurring for many decades, unfolding their observation stage of the invasion. We must add that between one another there have been non-terrestrial squabbles over who would become the dominant influence in the destiny of you and your planet. Eventually it came down to two main groups, and a lesser-known group, publicly speaking.

In the early 1950s, both groups made physical contact with your leaders. You can get more information about this from your books that focus on this matter.

But as a brief recap here with regard to your question, the benevolent Beings of these two groups of extraterrestrials came here and made contact with your leading governments of that time. Their generous objective was to freely offer their assistance to all Terrans, equally, for the purpose of helping the planet ascend, which would also assist Terrans to ascend. This compassionate group of extraterrestrials knew, even at that time, about the coming event of the Lower Triad folding-up. So, out of love and concern for their fellow Terran siblings, they went to your planet in a gesture of good will so as to help with the ascension event. In exchange for offering their assistance, the stipulation was that all weapons had to be destroyed so that peace would reign throughout the planet within a framework of love and altruistic cooperation. Otherwise ascension could not occur.

But, the other group of extraterrestrials, greedy and self-aggrandizing in nature, came here at about the same time, contacting the same country's leaders, but their miserly objective was to obtain natural resources from your planet, as well as collect DNA from your bodies and from some of your animals and plants. All of these substances would be used to fulfill their own agendas, part of which has to do with them trying to genetically modify themselves. And, in exchange for obtaining these resources, this particular group of extraterrestrials offered to the leaders of your planet some, but not all, knowledge of their own exotic technologies which, your leaders were told, could be exploited for purposes of war.

At a later time we shall elaborate more about why these extraterrestrials wanted your DNA. But for now we will say that from one simple look at your planet it is easy to conclude which offer your leaders chose to destine themselves and you into.

Your wellbeing, and that of the planet, and the opportunity of assistance to ascend, was duly sold-out by your leaders for a bit of knowledge about how to make better war weapons, as well as for the constant manufacturing of ever-increasingly more sophisticated gadgets and devices and goods that continually hold your focus of attention, thereby feeding your desires for the acquisition of more material stuff, thereby spending more and more money to acquire them. This focus of attention and conduct by you serves as an ongoing distraction from the negative faction's sinister motives, behavior, and agendas.

The 1950s era, in particular, is when yet another greedy group of extraterrestrials literally moved in, in-earnest, assuming the role of overlord to any Terran leader who was determined to benefit from such a position in life. But this is a very malevolent group that you do not hear much about, and they want to keep it that way.

These extraterrestrial overlords reside in underground facilities on your planet, as well as on their orbiting ships, some of which are stationed and hidden from telescopic view on the backside of your moon, and a few reactivated bases on the planet you call Mars.

From Contact to Ascension

Had your leaders chosen to accept the offer of the benevolent extraterrestrial Beings to assist with the ascension event of your planet and all on it, your lives would be very different right now from the way they have come to be.

Yours is the only planet whose leaders rejected the benevolent Beings' offers of assistance for ascension. All the other ascending planets and their inhabitants accepted it; consequently they are way ahead of this one. A few of them have already, most recently, made the ascension. And of the inhabitants of those planets who were not ready to ascend, they were willingly relocated to other planets that reside near the womb of the new universe. All of these souls are eagerly awaiting their new adventures as creators and technicians of the new universe. So, everyone is happy.

We wish we could say the same thing for the inhabitants this planet, but we cannot. All of our Volunteers, who chose to reside on this particular planet, understood the unusual and extreme situation that was developing once the leaders chose to accept the malevolent extraterrestrials offer. This is one reason why, Volunteers, your loved ones in the Upper Triad have been so tremendously concerned for you. Can you blame them?

The attempts of this now-well-established negative faction, currently a combination of Terrans and extraterrestrials working covertly together, has resulted in the creation of such technologies that are specifically designed to prevent all ascending Terrans brains from activating the areas that are responsible for accessing and processing higher frequencies.

This exotic extraterrestrial technology is based in the use of ultra-high, or super- sonic vibrations that interfere with this part of the brain's functions.

This particular sound frequency, that you cannot hear, first went online, so to speak, in a crude manner, in the 1960s, and that is an above-above-top-secret purpose for the launching of so many satellites around your planet – to create a planet-wide transceiver relay system for these frequencies. You also have them based on land with HAARP array technology, and which is the covert purpose of every cell phone tower which functions as on-the-ground relay systems for the larger array and orbital systems.

Is it any wonder, then, that cell phones, and all their spin-off devices, have pushed their way into your lives so quickly, coming to be in widespread use in all industrialized regions, and which is spreading to every other area of the planet? You cannot use the phones and other related devices without a tower nearby. So, as you would say, do the math.

Now, you must understand that these frequencies are geared to target the Terran brain, specifically, and they target a specific area of it, because each part of the brain aligns with different frequencies.

The extraterrestrials who have intently been studying your physiology since the 1940s, did extensive research on how your brain functions with the objective being able to have, eventually, absolute control over the degree to which you are able to "know thyself" – which, in this case, is to not allow you to go beyond the level of the intellect for academic purposes relative to being a slave to consumerism.

Over time this higher brain control, through frequency-jamming technology, has, within your past decade, been refined to the point where the higher functioning area of the Terran brain is becoming incapable of accessing and processing the higher frequencies that are all around you, and that are coming from the core of your planet and from your sun.

Now remember, we are speaking of the brain being affected. Keep that in mind.

From Contact to Ascension

Have you noticed, looking over the past decade, that for the most part people stopped progressing so quickly in their attempts to reach higher states of consciousness – try as they might to do so? They are finding that it simply isn't working as well as it used to just a few years before.

In an endeavor to "jumpstart" themselves, so to speak, they are hopping and shopping all over the place from one approach to another, from one external procedure to another, from one electronic apparatus to another, from one product to another – which has become yet another means of consumerism. There's big money in those expensive devices and products.

Perhaps now you know why they aren't working so well any more – they aren't meant to work for the purposes you have in mind for them. If they did work then why are you still here?

We are not saying that the devices and products themselves alone are at-fault, but your brains are becoming increasingly incapable of processing the vibrations coming from those things.

Also, we are not saying that these things do not help or assist the brains of unevolving Terrans for there can be some benefit obtained to these weaker vibrating brain areas.

But for Ascending Souls, these methods are quickly becoming obsolete, outmoded, and therefore futile endeavors.

So, what's an ascending Terran to do? Our advice, as we have stated before, is to remain attuned to your planet, for as you do, upon the ascension of the planet, you will be hooked into her soul and she will pull you Home with her. Like a transceiver, your planet is receiving and transmitting an ascension signal that your body harmoniously resonates with, naturally...but it is your mind, in particular your so-called altered ego, which is in your own way of allowing your body to access and process her signals that you are immersed in.

Your history tells of many cultures that were once vibrationally attuned to the planet through nature; and of spiritual groups who, through time-tested research, employed methods and ways of life that assisted them in staying tuned to the planet and to all of nature.

We suggest that you do some personal research about this topic and find the particular culture and spiritual focus that resonates with yourself the most, then emulate their ways as best and as fully as you can, adapting it to your desire and needs. Make it a way of life for yourself and you alone…in other words, do not impose it upon anyone else. If others resonate with it then fine, share in it with them.

Engaging yourselves in these time-proven focuses and actions that specifically attune, and keeps you attuned to the planet and its ascension signal is the best thing you can do for now in order to circumvent the effects of the frequency-blocking technology. It is your intention and actions of connecting and remaining connected to the planet herself that is going to lock you into her ascension Home.

In other words, you need nothing more than the planet that is right under your feet.

C: Are we Volunteers being affected by this frequency-jamming technology too, and if so what can we do? And how is it affecting our ability to do our job here?

A: As Volunteers originating from the Upper Triad, you are not as adversely affected by this technology, as are the Terrans who are trying to ascend. It is preventing Ascending Souls from progressing any higher through the use of the brain's capacities when using these external things.

As we have stated before, the manner by which our Volunteers are receiving the light-energy, that you are anchoring into the planet, comes in through your soul, not through your brain.

From Contact to Ascension

The soul is a far more spiritually sophisticated thus complicated component than the brain and the technological devices created for brain-mind control. Consequently, the creation of artificial and practical means of soul control, to any degree of success and accuracy, have all failed. That is why your presence on the planet has continued in spite of the frequency-jamming devices targeted at the brain.

That said, our Volunteers do have a Terran brain too. Have you noticed that you do not seem to be advancing much in your own attempts to generate accomplishment through your use of various practices, techniques, devices, and so on, for engaging your psychic powers to any degree of success? The part of the brain that houses one's psychic powers is aligned with the higher frequencies that the frequency-jamming devices are targeting in that area of your brain.

That is not to say that your psychic abilities cannot activate spontaneously at all, for they will activate when one or another local satellite and cell phone devices go down due either to maintenance issues or from storms, earthquakes, and such, interfering with their signal-relay transmissions.

During these times you will notice a brief phase of psychic activity, usually occurring spontaneously such as lucid dreaming, precognition, premonitions, and so on, but it will be only temporary until the signals go back online. It does not stay offline long enough for you to make any real progress with deliberately activating your psychic powers – just long enough to remind you that it is still there.

For non-ascending souls, they don't notice anything one way or the other since most of them do not give credence to such powers in the first place. Their skepticism and doubt is enough to keep the higher functioning part of their brains from activating.

Now, back to your negative faction's intentions; by virtue of the benevolent Beings' meetings with your Terran leaders, the Beings enlightened your leaders as to what the cosmic situation was, explaining that the universe is folding-up its Lower Triad, and that the best way to deal with this inescapable event would be to ascend the planet and as many souls on it as possible. Your leaders were instructed in this matter, how it worked, why it was occurring, and what the best solution was for the coming occurrence, reassuring them that there was enough time to prepare the planet and its inhabitants for the ascension event, or for migrating to the new universe, per each soul's evolutionary need.

We tell you about this because it illustrates why your leaders have gone to such length to create the frequency-jamming devices, which has been to prevent as many souls as possible from ascending. They knew long ago about the folding-up of the Lower Triad and the ascension of the planet. They also knew about the new universe that is being created, and that any soul who chooses to do so can migrate to that place as their next adventure in evolution. They knew that whichever path they and you choose, all will be well with you and everyone else.

Amongst themselves, the fear-ridden and self-aggrandizing leaders deliberated over which offering would benefit themselves the most.

In that many of these leaders were of corporate standing, and many others were of military standing, the collective mindset of the groups in each country – which was much larger in numbers than most give credit for being – could not see past the almighty dollar signs and the almighty barrel of a gun.

The overall prevailing fear of both types of mindsets concluded that they had nothing to lose by choosing to migrate to the new universe and, while they were at it, take as many souls with them as they possibly could.

In the meantime, they would receive knowledge from the malevolent extraterrestrials for making greater weapons of mass destruction, which appealed to the military minds, and for making more and better consumer products to profit from, which appealed to the corporate minds. And, in the meantime, if no such events as described to them by the benevolent Beings ever occurred, then they would still hold the world in their own hands. Why gamble it all away by choosing to trust in the benevolent Beings offering? By accepting the malevolent extraterrestrials offer, either way they would win – so far as they could see.

This is why you are in the mess you are now in on your planet. Your leaders gambled with your personal destiny and chose the one that they wanted for themselves.

But they did not understand that other plans were afoot for this planet and all of its Ascending Souls – an alternative strategy was, unbeknownst to them, being created by Ascended Beings in the higher dimensions of reality.

This is why our Volunteers are on this planet in such large numbers – to counteract the negative factions' efforts to prevent as many souls as possible from ascending.

Now you understand why you are having such a difficult time making progress with personally activating and controlling your higher powers, deliberately.

Now you understand why connecting to and remaining connected to the planet, through nature, is your ticket Home as you ride the planet to her new place of residence in the Upper Triad.

Again, we suggest that you do your own research to discover which mode of connecting to the planet is most aligned with you, and make it a part of your daily routine. It is your soul connecting to the planet's soul that locks you into her ascension Home.

This is what your leaders did not anticipate happening. They did not understand that blocking your brain's higher functions is only one avenue of ascending under this particular situation when the planet itself is ascending.

When your soul connects to the planet's soul, then you are beyond their ability to prevent you from ascending with the planet. Were the planet not ascending, and you were endeavoring to do so on your own power, then you would have a problem. But you're not doing it on your own, so utilize the spiritual manner that we have suggested and your ascension will still occur.

This goes for our Volunteers as well for it is your job to remain connected to the planet until the job is done. Develop a conscious connection with the planet, even though your souls have you connected unconsciously.

Your planetary controllers cannot prevent you from developing this soul-to-soul connection with your planet. They cannot control it. They cannot take it away from you. But it is purely up to you to make the connection and maintain it.

Now, we will shift our focus upon the identity and nature of our Volunteers themselves, and how you can know the difference from who you have thought you were.

Because all our Volunteers, as souls, originate from the Upper Triad, it means that these souls have already ascended, eons ago, above and beyond the Lower Triad. It means that these souls are already free of what you call karma – and that's another topic of discussion for another time.

Because we, of Intergalactic Board of Council, exist in the Upper Triad, we know that these Volunteer souls are what you would consider pure in their nature – they have no issues or problems or hang-ups or any such contradicting vibrations within them that would obstruct or interfere with their higher vibrations. The reason for that is because once you have ascended from the Lower Triad into the Upper Triad, you are then out of that which is the triad of duality, of opposites. We shall explain.

When our Volunteers chose to make their journey back into the Lower Triad, they knew that their souls could hold the higher energy onto and within the planet. They also knew that while their souls were doing that job, that upon incarnating into the Lower Triad their souls' memories of who they truly are and why they are on their planet would not be consciously retained. That is a particular phenomenon of the Lower Triad as a function of duality.

The Volunteers, when they incarnated onto their respective planets, were born without the memory that they are Volunteers, their souls are still capable of holding the light onto the planet – it does not require that the Volunteer consciously remember who they are in order to hold the light on the planet. It simply requires their presence, having the soul on the planet in a physical form that is a vibrational match to that of the planets'.

Consequently, once they began to grow older with years they became indoctrinated into the perspectives, beliefs, thinking, and the behavior of their fellow native Terrans. It could not be helped. It was just the way it was, yet this created a struggle concerning their identity, because, on the one hand, the more they grew and matured, the more they became aware that they had an identity other than the one which they had been immersed into on the planet.

Now, some of our Volunteers are more awake and aware of who they truly are than others are, and it is for this reason that we deliver this information at this time – to help with the awakening and remembering of all of our Volunteers.

Because the native Terrans who are evolving on the planet have their own perspectives, thinking, and beliefs about what life is for them, they do not resonate with our Volunteers as they become more and more aware that they have another identity, another perspective on life that it is wholly unique so that it has nothing to do with the Terrans' identity and perspectives. It has nothing to do with Terran beliefs. It has nothing to do with Terran behavior.

So, our Volunteers are waking up and realizing what it means to be a Volunteer in this mission. What they need to understand, though, is that within the nature of the Upper Triad from where they came, which still exists within their souls, the soul has no tendencies or propensities to think and be and live like a Terran. Their soul has none of that. Yet the conscious mind – there is a part of it that you call the altered ego that has developed since you were born – the conscious mind is that part of you that is contradicting and impeding your true identity and the true nature of your being as an Ascended Being.

The altered ego is a repository of information that you have adopted and collected over time from the Terrans around you who are telling you who you are, who are defining you for you, who are giving you the roles that, according to them, you are supposed to play. And so without question, most of our Volunteers bought it all, yet their soul is saying something very different within them. So, our Volunteers have been in a kind of internal struggle of identity and manner of being.

Now the time has come for you to recognize your true identity and your true nature. The reason for that is not that you have to do so in order to anchor the light any more than you did when you were born here, but it is that when you become consciously aware of who and what you truly are and why you're here, that you can then consciously cooperate with your light-anchoring job, and deliberately do your job that in-turn enhances the effect of the light that is coming into you for the improvement of your personal life.

It's sort of like, the light that you brought in with you is being hosed into the planet, possessing the amount necessary, as it is flowing through you to do, that job effectively. But being conscious of it puts you in the place of being the one who can literally turn up the volume of the flow – not that you have to do that in order to do your job effectively, but that doing so enhances not only the light going into the planet but it also enhances your personal life as well.

So, we would like you to understand that all of our Volunteers in their souls, have no, what you call, issues. The issues that you believe you have, that you have thought were yours, you merely adopted them from those around you and made them yours. But they did not originate from your soul therefore they are not who you are. Those beliefs belong to another world that is not your world. They belong to another species, even though you're in the Terran bodies.

Terran souls are evolving a species as well as themselves as souls, and because you're in one of their bodies you do have cellular memory of the species as well. But that memory is not who you are, nor is it your true nature.

We want you to understand that because our Volunteers, in their souls, are attuned vibrationally to the Upper Triad, there is a level of power within you that is not commonly available to the native Terran souls on the planet. The ascending Terrans are increasingly coming in to it for themselves, but you have it fully in the soul already. It has just been suppressed. When this power of true identity and nature fully integrates with your conscious mind, in your brain, it can do some very phenomenal things.

It can, for instance, draw information from the soul of another Being on the planet and connect with that soul and begin to understand that soul and what it has gone through, who it is. That information, then, is brought back to you, the Volunteer, and you "remember" that information even though it is not yours.

Many of our Volunteers are misinterpreting that information, retrieved from the memory held in other souls, as pertaining to themselves in some way; that it must mean that the information they accessed occurred through their own personal experience, from a past lifetime on this planet. But we're telling you that it did not – not as your past lifetime because as Ascended Beings you have been out of the Lower Triad loop for a very long time, from all that is going on on this planet. Most of our Volunteers have never even been here before so they have no past lifetime memories of their own on this planet.

Other Volunteers misinterpret the experiences, accessed from another soul, in the sense that they are somehow now either possessed by that soul, or that they are a "walk-in" to the body.

But that is not the case for our Volunteers, because when you incarnated here on this planet as a Volunteer you remain, always, just that. You are a Volunteer for the duration. No soul swapping, no body snatching occurs, no possessions occur. Your identity does not change, your soul does not change, and if you think it has then that is a belief you have adopted from the native Terrans around you and live within the confines of that illusion.

We wish you to understand that your job was not to come here as a Volunteer and then abandon your post and allow someone else to come in and take over your embodiment, or your life, or swap places with one another, or allow yourselves to be possessed in any way. That's not the way that the Volunteer program itself, nor you as an Ascended Being, works.

When you came here, you did so knowing full well who you are and you knew what your job is. You knew that to abandon your job for any reason would be paramount to abandoning your mission of holding the light here on the planet.

Now, what we are saying is that even though your soul is of the Upper Triad, your consciousness may not be aware of that fact so that your personal lives do not reflect it. You see?

When your consciousness becomes aware of that fact, then everything fits together. It all aligns and your power returns, your memories from your soul will, what you could say, upload into the conscious-brain-mind so you begin to understand how it all works as a Volunteer.

You have no issues in the soul; you did not come here with any issues. You did not come here with any kind of karmic problems in the soul to work out. Your souls were pure. You're still pure in your soul. It is the conscious mind that has adopted the concepts, beliefs, attitudes and behaviors from the native Terrans around you that has, in-turn, caused you to create an experience of it for yourself, even though those experiences are, for you, completely illusion-based. That doesn't mean that it is true, of you. It means that you are living a Terran-based misidentification of who you really are.

D: So there is a conflict between the original soul or blueprint, and what our physical body is – it's like two different things?

A: No. The physical body has its own ideal blueprint and it was created by your soul, so those two parts of yourself are in complete harmony with one another. Your blueprint and your soul are in harmony. So the body that you have, which you came in with, that was based upon that blueprint, it is the same body-blueprint that you have now except that the body, not the blueprint, has been altered from the blueprint because of your immersion into the Lower Triad beliefs of the native Terrans. This has created the health issues because the beliefs of the native Terrans are based in duality of health and unhealthy, as well as rich/poor, have/have-not – all of that.

So as long as you believe that the Lower Triad's nature of duality is who you are, that it identifies who you are, and you relate to it, then you will live that as an illusion of who you are not; you will experience it regardless of your soul knowing otherwise.

The purpose for this topic of discussion is to help clear up all of this so that you can pull yourself out of your adopted Terran identity and become who you truly are. When you do that then you are in conscious alignment with your soul, and then you are in conscious alignment with your body's ideal blueprint, and then you are in conscious alignment with your power. So it all lines up. You see?

But you cannot line it up until you get rid of your adopted baggage, so to speak, of all Terran-based beliefs. As ascended souls from the Upper Triad, they are not yours. You have mistakenly taken them on, and that is very understandable given your situation.

Our oracle did the same thing. Only recently has she awakened to her true identity and what it means to be a Volunteer. She sort of knew what that was, but then she realized that her identity as a Volunteer is something very different in nature from her misidentity as a Terran. When she began to examine the difference between the two, she saw that it was like the difference between day and night.

The identity of the Terran is of a 3rd dimensional understanding that is based in duality. The identity of the Volunteer soul is of a 5th dimensional identity that is based in what we call the Singularity. Consequently the two natures are very, very different from one another, like day and night. When you start examining that fact for yourself, you will clearly see it.

When you start questioning your own identity and asking yourself, "Is this really me, or is this something I adopted from those around me who, because they didn't know I am an ascended Volunteer, told me that's who I am and what I should do?" They have had no idea what a Volunteer is so how could they inform you to know and be and do otherwise?

C: So, where did the Volunteers come from? Where is the higher dimension or the 5th dimension?

A: The 5th dimension is part of the Upper Triad, and the Upper Triad itself exists everywhere around you, throughout the universe, and so does the 3rd dimension as it is part of the Lower Triad. You have to understand that all dimensions and all Triads – and there are 3 triads, each Triad being composed of 3 dimensions – they are superimposed one upon the other. It's like ghostly images that can walk through one another and you never know it.

The 3rd dimension exists throughout the entire universe, just as the entire Lower Triad does. And the Upper Triad exists throughout the entire universe, as well as the 5th dimension, and the 6th, and so on. The difference between them is in the energy frequencies that configure thus dominates each of the Triads.

As we have discussed before, the particular energies that compose the Lower Triad are separated from the particular energies that compose the Upper Triad by a 4th dimensional barrier that protects the energies of each Triad from mixing together and losing their coherency within that Triad. It's a complex understanding that gets deep into meta-quantum physics. Need we say more? We're not here to give you a science lesson but to help you remember, understand and cooperate with your true identity and purpose here so that the true nature of your Being, as an Ascended Being, can begin to be resurrected from your souls.

Specifically which dimension you originated from within the Upper Triad depends upon the information coming from your own soul, which possesses that information. If you want to know it and understand it, just request that information to come forth from your soul, then listen to and heed its response.

The Upper Triad, as we discussed before, consists of planets that have been ascended, and it consists of all the nature on those planets. And the Upper Triad consists of ascended suns and moons, just like you have here in the Lower Triad, except that these objects in the Upper Triad are not based in duality, what we would call opposites in nature, and they have no atomic basis. They are based in the Singularity that constructs a non-atomic physicality so that all life in the Upper Triad is always going forward into a refinement and an enhancement of itself.

That is a major difference from what exists in the Lower Triad where you have duality and atomic structure based in life and no-life. You have the opposites in the physical level because you have the opposites in consciousness that we prefer to call duality. The opposites in nature, we call organic opposites. We distinguish between the duality in consciousness and the organic opposites in nature.

These differing states of being do not exist in the Upper Triad, so when you came from there, to your planet here, you came from a beautiful place of existence that's always going forward, that never reverses itself, that never opposes itself, and your soul is still of that nature – it hasn't gone anywhere.

The Upper Triad consists of dimensions 5, 6, and 7. You were of a 7th level of understanding. So, that's what that means when they said, 7th heaven. They were simply using a different word for the same thing.

All of our Volunteers long to return Home, regardless of where they originate from in the Upper Triad. They all long to return Home, and that longing becomes stronger and more intense as they increasingly remember who they truly are. Yet they increasingly remember why they are here, that they have a job to do, which in-turn makes remaining here on the planet a bit easier to deal with.

Part of what we're trying to clear up here, is the fact that none of our Volunteers have any karmic issues to clear up with one another. You do not have any issues with one another that you incarnated with. You did not come here with such a need in your souls; no hang-ups or unfinished business because you came here pure and free of all that karmic stuff. You came here as Higher Dimensional ascended souls who no longer existed in the consciousness of duality wherein karmic issues occur. But when you immersed yourselves in the consciousness of Terran duality, that's where your misidentifications and your misunderstandings have comes from. You now have false beliefs that you adopted from your Terran misidentification. It is all in your head as an illusion, not in your soul wherein dwells the reality of who you truly are as an Ascended Being.

You have a saying, "When in Rome, do as the Romans do." So, this is how you've been treated ever since you got here, because no one knew you were a Volunteer and you had forgotten you were a Volunteer.

Yet, intuitive senses do come out to Volunteers at various times in their lives, about who you truly are. That's when your true identity really started surfacing from soul memory. But you've been doing your job ever since you took your first breath – actually even slightly prior to birth, but not before then. The reason for that is because our Volunteers souls are vibrating at such a high frequency that when the soul enters into the mother's womb too early, it can cause an aborting of the fetus.

For our Volunteers, if their soul tried to enter the fetus too soon before it's birth, then there is too much energy coming into the mother's womb, from the Volunteer soul, for the mother's body to handle.

But, this is not what occurs for native Terrans entering into the fetus any time prior to birth, when the mothers are carrying the souls of native Terran babies. The Terran soul can enter the fetal body at any time and things can go just fine because the unevolved soul does not possess the higher vibrations that an ascended soul possesses. You see?

But when we have ascended souls possessing Upper Triad frequencies coming into these Terran fetuses, and into Terran mothers whose souls are not yet of a Higher Dimensional vibration themselves, the early entrance of that ascended soul can cause problems because the frequency is too intense for the biology of the mother to bear.

So with regard to the First Wave of Volunteers who had to incarnate through native Terran mothers, after several aborted attempts, it was determined that the Volunteer souls had to enter into their embodiments at the moment of labor or birth, and no sooner. So they were held back, so to speak, from entering into their Terran embodiments until that moment. And even then, after birth, your soul did not enter fully into the body until later, well into your first year, so that your Terran body could gradually adapt to your soul's high-energy capacity.

Now, we wish you to understand that as your souls came into these bodies, and your consciousness began to grow along with your bodies, your Terran-altered identity began to grow as well.

So, we feel that it is important that you understand clearly that you are not everything that you have thought you are. We know that this can be quite disturbing, to let go of the Terran identities that you have related to so strongly, and so very long throughout your time on the planet.

But once you understand that as you adopted Terran beliefs and attitudes you created for yourselves, through your altered ego, false Terran identities. These identities are not who you truly are, and while you're on this planet they are truly holding you back from being all that you can be as ascended Volunteers. Once you understand this then it's no problem to let go of your false identity because at the same time you are taking on your true identity as the memories are released from your soul.

If any part of your identity originates from here on this planet rather than from the soul, that identity is not yours. What we are talking about with this is belief systems and manners of behavior, adopting these ideologies that the Terrans embrace for themselves regarding who they are, how they are, what the nature of their being is, which is duality-based. We are not talking about just religion-based beliefs and attitudes, but physically and psychologically as well.

Let me give you an example. One Terran ideology regards the matter of health. You have adopted the Terran beliefs in health and sickness.

Our point here is that you don't have to work on being healthy. You are it! Your soul possesses that nature of absolute health and wellbeing. That's the thing.

We want you to understand that you already are absolutely healthy, because as an ascended soul there is no opposite involved – there is only health, there is only wellbeing. So, what we're trying to get at is the Terran-based idea that you are vulnerable to being sick.

Now, we would also say that the same thing is correct for Terrans themselves because it is a belief and they must learn how to shift out of that falsehood in their consciousness.

But we are saying that it is absolutely not true for our Volunteers, contrary to what you've been told, because you originate, again, from the Upper Triad where there is no disease, there is no sickness, there is no opposite to your wellbeing. Health and wellbeing already exists within your soul and all you have to do is remember your Higher Dimensional nature that composes your soul and you become it – and you become it to the degree of your remembrance and allowing it into your conscious awareness.

When you do, your body will automatically change course. It will get of off the genetic-inclined course laid out by Terran-based beliefs in illness and sickness, and aging and death, and it will shift over into alignment with the truth within your soul where absolute health and wellbeing exists. And your body, biologically, will begin to reverse itself. It has the capacity to do that, but you have been taught to not believe it.

What we're saying here, as we started out saying, is that your body's ideal blueprint is in alignment with your soul, and your soul contains that blueprint. It is there. It's a soul memory.

So, when our Volunteers start letting go of the beliefs of the non-ascending Terran species, and you start embracing the identity contained within your soul, as an Ascended Being, then the body then responds to that fact. The body then becomes the ideal blueprint so that aging process stops because there is no aging contained in that ideal blueprint. There is no aging in your soul. There is no aging in the Upper Triad.

C: So, you're saying that with your own blueprint being pure and perfect, that we just need to fully accept that the body can function perfectly?

A: Exactly. It will regenerate the cells of your body in accordance to its ideal blueprint relative to your degree of remembrance and allowing that fact to become the basis of your reality. The more you remember who you truly are and allow the facts of your blueprint to become the literal reality for you, the quicker the regeneration processes occur. You see?

You will notice these things occurring because of your conscious shifting from a false identity as a Terran, to your true identity as an Ascended Being who's simply on a Volunteer mission here.

But, mind you, these changes are also happening because the ascension event itself is happening. And in-lieu of that, as Ascended Being Volunteers you possess the capacity to enhance or amplify the results by consciously identifying yourself with your True Identity, therefore the true nature of your soul.

Our point here is for you to understand that you, as Volunteers, already possess this state of being in your soul, while Terran ascending souls are developing it, and non-ascending souls are not developing it at all. You do not have to develop your soul into possessing that Higher Dimensional nature. You already own it.

In-lieu of that, you need to understand that when you come into alignment in consciousness with your ascended soul, then everything falls into place because there's no longer the internal struggle going on between who you are truly and who you thought you were that you really aren't. It is who you thought you were that has generated the biological tension and stress that creates the diseases, the illnesses, which creates the susceptibility and the vulnerability to these diseases, thus aging, thus death.

So, once you know implicitly that you are already an Ascended Being, and remember that that memory is already in your soul, and then everything changes for you. It's not just your health that changes. It changes your life, the way that you live; and what you want begins to come to you, to manifest more easily and quickly, because now you're in alignment with your power to manifest as well.

Due to your ascended nature, it can occur right here in the place you are dwelling at right now. In the Upper Triad there is no distinction. The consciousness, the body, and the soul are perfectly integrated with one another, so there is nothing that distinguishes one from the other. And, there is nothing that opposes one between the other. They are all in perfect alignment with one another so that life as you would like it to be here on this planet, is already that way in the Upper Triad. It is the nature of where you came from.

C: That's why they say, "Even before you ask, it is given", because it is your desire, so it comes quickly.

A: Yes. That is true but its quickness all depends upon how open your mind is to actually receiving that desire. What you have called instant manifestation occurs all the time in the Upper Triad. No one has a resistance to receiving their desires, nor are there any energies opposing its manifestation.

You've heard ancient scripts of examples of that. The Beings who were demonstrating that fact were souls who had come here from the Upper Triad, to try to help the Terran species along, to inspire them. They did demonstrations to show people their own potential as a soul and as a species.

Now, we shall end our discussion here and continue it in the next communiqué.

We hope this communiqué has brought further clarity with regard to the true identity and nature of our Volunteers, information to help you discern the difference from your misidentification as a Terran, so you can become who and how you truly are. Know thyself!

Q: Please clarify more about the subject of disclosure and contact. To begin with, other ships have been observed for decades, but not yours. Why not?

A: We will clarify this for your sake. The ships that you have been seeing already are those of the Beings who exist in the Lower Triad. There are Beings in the Lower Triad who you call extraterrestrials whose cultures, societies, and species have been around far longer than the ones on your planet. They have become very technologically developed. They have developed what Terrans here have called exotic technology – exotic only because it is something that is not common on this planet. So, they have the technological ability to travel from one galaxy to another very quickly, with no problems.

You hear your scientists say that doing such a thing is not possible. Well, we're telling you that it is. Some of these scientists are either covering up the truth, while others simply don't know the truth about it.

So, these Beings, who live in other galaxies, can come here in their ships and observe you. They're curious.

C: Is it true that some of them are responsible for us having exposure to the technology we have now, helping us along?

A: The technology came about through extraterrestrial sources, whether they were deliberately put here or through accidents that had happened, it matters not. But the technology that has advanced your culture so quickly in such a short amount of time was obtained from these ships, and not all of it came from crashed ships. Some of it came through ships that your scientists were allowed to examine.

Now, regarding some of the technology that has been given to your people, some of your scientists were given it through, shall we say, telepathic communications or through inspiration during dreams, where they pick-up on that information and they go about developing what it was that was given to them, assuming that they are the inventors of it.

So, you have many different species who are coming here and visiting for many different reasons, and that has been going on for a very, very long time.

Now, for the sake of clarity, please understand and remember that these are the Beings we refer to as extraterrestrials, who originate and currently dwell within the various dimensions and sub-dimensions composing the Lower Triad. Though they may be technologically advanced, most of these Beings are not spiritually evolved to the point of ascending out of the Lower Triad, although some groups of their species are ascending, such as those amongst your Terran species who are ascending.

Any of these extraterrestrials that you hear about, who travel in ships of physical density of one level or another, are residents of the Lower Triad. Any species that you hear of who have religions, or belief systems wherein they venerate or worship other Beings as their gods or as their gurus are of the Lower Triad, for there is none of that going on anywhere in the Upper Triad. No entity who has ascended to the Upper Triad needs religion, does not venerate or worship others, or has external belief systems. In the Upper Triad, life simply is, and it is accepted, understood and interacted with as it is — which is different than how it is in the Lower Triad.

IBOC Communique Session 003

The Beings who come here, to you, from the Upper Triad into the Lower Triad, such as the ones who are heading up and participating in this mission here, their ships are of a meta-quantum kind of light energy. In the blink of an eye, their ships are capable of going from a frequency that cannot be seen by your eyes to a frequency that can be seen. It is these ships that are of the Upper Triad. They are not here to interfere in any way with the Beings who exist in the Lower Triad.

C: Who are the ones here who are protecting our planet from the negative factions in the Lower Triad?

A: They are the ones who are participating in this program here. We have not shown you our ships because we are not here to interact openly with your populations. We are here to protect your planet from the ploys of the negative factions so that it can ascend, which in-turn protects you while you assist its ascension, which in-turn assists all souls who are ready to ascend with the planet.

When disclosure and contact occurs amidst your masses, most of the ships and Beings you will see are those of extraterrestrial origin, current residents within the Lower Triad.

We Ascended Beings will make contact only with Ascending Souls and our Volunteers, and only they will see our ships.

Please understand that we do not deliberately reject making contact with non-ascending souls but it is they who would not benefit from our presence for it is not in alignment with the destiny that their souls have chosen, which is to migrate to and become the residents of the new universe. The Prime Directive that we live by, which is of the Upper Triad consciousness and energy field of configuration, guides us away from intervening or interfering in any way with personal soul preferences.

The Ascended Beings are the ones from the Upper Triad who are protecting your planet insuring that it has the freedom that it needs, meaning the physical stability, in order to ascend. They are protecting the planet and all of nature on it, as well as the Terran species, from being destroyed by the negative factions who know we are here - a fact you've not been privy to know about.

D: One of the things I've noticed over the last 10 or 12 years is that even our animals seem to be much more intelligent and much more gifted than they were when I was growing up.

A: They are, because they are ascending, because they are the nature that composes this planet, so all of nature is ascending. That is a sign that ascension is occurring. And not only that, but you have also heard of, if not witnessed yourself, strange animal species pairing up with each other, who are sometimes predators or prey of one another.

Your script has a saying that in the last days the lion shall lie down with the lamb, and this is what it means. It is a sign to you in this current time indicating that the planet itself is ascending because all of nature is ascending with it. It is shifting its consciousness, thus energy, out of the consciousness of the Lower Triad where the energy of duality exists – the prey and the predator. It is moving into the consciousness of the Singularity where there is no prey and predator, there is only, "We're all friends! Let's have fun!"

C: Now, we have a few more questions for you. Clarify more about the planet that the non-ascending souls are taking with them into the 2nd density. What is that event like to them, and to us? Is it a ghost planet?

A: We would agree to that to some degree, yes, because the Terrans who are not ascending with the physical planet, they are collectively retaining within themselves a sensationalized image of this planet. As they shift from 3rd density into 2nd density, the non-ascending souls remain locked-in-step with the lowering of their collective vibrational frequencies, from 3rd to 2nd density. Their vision of the planet changes in a sort of reversed mode with the changes that the physical planet is going through as it ascends, so that what they are seeing of the planet appears to remain the same according to their collectively generated perspective.

We would like you to recall from our previous discussion, that what they are perceptually retaining for themselves as being their planet is what we refer as the phantom-limb effect, to use an analogy that you can relate to. We call this sensationalized image that they are creating, the Phantom Planet.

If you had a Kirlian photography camera large enough you could actually see this image being developed. Last fall our oracle took some photos of her family that shows evidence that this phantom affect that is indeed transpiring. It clearly shows the fading ghost-like effect of some things overlaid on top of objects that are more solid.

So, the Phantom Planet seems to them to remain just as interactable as it ever did. Just because they are not ascending does not mean that they lose their perspective of what they expect is real for them. As the planet ascends and loses its atomic density, the non-ascending souls are not aware that it is losing atomic density because their belief in a physical planet sustains their ability to interact with the collectively generated Phantom Planet that they are creating, but which serves a substitute planet for the real one that is actually moving further and further out of their range of frequency.

Simultaneously, those of you who are ascending, you are collectively seeing thus experiencing the ascension of the physical planet as it loses atomic density so that it becomes a 5th dimensional density.

We could say that according to the experience of those who are not ascending, their event is ascension in the reverse, and the term descension would appropriately apply, to give you a new word.

The creation of the Phantom Planet is the product of their collective expectations that generates a collective effort to retain a level of physicality that appears to support their belief that nothing out of the ordinary is occurring when in-fact it is, and it is, in-fact, beyond their control to do anything about except to hold on to an illusion of what they once knew as real.

As the non-ascending souls themselves descend in vibration from the 3rd to the 2nd density, their collectively created Phantom Planet gains more density as it moves from its frequency as an idea in consciousness, as pure thought energy, to materialize only so far as the 2nd density and no further. The Phantom Planet densifies no further than the 2nd density, which is a sub-atomic density state, because the non-ascending souls are, at the same time, descending in density to the same sub-atomic state. At this point of 2nd density the "2 parties" converge, they meet up with one another. But this point has not yet been fully reached. The descension process is still being generated as the physical planet continues to ascend to the Upper Triad.

C: So this is kind of like our scripts that say that one will leave, one will stay; meaning one soul ascends to the Upper Triad, and one goes into the 2nd dimension?

A: Precisely. There is a parting of ways for all sentient souls on the planet, but the manner by which this is occurring is not what has been supposed by many people who assume that two physical planets are coming forth out of the one.

Only one planet is physically ascending. The other one is the sub-atomic Phantom Planet that is moving, shall we say, into the frequency where your deceased exist, which has a 2nd level density.

But do understand that while the Phantom Planet is generating itself into 2nd density, according to the non-ascending souls their Phantom Planet is not dying. The Phantom Planet, so far as they are concerned, is still very viable and real to them because the densification-dedensification process of both parties remains locked-in-step with one another so naturally nothing out of the ordinary is noticed by the non-ascending souls.

You are aware that what you call the phantom-limb syndrome, of a person who has had an arm severed, they still feel their arm. For them it's still there. From our perspective, this is what is happening with the non-ascending souls as they descend into a 2nd density and their Phantom Planet is materializing more, from pure thought, into 2nd density.

C: Now, the next question; Clarify the matter about soulmates with regard to your previous comments of "split-apart souls", and why the integrated spirit had to split itself into polarized charges.

A: We shall clarify what we briefly mentioned before.

Before any of us ever came into the Lower Triad, we were fully integrated spirits existing as the vibration known as the Singularity. We came upon the energy barrier of the 4th dimension, which is between the 3rd and the 5th dimensions, and, as integrated spirits vibrating relative to the Singularity, we discovered that while we could pass through the barrier we could not interact in any way with anything in the Lower Triad.

We soon discovered that in order to do so we would have to become the nature of what the Lower Triad is, which is the polarities of the opposites. That is the fundamental nature upon which all things in the Lower Triad are formed, at the basis and the root of it all.

If a spirit wanted to interact with, thus personally understand, the nature of the Lower Triad, then that spirit needed to become like it in its nature. You cannot personally understand something until you have become the nature of it. This is the point for evolution.

So, it came to be understood by each integrated spirit that they must split a part of the spirit-self into the 2 existing charges that are opposites of one another, otherwise the spirit cannot interact nor, consequently, gain an understanding of life in the Lower Triad – it would not evolve any further.

As the spirit took a part of its self to be split apart, half of its soul became the positive charge of energy that you refer to as the masculine force, and half of it became the negative charge of energy that you refer to as the feminine force.

As an analogy, you have 2 halves of your brain that function differently within these 2 polarities, yet your brain remains intact as the information provided by both halves is shared and integrated into the overall brain. Apply that analogy to the splitting apart of your spirit into 2 differently charged soul aspects.

While your spirit remains eternally integrated in its innate state of Singularity, it is your soul that was split into 2 charges, and these 2 charges compose, forever, the one spirit that you are. You are a Singularity. These 3 aspects of you are forever linked together into a triad – and here we have triads again – composing the 2 soul aspects of the 1 spirit. The spirit is always linked to the 2 charges of its soul.

When we, as split-apart souls, had created life in the Lower Triad to the point we could incarnate into the life forms, when our souls incarnated into the bodies, our spirit always remains in the Singularity, always connected to its 2 soul aspects that incarnated into respectively charged male and female embodiments.

Our adventures in this type of experience taught us that what one soul would experience during its lifetime, that information would feed into their mutually shared spirit where the other soul would pick up on that information, literally generating a shared experience. One soul would gain the wisdom from an experience and, through their spirit; the other soul would pick up on that wisdom which automatically becomes integrated as the wisdom of each soul. You see?

So, this kind of evolutionary experience, it was discovered, amounted to our spirits being able to evolve us twice as fast because the one spirit is now having 2 very different experiences at the same time. The 2 experiences are coming from 2 different perspectives – the perspective of negative charged soul, and the perspective of the positive charge soul.

So you, as one spirit possessing 2 soul aspects, you have a soulmate, who is somewhere out there, with whom you share a common spirit. You are never separated from your soulmate – you may be physically separated, but never ever spiritually separated. That is the reality of soulmates.

The female soul will always experience what her male soul is experiencing, and through their shared spirit she picks up on him and vice-versa, he picks up on her experiences.

This doesn't mean that the female soul is a male soul, having his experience – it means that the female soul is picking up on what her male soulmate is experiencing, and vice-versa.

The one spirit's 2 souls do not switch places nor switch charges with one another for there is no need of such vibrational redundancy because both souls exist simultaneously together as they continuously share and integrate experiential information with one another. So, what purpose would it serve for a spirit's souls to switching genders serve when that act is nothing other than switching charges, when the information from every experience is constantly shared and integrated by both anyway.

So there is this continual trade-off of information flowing between you and your soulmate, for evolutionary purposes, that is going on. As one soulmate evolves it helps the other soulmate evolve, so you are assisting each other in the evolution of the one spirit that together you are.

Now, when you're having insights and inspirations and wisdom, and even some lucid dreams, sometimes what you're doing is receiving what your soulmate is experiencing, you're picking up on it through your common spirit.

Even when you are an Ascended Being you're still picking up on what your soulmate is doing, wherever they are.

Right now, with you serving as our Volunteers on this planet, your soulmates are picking up on what you're experiencing here, and they're getting some very weird stuff that you're undergoing. They are indeed still in the Upper Triad, and as Ascended Beings they understand what's going on. They are aware of you and where you are. When you're in the Upper Triad you know where your soulmate is at all times. There is no separation in consciousness such as occurs in the Lower Triad.

One point we want to make is that the one spirit of 2 soulmates' never intended to rejoin its soul mates into one soul. There would be no point in doing that because the 2 soulmates are enriching the spirit by being 2 differently charged aspects of itself rather than 1. You and your soulmate are contributing to the evolution of your one spirit in a much greater capacity than would otherwise occur within the Lower Triad. It would be like you having only 1 hemisphere of your brain for perceptual and *perspectual* analysis. You could do it, but your assessment would be limited and slanted.

Question: When soulmates ascend, do they each still possess the 2 opposite charges, which you say is relative only to the nature of the Lower Triad? How can they ascend while possessing these Lower Triad polarized charges?

A: Upon ascension the 2 soulmates remain as 2 distinctly individualized aspects of their commonly shared spirit, but "once you're out of prison then the charges are dropped", to use a pun on words for you. In other words, once ascended, the Lower Triad's positive/negative charges are transformed into the stabilized energy of the Singularity, yet as 2 Ascended Beings, still being male and female but now per the nature of the Singularity, you retain your own unique perspectives and perceptions of the ascended way of life that you continue to experience in the Upper Triad. While each soulmate will retains their own male and female individuality once ascended, the higher vibrating nature of the Singularity overrides and replaces the lesser vibrating nature of the duality that sustained your souls in the Lower Triad. You see?

Now let us shift focus for a while to translate this sharing of information between souls to how it affects you as, say, a Volunteer whose soul still holds the memory of its abilities in the Upper Triad.

Memory can lodge into your body so that the memories of others appear to be yours, but at the psychic level where, as we said before, you can tune into the experiences of another Terran and misinterpret that as something that you are experiencing or something you had experienced in a past life, but you never personally did. You're just psychically picking up on what somebody else has experienced.

Now, for instance, this example is going to demonstrate the ability that your soul has.

Our oracle experienced being her granddaughter 2 months before she was born. She experienced the day that her granddaughter was brought home from the hospital. She became her granddaughter in this experience. She was her granddaughter who was sitting in the back seat of the car, and she heard the thoughts of her mother who was upset because her father was upset from having a bad day. So, experiencing herself as her granddaughter she, the baby, was aware of what was going on with her parents. She was aware that they were not in harmony with one another. At 5 days old, she was able to tune into her parents and know what was going on and she, the baby, reassured herself that she would be OK because they were young, and they would learn and grow. Then she telepathically heard her mother talking to herself about how sweet her new little daughter was, and how much she loved her.

That is what our oracle experienced long before the child was born. It wasn't merely a dream; it was a literal experience that had our oracle a bit confused.

Now, about 2 months later on the day that that event actually occurred, physically, our oracle was present with her daughter for the birthing of her granddaughter, but it wasn't until the next day that she remembered the experience she'd had 2 months before, of being her granddaughter on the day she was brought home from the hospital.

When our oracle told her daughter about it, conveying to her daughter what the baby had heard her mother say to herself, her daughter said, "That's exactly what I was feeling! That's exactly the words I was thinking." So, our oracle was able to use this experience to reassure her daughter that everything would be OK, and that her baby felt safe and secure in her parents care.

This is an example demonstrating to you the power that you are. Understand that at first our oracle misinterpreted this dream-experience as being about herself as a baby, when she was brought home from the hospital. It was after the actual incident had occurred with her granddaughter that our oracle realized that she had tuned in to a future event that happened not only exactly as she saw it, but also exactly as she experienced it from the perspective of another soul.

Her initial misinterpretation of that event was understandable, but we want you to understand that you have the power within you to do these things that are phenomenal, that you're not used to doing, and you're not used to interpreting correctly. Even though it's within your soul to do them, your conscious mind has not been taught to properly understand these things.

So, when some of our Volunteers feel as though you've gender-swapped, soul-swapped, body-swapped, therefore you assume that you actually are someone else's life, and you take it upon yourself to mean, "Oh, this must be me. I experienced that myself as a child, or, I experienced that in a past lifetime, or, I'm experiencing myself as the other gender", we are telling you 'no', that is not the case if you are indeed an Ascended Being. Ascended Beings do not gender-swap, soul-swap, body-swap, body-possess, or do any of those things simultaneously for there is no need to do that. Such is the erroneous assumptions about life that is coming from non-ascending souls trying to make sense of such nonsensical concepts, most of it being hogwash fed to you by your negative factions as more ways to keep you confused about who you truly are so that you do not know how to be who you truly are.

We are telling this to our Volunteers, and all Ascending Souls, because we want you to really get into thinking about these things so you understand what is the Terran identity that you have adopted for yourself, and what is who you truly are that resides within your soul. Then you will no longer be creating that stressful tension in your body at the biological level, so then you can come into alignment with your ideal blueprint, with your soul, with your conscious mind, with your power all lining up.

D: What's the purpose of having a premonition, of the future? What's the purpose of that information?

A: Simply because you have the ability to do it. It's a carry-over of the soul from its former ability as an integrated spirit of the Singularity.

D: I understand that some of these things happen in order to show us that we can do this, that we have this ability. But when this information does come to us a lot of times, we're sitting down and asking, "What is this for? What do I need to do with this? Why do I need to know this?"

From Contact to Ascension

A: To answer that I will give you another example of what happened to our oracle many years ago. She had a dream — she is a prolific precognitive dreamer, being open to receiving information from unusual sources and people. She had a dream that her girlfriend's boyfriend was in a car accident, even though she'd never met him before. She saw him out of his car and lying on the ground, and she saw that the lower part of his body was in a watery kind of appearance. She recognized the place where the accident happened. She wondered what to do with this information — to tell her girlfriend about it or not. She chose to tell her about it, serving simply as a conveyer of the information, not whether or not it would occur.

When she told her girlfriend about the dream, neither of them was sure whether or not the dream information should be relayed to her boyfriend because after all, would it be protecting him or would it be planting a seed for it to happen? Our oracle left it up to her girlfriend to decide what to do.

Her girlfriend decided to tell him and, as you can imagine, he laughed it off as nothing more than just a foolish dream. But two days later, he had a car accident at the exact place that our oracle saw it happen in her dream. He was thrown out of the vehicle and his legs were injured, which, in her dream, was signified by the watery appearance of his lower body.

She has had precognitive dreams many, many, many times, and we want you to know that for the untrained person, it is difficult to know what to do with that information because you are on a planet where duality exists in a massive intensity, where if you share that information and someone is receptive to it and will take it seriously, then that is good. But there is also the opposite result where they receive it and do not give it any validity, thus do not heed the warning, as her girlfriend's boyfriend did.

So, it is sometimes difficult, yes, to know what to do with this information, so you need to get in-touch with yourself and the other person or persons involved and, shall we say, feel it out for what to do with it.

C: That is good advice. The next question; Clarify how and why the Creator-Source is ascending relative to why the planet is ascending, relative to why the universe is ascending.

A: Going back to our previous discussion of how universes are created, and that universes give birth to universes: When they do that, their lower section of energy, shall we say, is what goes into the new universe, serving as the raw material that will be used to create the new universe. We also have souls who go into these new universes to be the creators who will make use of that material. These souls become the Creators, and they become the Source from where everything comes into existence within that universe.

This is how this universe came about. All of us who are here in this universe existed in another universe before we came into this one. We decided not to ascend with that other universe – we can call it the mother universe of this one. When we were there in that one, we chose to migrate into the new universe that was being created by the mother universe.

So, ever since that new universe was birthed we have been here. We have been creating, and experimenting, and exploring. We have been having fun!

Because we have created everything that is here, we are, hence, the Source from where everything came into existence. And yet, as we are continually ascending we are everything that is also ascending. As we ascend, that which we create ascends too.

As we shall explain, the ever-weakening energy within the Lower Triad that is outmoded for ongoing creation becomes the raw material for the new universe.

From Contact to Ascension

Consequently, there is a connection between that which we are as Creators and that which we are as the Source, Creator-Sources who are ascending – an evolutionary process that we cannot stop, nor would we want to, even for those who are descending into the new universe; either way, we are all still continuing our evolution and ascension.

By being here in this universe, the very fact that we are the Creator-Sources who are ascending the universe itself, the Upper Triad is ascending as well.

The universe has reached a point in our creation of it to where new energy needs to come in with which to continue creating. So, as we bring in the new higher energy, the older, lower energy becomes unnecessary, it becomes obsolete and outmoded. It is no longer useful to what we are now creating.

To give you an analogy of this we will say that when you build a house, you have a house plan. You draw it up and you build your house according to this plan. And when the house is built, the plan is no longer useful. The plans of most houses no longer exist. So for those plans that do exist, the plan itself becomes, shall we say, stuck away and forgotten about for many, many years, decades. And it rots, deteriorates and it's gone. And this is how the plan for the creation of the universe works.

This is not the first time that the lower frequencies of the Lower Triad have been eliminated. The first time occurred when the original fundamental layer of plans for this universe, that we created, were no longer of use to us. Our non-use of them, our non-attention of them, allowed the energy of those plans to go inert, deteriorate, diffuse.

The original energy that was used to create the basic plans of all that would exist in the universe was no longer of use to us, so we moved to the next level of energy so as to engage the current energy of the creative plans. These energies have now run their course too. We can do nothing more with them for the continued evolutionary purposes of this universe. To hang on to them is to spin-our-wheels, as you would say, generating only redundancy and stagnation for the entire universe as a whole. This is why they are currently, and permanently, being released.

We know this is a difficult evolutionary concept to grasp. It is much more complex than this simplified rendering.

Suffice it to say that the current state of this universe has reached a point where it is time to bring in more new higher energies because the lower energies are no longer serving a purpose for ongoing creation. These lower energies are increasingly becoming the raw material with which to create the new universe.

So, with a new universe being created, we could say that our universe is pregnant, and this explains why your scripts depict the universe as a woman inside an egg, or as a pregnant woman. The significance was meant to convey fact that universes give rise to new universes, hence they are considered female in nature.

The lower energies flow into the universe's womb, and non-ascending souls migrate in spirit to this womb in order to become the creators of that new universe and the source of all that exists in it.

When the universe's womb has developed to the point where it can sustain itself on its own, the new universe detaches itself from its mother universe to become an independent universe in and of itself, growing and expanding through the creations that are being done by the spirits within it.

Meanwhile, the mother universe continues to grow and evolve and expand and becomes something new, and more than it was, because the new higher energies have come in.

But, we must clarify, with this particular ascension event that is currently transpiring for us all, the new state of the ascended universe will not contain a Lower Triad or its nature of opposites and duality thereof. The ascended universe will exist strictly in a state of the Singularity. It will not revert back to a duality state.

So, this is what is happening. This is why our Volunteers are here in the Lower Triad, to help bring as many planets as possible into the Upper Triad. Along with the ascension of these planets comes, at this time, all souls who are ready to ascend with them.

This kind of planetary mass ascension event hasn't happened before because it didn't need to happen this way before. But now we're getting close to the time when the universe is folding up its Lower Triad, where the lower energies are increasingly flowing into the new universe.

Consequently there is a, let's say, not a rush, but a need to bring as many planets as are ready for their ascension into the Upper Triad as is possible. And by so doing all of nature on each planet ascends with it. And by so doing, all souls who are ready for ascension are going for the ride as well.

All of this is coming together in a very musical fashion. It's very orchestrated. It's a very beautiful dance that's happening.

C: Thank you for that information. The next question is: There are some claims being made that the ascended souls, once they've ascended, will take their ascended bodies into a state of being pure light energy. Please clarify whether this is correct or not.

A: We have been aware that some people believe that when you ascend with the body, that once you are in the Upper Triad, that you will no longer need the body and will take it from its form in density into a pure light form in consciousness.

What you need to understand, though, is that the physical bodies in the Upper Triad are already in a state of light. Everything, everywhere, is already in a state of varying degrees and densities of light.

The Beings in the Upper Triad have the ability to, shall we say, accommodate their physicality upon whatever dimension they are expressing themselves on. So, if they want to go into a lower dimension, such as to come into the 3rd dimension of the Lower Triad, they have the ability to lower their density and become equal to the density that is here. If they want to go into a higher dimension, they have the ability to raise their vibrational frequency from where they are, let's at the 5th dimension and go into the 6th dimension, and interact with the physicality that is there.

This dimension-shifting process takes the current density of the body into its pure thought form as held in the consciousness of the host, and then redensifies the body to be the relative density of the dimension they wish to be on.

So yes, all Ascended Beings possess the ability to take their bodies from the current state of density into pure thought energy, but they do so only as a means that allows them to shift from one given dimensional density to another. They never remain in their pure thought form because every dimension and sub-dimension has a given type of density of one degree or another.

There is a misunderstanding about that whole notion of ascending your body and then giving it up, when in reality there is no need for doing that in the Upper Triad. To remain in pure thought form is to render oneself incapable of interacting with the kind of life that exists in each unique dimensional realm because each one has its own level of density.

If, for instance, you are in the 5th dimension, in your 5th dimensional body consisting of a 5th level density, and you want to explore something in the 6th dimensional density, all you have to do is shift your vibrational frequency and you're there. When you're done doing what you were doing there, you lower your density back into your 5th dimensional density body and there you are. It is a complex process that when engaged by Ascended Beings occurs instantaneously.

You can take your body from its physical form into a pure light form held in your consciousness, and travel to wherever you want to travel, and then rematerialize your body. You don't need a wormhole. You don't need a stargate. You travel as a Being of light. It is all done through the power of the mind.

And when we say 'travel' we mean that you travel in consciousness. You're not traveling anywhere directionally through space as you think of it. You travel in consciousness, which is space, from one localized point in thought that you were focused upon, to another localized point in thought that you are focused upon, and yet you have gone nowhere as you think of it, but still you have shifted locales which actually are points in consciousness. It is done instantaneously.

Since you travel in consciousness, you cannot call this time travel because there is no time involved. The notion of time travel is a misnomer. It is not time travel, it is consciousness travel.

So, the whole idea that you would ascend your physical body and then give it up only to reside forever as pure light within your own consciousness – why would you do that when everything that has been created has its own relative degree of density, and in order to interact with it you must be of the same density. This brings us back to the very purpose of our spirits wanting to enter into the Lower Triad and becoming the same nature that exists here in order for us to evolve. If you want to reside forever as pure light in consciousness then you do not have access to the catalysts of density that generates p within each dimension. Why would you do that to yourself? There is no need for that.

IBOC Communique Session 003

We hope that we have clarified that question. We hope that we have addressed things that are helpful to you. We ask that if you have any further questions now, to please ask at this time.

D: I am just curious…why did the Terrans or the earthlings make up religious stories and belief systems about heaven, hell, and make up all these religious ideas?

A: The original stories, so to speak, were based upon truth. The truth came to the ancient cultures long, long ago, through Ascended Beings who had come here to help the Terrans evolve. But then during a later time, when negative factions overran the planet, the truth contained in those scripts was deliberately censored. Those in control confiscated all truth everywhere that they could find it, and in its place they gave you the distorted stories that you now have. There is very little truth left in these stories that have been specifically designed to confuse you in order to lead you away from knowing who you truly are. And their scheme has worked beautifully for them, hasn't it.

Control has been the purpose. That's why these stories seem so nonsensical to you, because you have already evolved beyond them. You know that they are nonsensical. They do not serve a purpose in your life because you have chosen ascension.

But the non-ascending souls are still evolving within themselves to gain an understanding of what the truth really is. And they are having a hard time with doing that because the truth is being kept from them, and it is being replaced increasingly with a new kind of religion called materialism. The reason for this is that the age-old religions are loosing ground so far as being control tactics, so they must be replaced with something more updated and modernized. Even those people who consider themselves very religious or very spiritual are allowing themselves to be cleverly seduced into being subtly "materialized" by the negative faction who is constantly producing more enthralling stuff that captivates your attention and energy, hence your life. Mind you well that word, captivate.

Yet, on the other hand, this seeming madness is serving a divine purpose for all non-ascending souls because it is allowing them to make their decisions regarding where they want to go with their personal evolution.

It's sort of like being in a play wherein the story itself is not really happening – it's just an enthralling story but it's captivatingly entertaining enough to keep you distracted from where you are not, and focused upon where it is leading you. Consequently, to the non-ascending souls who are pretending to be part of this seemingly bizarre story, for them it's a perceptual means resulting in a self-created conclusion that magnetically draws them into the new universe.

So indirectly these ancient stories, and the current transforming of them into something new and improved, do have a divine purpose for they are designed to not allow non-ascending souls to evolve and ascend, but instead to migrate into the new universe where they want to go as their new soul destiny.

Every Terran soul is free to evolve if they want to. If that is what they choose to do, then they will do that and they will recognize those stories for what they are, and not be bothered by them but will let them serve the divine purpose for other souls who have chosen to migrate to the new universe. So these souls are using these control tactics as "tools" to help keep them migrating there. In that sense then, there is nothing wrong or bad about it. You see?

We wish you to understand something. It takes an awful lot of souls to create a new universe. So it's really no surprise that most people on this planet, and other planets, are not ascending. Most of them are migrating into the new universe because the new universe requires that the more souls who are there to create diversity in that universe, the better. And the souls who are migrating there know this. They are choosing that. They are happy with that choice. They are eager to get on with it because they are just as bored as you are with being in here the same old Lower Triad that's now going nowhere, as we have explained.

You are wanting to ascend with this universe as much as they are wanting to go into the new universe, so everyone's is sort of saying, "Let's get the shows on the road!"

We hope that we have clarified this matter and helped you to see the difference between who you have thought you were, and who you truly are. We wish you to take this information and use it for discerning the difference, because when you do then you will begin to align with your soul again and, for you Volunteers, the memories will come forward regarding what it is to be an Ascended Being, which is very different from being a Terran Being.

When you come into this understanding you will be able to align with your power, and align your ideal blueprint with your body, so that it's all wrapped up together. The only thing that has been missing from your lives is knowing who you truly are. Once you let go of the misidentification of being a Terran Being, and know clearly that you are an Ascended Being, and then everything changes. This is what we are wanting for you as Volunteers, because by so doing it will enhance your personal lives considerably.

Our advice on this matter; Know thyself so that you don't worry, you be happy!

We have immensely enjoyed this time with you. We feel that the time has been well spent, and we look forward to our next get-together.

An T'na answers some reader's questions

Q: An T'na, in the previous communiqué, you said that of all the ascending planets, this one, Terra, or Earth, is the most difficult case due to the activities of the negative factions who have created frequency-jamming devices that have been stationed on and around our planet; and that these frequencies are preventing the respective part of our brains from accessing the higher frequencies. You also said that other planets' ascension processes are ahead of the progress of this one. In-lieu of that, I am unclear as to how this is affecting our planet's progress as it attempts to ascend. Would you offer us further clarity on this matter, please?

A: Yes, thank you for your question. We did say that the frequency-jamming signals are targeted at the part of your brains that access higher frequencies. That is correct. You, on the other hand, might counter us with the assumption that you possess the power to override these signals, but we tell you that in order to do that you must use that part of your brain that the signals are targeting, which is the same part of your brain that generates those functions necessary to override the signals. How do you access the part of your brain that is being restricted from accessing the frequencies to override the signals? So you see, it is a catch-22 situation, as you would say.

This is why we clearly advise you for now to make a strong personal connection with the planet herself because she is not affected by these signals. We said that by doing so you lock yourself into her receptivity of the higher frequencies coming to her from deep space through our Volunteers as they access the higher light-energy originating in the Upper Triad then anchoring it into her core. These higher frequencies are not being blocked from her, neither through her own doing, nor through the deeds of the negative factions who do not possess the technology that could possibly harness enough energy to block her receptivity of the light-energy. They did try, but after years of attempts, they utterly failed.

Q: OK. That makes sense. So, if our planet is still receiving the light-energy and is ascending, why or how is it, as you said, that the other ascending planets are way ahead of ours? Why have some planets already ascended but not this one? Compared to them, what has set us back so far?

A: Thank you for asking. That situation is not a matter of your planet being behind in its ascension progress, for it is on-schedule as planned, so to speak, but it is a matter of the other planets' occupants having accepted the assistance of the same group of Advanced Extraterrestrials and Ascended Beings who approached yours too. The leaders of your planet rejected that identical offer, as we discussed in the previous communiqué.

The leaders and common people of those other ascending planets collectively chose to receive an education about what is transpiring cosmically, which is beyond their control per the folding-up of the Lower Triad which, in-turn, generated a need for us to get as many planets as possible ascended into the Upper Triad before that event occurs.

This education that they are receiving includes meta-physics lessons about how and why this cosmic event is occurring. This provides a fundamental basis upon which to gain essential knowledge that removes any sense of fear about what is transpiring for it is indeed a completely natural-occurring process of the ascending universe. Knowledge vanquishes fear. That is a fact.

Because the Source that we are never creates an event without presenting us with options, the education they are receiving includes an extensive, graphic description of the 2 available options regarding their personal experience of this event. The 2 options are to ascend into the Upper Triad, or to migrate into the new universe.

It is accepted by everyone – even the skeptics who eventually became convinced by the evidence presented to them – that of 2 these options to choose from, neither is better or worse, right or wrong, more or less divine than the other, that each option exists for the purposeful good of the evolution of each soul.

From Contact to Ascension

Everyone thus wholly understands that the option that person chooses is the right one for the evolution of the soul. Consequently there are no negative attitudes toward one another, but instead there is absolute allowing and acceptance, which is that which you call unconditional love.

If we could give you an analogy of how they are handling the situation, it would be one like unto that of your graduation day from a university. All of your graduating schoolmates have gathered together for the event, knowing that everyone is going to go off to one career or another, and everyone is happy for everyone else's career choices. There is no judgment or criticism. There is only acceptance and encouragement amongst everyone present. The prevailing atmosphere amongst all is one of great excitement.

This is how the people of the other ascending planets are experiencing the cosmic event that is unfolding before us all. Through an extensive education, generating a knowledgeable understanding of the situation, everyone is happy for everyone else's choice in the matter because they know that each choice made is for the purposeful good of their soul's evolution. So then, where is the right or wrong, good or bad, divine or undivine in it? You see?

Regarding ascension, there is only a loving cooperation amongst these people and, thus, with the planet they reside on. It is this collective cooperation on a global scale with the flow of ascension that has accelerated their planet's own natural progress, you see.

So it is not that your planet is lagging behind due to the actions of the negative factions or to anyone or anything else, but it is the fact that these other ascending planets are being accelerated in their natural progress by the collective cooperative forces of their occupants adding to and enhancing the ascension processes of their planet.

While these planets are receiving a beneficial global scale boost from their cooperative occupants, your planet is currently receiving no such additional boost from its occupants. But this does not impede or retard your planet's ascension progress, it simply does not enhance thus accelerate it. Do you understand?

Q: Yes. This is very helpful information and explains a lot. But is not the presence of your Volunteers on our planet contributing to an acceleration of the processes?

A: No, not in the way that we are explaining here. Let us go back to the time before our Volunteers incarnated on their respective planets.

It was known by the Councils of this mission, which is to ascend as many planets as possible, that the cooperation of any leader and common people of any planet was not guaranteed. Your planet turned out to be a prime example of non-cooperation, but due to free will, it was not known ahead of time which planet's occupants would accept the assistance and which would reject it.

So, it was decided by the Councils to place Volunteers on each planet that was determined to be suitable for ascension.

We must remind you that in order for planets to ascend, which includes all lifeforms on it with the acceptance of the sentient Beings residing on it, that these planets and lifeforms do not possess the necessary aptitude within themselves to ascend into the Upper Triad, that they require the assistance of Ascended Beings who possess the capability of infusing them with enough higher frequency light-energy from the Upper Triad, to be anchored directly into the planet or lifeform for its ascension.

It was for this particular reason that our Volunteers were placed upon each planet found to be suitable for ascension. Their ascended assistance was required. The presence of our Volunteers on the planet initiates, sustains, and maintains the processes of its ascension – their presence does not accelerate the process.

From Contact to Ascension

While our Volunteers are present on the planet, having ignited the planet's ascension processes, the acceleration of those processes occurs only when that planet's sentient occupants collectively cooperate with the ascension event that our Volunteers initiated and sustain.

While your planet, like all the others, received the presence of our Volunteers to ignite the planet's ascension processes, the occupants of your planet have not come together in a collective cooperation amongst themselves that would in-turn enhance thus accelerate the ascension processes of your planet, so that your planet would then enhance thus accelerate the ascension processes of its occupants. You see? It works in a synergistic feedback-looped system when it is all working together harmoniously.

Such is not the case on your planet. That is why the planet is not receiving any additional boost from its occupants – at least not right now. Were it not for the presence of our Volunteers on your planet, the planet would not be ascending at all. Our Volunteers are the initiators and maintainers of your planet's ascension.

The planet's occupants are the ones who could, if they so chose to do so, accelerate the processes that our Volunteers are sustaining because then you would harmoniously create that synergistic feedback-looped system that you and your planet would benefit from. But the people of your planet are not educated in this matter in order to make this collective venture a reality.

Q: Are other ascending planets in a similar situation as ours?

A: Most of the ascending planets occupants readily accepted the offer from the Advanced Extraterrestrials and Ascended Beings. In the beginning when our Volunteers incarnated onto a few other planets chosen for ascension, not all of those planet's occupants wanted to receive the education from the Advanced Extraterrestrials and Ascended Beings. They were in fear that the presence of these Beings was up to no-good. It took a while for the leaders to convince these fearful people and, in a couple of other cases, for the people to convince their leaders, that accepting the offer of assistance presented no threat.

We are talking about the majority of people on these planets who have evolved to become fundamentally peaceful in nature, and who, except but the few unevolved souls, were able to recognize impostors when they met them. It took some time for the fearful folks to come-around, but once they received the same education that everyone else received, it was enough to convince them to cooperate with everyone else, given that the cosmic situation itself offered them no other choice but to learn what their own options are.

Of these other ascending planets, their occupants' initial resistance was more quickly overcome than has been the case on your planet.

But all is not lost since your planet is still ascending due to the presence of our Volunteers, as explained earlier in this communiqué, and, as we have already stated, all Ascending Souls can circumvent the frequency-jamming signals and still ascend by making a personal connection with the planet. Refer to our communiqué in Session 3 – Part A for a refresher about this.

We will also say that there is a plan afoot, by a group of Advanced Extraterrestrials and Ascended Beings, to disregard your negative factions' rejection of their offer of assistance so that the common folk can go ahead and receive a much needed catch-up crash-course in the education that has been taught to the people on the other ascending planets.

Now, some people on your planet would whine about us coming in with this plan as a violation of the cosmic Prime Directive, but we have said before that the Prime Directive as defined by your fiction stories and presumed to be real is indeed fiction. We said that the real Prime Directive is all about not interfering with the evolution of souls, and that has nothing to do with assisting the common folk of a planet when its leaders are tyrannical and oppressive such as are yours. These tyrants are the ones breaking the divine Prime Directive as they continually, deliberately interfere with the evolution of the souls who are residing on the planet with them.

Now you see why the negative factions have given you a false definition of the Prime Directive. They twisted the facts of true Prime Directive in order to redirect your attention and blame off of themselves by replacing it with a fictional Prime Directive aimed at us. The definition of the true Prime Directive blatantly gives them away as the thieves-of-evolution that they really are.

So, this plan that is afoot will occur soon. And yes, I know, you are thinking that "soon" is always the operative vague date used by us, but we refuse to divulge precisely when this plan will occur so that it will take the negative factions by complete surprise so that, for your sake, they do not have time to create a counter-plan. Is this not reasonable?

Q: Yes, it is, thanks. Is there going to be enough time for the occupants of our planet to "get educated" well enough so that it begins to accelerate our planet's ascension, thus our own in-turn?

A: Yes. As we have stated before, this planet is not ascending next week or next month or next year, but it will occur within your lifetime, just as we have said. Without the collective cooperation of your planet's occupants the ascension of the Ascending Souls into the Upper Triad, and the migration of the non-ascending souls toward the new universe, their journeys would be difficult to experience – let's say it wouldn't be nearly as pleasant as that happy event of the graduation analogy we described earlier.

Contact will occur very soon, and during the years to follow until the Lower Triad folds up, this planet will receive the education that will give it that beneficial boost such as described earlier, thus you in-turn.

IBOC Communique Session 003

Many people are mistaken that this coming contact event will result in your planet being inducted into a galactic society. To some extent this is true, but not in the context that they are assuming it to be.

Once contact has been made and your education begun, your planet's occupants will join the throngs of people residing on the ascending planets neighboring your own – some of their occupants are ascending to the Upper Triad, while others are migrating to the new universe, and whichever option one chooses, it is all accepted as a grand and purposeful event. Bear in mind that there is no right or wrong choice in this matter.

There will be a sharing not of technology but of knowledge, which will take place between them and you. Technology has no place in the Upper Triad, nor can it be taken into the new universe.

There will be travel between their planets and yours for further educational and acquaintance purposes. But your contact with them will not entail the wild adventures such as those found in your fictional stories you call Star Wars, Star Trek, Stargate, and so on.

Your planet will also be contacted by other extraterrestrials who are not ascending souls but who are migrating to the new universe. All occupants of your planet will be respectfully allowed to choose which group of Beings they relate to who are souls relative to the evolution of their own soul.

If some people on your planet feel more comfortable in the presence of non-ascending extraterrestrials, then they will be free to interact with them, to even leave your planet and travel to the planets of those extraterrestrials.

For those Ascending Souls who feel more comfortable in the presence of Advanced Extraterrestrials who are ascending and Ascended Beings who have already ascended, then you are free to interact with them.

From Contact to Ascension

Our point here it to make it clear to you that both groups are on equal footing so far as it pertains to the necessary evolutionary direction of each soul. In that understanding there is, then, no judgment, or criticism, or condemnation for making what might be a wrong, bad, or inferior choice, because that concept simply doesn't apply to this situation that we are explaining. Do you see?

Your people will also receive the assistance of the Advanced Extraterrestrials and Ascended Beings that will return your planet and all of nature to its pristine state of being.

You will receive assistance that wipes out disease, aging, death, and the tremendous disparities created by your negative factions that have generate war, crime, homelessness, hunger, poverty, illiteracy, intolerance – if we may coin such a word; that wipes out the inequalities of race and gender and employment, and so on.

All fields of life shall be leveled and revamped so that all people are on equal ground, and global peace shall be the outcome. That is when a collective cooperation of ascension begins.

In what was your 1950s, this wonderful existence is what was offered to you by the Advanced Extraterrestrials and Ascended Beings.

Q: Yes. That being what it was, why did the Ascended Beings and Advanced Extraterrestrials at that time not engage this plan-of-intervention of disregarding the negative faction's rejection of their offer that instead, all this time, plunged us common folk and the planet into the mess that we are currently in now, which is the result of our ruthless leaders accepting the destructive offer of the malevolent aliens? Why engage this plan you speak of now, rather than back then?

A: We have stated that we knew that once our Volunteers were present on your planet that the planet would ascend, and it still is. We knew that most Ascending Souls would continue ascending, while some have lost their way. We have said that the planet and its Ascending Souls would continue to ascend together. And they are. These were known factors at the time, back then.

Free will being what it is, at that time we did not foresee that your negative factions would, more recently, be given technology from their diabolical alien overlords that would be used to directly impede the part of your brains that accesses the higher frequencies for ascension purposes.

As we stated in our previous communiqué regarding this matter, this sinister ploy went online through your satellites and cell phone towers only within your past decade. This evolution-threatening exploit was unmistakably a violation of the true Prime Directive. That is when we decided it was time to step in and create a plan of intervention on the behalf of the common folk.

Now, you wonder why it took nearly 10 years for us to merely formulate this plan-of-intervention, and the answer to that is that there is a time-difference between your time and ours. So, by the time we devised a working plan, many years had passed by in your timeframe. It wasn't that we were dragging our feet on it, as you would say, but the time factor is involved. This is why the word "soon" as a date is relative.

We do have a working plan now, and it will be implemented in 1 year, on the 3rd Sunday of your May, at 10 minutes past noon. …. No, really, we are teasing you regarding the matter of time. Just a bit of humor.

As we said, and for the reason we explained earlier, we refuse to be precise as to when this plan will be implemented. Just rejoice knowing that it is forthcoming, at a theater near you … soon!

We know that all of this is a new perception for you to grasp, and if necessary, do reread this communiqué in order to "get" what we are "getting at".

If you have further questions, please present them to us and we shall respond.

Disclosure and Contact for Volunteers – Who They Are

Q: Please clarify more about disclosure and contact by the people who the Volunteers are associated with in their work on Terra.

A: In sessions 1 and 3 we touched upon this subject briefly. We would like to add more about this matter for your greater understanding of what is transpiring and what you can expect.

We spoke of our ships being composed of varying light frequencies, which can instantaneously raise and lower density thus the visibility of the craft. Most often you will not see them in your skies and the reason for this has been that it has not been time for them to make their appearances, and by "them" we are referring to our lightships, not the craft of others we shall discuss herein.

Our lightships are massive in size yet if they do not want to be seen they can disappear from sight in less than the blink of an eye. They are not zipping around through space at high velocities in order to escape your view. When they disappear from sight they remain stationary and simply raise the vibration of the craft to the frequency of the Upper Triad.

Our lightships and their occupants who are the ones cooperating together in the ascension mission are not hanging around your planet for there has been no purpose for doing that at this time.

We do observe and monitor from a distance what is occurring on your planet. Our observation and monitoring process occurs through the engagement of our minds, and is not done through the use of electronic or other hardware devices. We need not move our lightships closer and further away from your planet. As Ascended Beings, our minds are capable of tuning-in to any given area of your planet in order to assess what is transpiring.

If we detect any major trouble occurring at a given location, then we dispatch a lightshuttle, so to speak, to the area and immediately neutralize the event. By "major trouble", we mean attempts by your negative factions to generate any kind of globally destructive event. By so doing we are endeavoring to keep this planet alive and viable as it ascends. But there are those who are endeavoring to counteract that by unfolding their genocidal agendas through global destruction. We have been, and will continue to closely monitor these activities and neutralize them whenever critical action is taken by them.

As Volunteers, you are on the planet to hold Higher Dimensional light into the planet to assist its ascension. Your job was never to monitor and diffuse the actions undertaken by the negative factions. You knew that this would be the job of those of us who are working in-tandem with you but doing so in another area of activity – that of protecting you and the planet that you are bring Home with you.

Our lightships are stationed around your solar system and some beyond it who are sentinels guarding the perimeter, for there are other negative factions in your galaxy who have attempted to move in and assist the negative factions already on your planet.

The lightship, which I, An T'na, am working from, is stationed near the rings of Saturn. Our oracle Gesanna has been there several times, visiting family and friends, but her memory of these visits was suppressed. Even then, some of those visits have surfaced from soul memory to conscious awareness, and when they did that it made her very homesick.

We learned early on, in this mission, to restrict all interactions with Volunteers by family members, mates and friends. Even when visitations occurred for necessary purposes and the memory was suppressed, we discovered that the innate nature of the soul of

From Contact to Ascension

Ascended Beings is not to keep memory suppressed but to allow it to surface freely. So it has proven difficult to keep all memories suppressed. Because of that, visitations with all Volunteers became limited to volunteer program team leaders who regularly monitor their wellbeing.

Gesanna has been one of our Volunteers whose soul has been very insistent upon keeping her memories readily accessible and flowing more freely than has been for her own good as a Volunteer. Her sometimes very vivid memories of her ascended life have made it especially difficult for her to desire to remain on Terra and do her job. She has been extraordinarily homesick, more so than a lot of our other Volunteers.

This contributed to her ongoing unreadiness, over decades, to engage the work she is now doing as our oracle. It is only within the past month [first month of 2013] that her soul memories began surfacing regarding her role as a Volunteer on Terra which gave her the clarity of mind to understand why she is on the planet with a specific job to do. The memories she called forth before were focused on her personal life as an Ascended Being in the Upper Triad, and upon the people who she knew and interacted with in all areas of that life. These memories made her homesick for that life and her people.

Only recently did she resign herself to the fact that the job she came here to do has not yet been completed, so she called forth from her soul, the memories associated with being a Volunteer and the job she agreed to do. As this came forth, it all began to make more and more sense. She began to realize that the wonderful life and loving people she left behind are still there where she left them, but they are not waiting for her return Home so much as they are, for now, encouraging her to engage her job consciously and see-it-through because it is a critical part of the mission. It was when she remembered that her very presence on the planet is what is "doing the job". She remembered that the job of assisting the planet's ascension couldn't succeed if she and most, or all, Volunteers withdraw from their presence off the planet. She then remembered that she "signed up for the duration", which means to remain on the planet until it has been ascended to its new Home in the Upper Triad.

Our point on this matter of contact is to clarify why you have not had any conscious interactions with those people you left behind. We do regret that it has had to be that way, but now you understand why.

Yet, things on the larger scale are now reaching a point where that will change in your near future. As we discussed previously, as the planet ascends to higher levels of frequency and becomes less dense, it gradually meets up with the level of frequency that our lightships are vibrating at, which is just beyond the detections of your most sophisticated instruments. The minds of our Volunteers, and Terrans who are ascending, will be detecting them far sooner than will their eyes.

Non-ascending Terrans will not be detecting our lightships and will not be encountering us, but will be encountering ships and Beings that we refer to as extraterrestrials, who still exist within the Lower Triad of life. We discussed this somewhat in session 3, but we want to clarify here that we are not members of the extraterrestrial communities or societies, as has been the common definition and description of such on your planet.

We refer to ourselves as Ascended Beings, not as some position of rank in a divine hierarchy – that is Lower Triad thinking – nor as a cosmic status symbol – that is Lower Triad thinking too – but because that simply described what we are. As Ascended Beings we have already evolved out of and beyond the Lower Triad, which is why we are not part of the extraterrestrial societies or communities or federations and such that are hanging around your planet, and some already in your planet.

These are the ones who non-ascending Terrans are and will continue to see and encounter on an increasing basis, because the opposite experience holds true for them as for our Volunteers and Terrans who are ascending, to where all non-ascending Beings throughout all of the Lower Triad, and there are many, mind you, countless numbers who are not ascending, are migrating with one another in lock-step-fashion toward the new universe, so that as the Lower Triad looses density and folds up — opposite to what is occurring to the ascending planet and its ascending Terrans — then these extraterrestrials ships will be increasingly seen and their occupants will be increasingly encountered by all non-ascending Terrans because they are a lock-step vibrational match with one another.

So, we want you to understand the disclosure and contact will occur relative to which direction you are going in your life — into ascending with the planet, or migrating into the new universe. It is this self-chosen direction that determines which kind of experience you will have.

Now, we warn you, do not expect any disclosure about us from your media. Your negative factions know we are here, but they are keeping that fact to themselves, and rightly so because our presence here has purpose only for the select group of ascending Terrans and our Volunteers, just as the extraterrestrial presence has purpose only for the select group of non-ascending Terrans.

Keeping all of this in mind, call forth from your soul, the understanding of the difference and you shall not be led astray into thinking-like-a-Terran who is expecting something very different to occur.

Volunteers as Ascended Beings - The Two Levels of Volunteers

Per our session, which you have numbered as 3, we wish to impart further clarity regarding who you are as Ascended Beings having taken on the role of mission Volunteers.

We want you to understand that there is another level of Volunteers who are on your planet also, and it is imperative that you learn to discern which one you are part of.

First of all, we discussed in session 3 the fact that as Ascended Beings you had already resolved all issues in prior lifetimes that you engaged while existing in the Lower Triad. In order to ascend beyond the Lower Triad you must resolve all issues and have absolutely no attachments to any situation, to anything, or to anyone that exists in the Lower Triad.

Just before your personal ascension out of and beyond the Lower Triad, you had reached a place in yourself where you were completely fulfilled with all that could be offered to you through your immersion in the Lower Triad circumstances. Upon your last lifetime on your particular planet, you had no further desire to put yourself into a new or different situation, or even to continue in the one which you were currently immersed in, for you had come to understand clearly that it is all designed to stimulate personal evolution through an immersion into duality.

You came to understand that the Lower Triad is based upon the natural principles of polarized opposites, and that whatever life-situation you immersed yourself in, in whatever lifetime of experience, of past, present or potential future lifetimes, you knew that all of your life-situations would be based in patterns of duality that you would have to deal with over and over and over again — different faces, different places, different times, different circumstances, different stage props, so to speak — but all of it always couched in the same patterns of duality of right/wrong, good/bad, superior/inferior, divine/evil, love/hate, peace/conflict, have/have-not, and so on.

You knew that another lifetime in the framework of the Lower Triad would offer you nothing beyond duality in which to continue your evolution. You had reached a point in yourself where you knew you had experienced all of those patterns of duality, and that you had come to terms with all of it within yourself; you came to understand it all and reached a point of peace with it all within yourself.

From Contact to Ascension

Upon this examination, you then realized that the kind of life offered in the Lower Triad no longer offered any further stimulation for further evolution of yourself. You had come to the end of this road, so to speak. Consequently you understood there was no other option but to move on from the Lower Triad's School of Hard Knocks, so to speak.

So, you ascended out of the vibrational field of the Lower Triad and entered into the vibrational field of the Upper Triad where the kind of life there offers new stimulation for continued evolution, except that in the Upper Triad the type of stimulation is free of all patterns of duality. Evolution in the Upper Triad is stimulated by patterns of creative curiosity.

Now, there is that pattern in the Lower Triad also, but to a limited degree and to a degree where the opposite of that which has been created is destroyed by an opposite force. So in the Lower Triad, that which is created there has a limited life span, if you will. You have a saying that "Nothing lasts forever" and that is true in the Lower Triad.

But in the Upper Triad, that principle of opposites simply does not apply because it does not exist there. There is nothing opposing the life of anything that is created, as we have already discussed in previous sessions.

So, you ascended beyond the Lower Triad and entered the Upper Triad where you would continue your evolution based upon a whole new framework of existence. Once you entered the Upper Triad, you were absolutely free of any and all issues, desires and attachments of all your former existences in the Lower Triad. You were indeed "set free" as your scripts say.

So, for what you would consider a very long time, you lived your life in the Upper Triad as an Ascended Being, for you are indeed a Being who had ascended out of the Lower Triad. So the term applies as a means of describing your life, what you have done. It is not a term of rank or status.

So, living as an Ascended Being in the Upper Triad, you had no hang-ups or issues about anything you ever did or encountered. You were beyond all of that, and such things simply do not exist there to be done or encountered. You were immersed in your creative endeavors and enjoying it immensely.

Then you heard the call to join a cosmic effort to assist the ascension of many Lower Triad planets in order bring them into the Upper Triad. This effort is the mission you signed up for as a Volunteer. So now you were an Ascended Being engaging the role of mission Volunteer.

While in the Upper Triad, before you came here, you were all briefed thoroughly on the mission objective and on your duties as a Volunteer of it. All who applied, with the expectation of joining the mission had the right to back out of it at the last minute if they so choose to. Some did back out, most didn't. And of those who did back out, they were not looked upon as having failed nor any such attitudes of duality placed against them for behavior that does not exist in the Upper Triad. They simply continued with their lives as usual, just as honored and respected and loved as ever.

Those of you who chose to join the mission are those of you who are here on this planet, while there are Volunteers on other planets that are being ascended as well.

When all of you incarnated into your respective lives on your respective planets, you did so with absolutely no former lifetime hang-ups or issues or attachments. You entered back into the Lower Triad with, shall we say, a clean slate in the soul. You had no, what you call, karma.

So, you came into your life here on this planet and, as we discussed in session 3, you were indoctrinated into the Terran mindsets of belief systems, attitudes, concepts, focuses of attention on some things and not others, so you began to think and behave just like them. You adopted their ways and you walked their walk, talked their talk.

As you adopted their concepts about life and who you must be according to that, you created for yourselves misidentifications of who you are and why you are here. You adopted their concepts that are supposed to justify certain behaviors of conduct and specific conditions of body.

You need to know that of those Volunteers who believe you are homosexual or walk-ins or in any other such manner of mind, body and soul disturbances, you are not, not if you are a Volunteer from the Upper Triad. You cannot be both, and we must be clear about this matter.

No Ascended Being Volunteer came into their life here with duties that put you into such circumstances, nor would such duties even allow for it. No Ascended Being would allow themselves to be placed into such states of being that would regress them from where they had already evolved to – which is beyond all of that.

The only way you could possibly be a Volunteer and be in such states of mind, body and soul at the same time is if you are a volunteer for a group of extraterrestrials who exist within the Lower Triad, for even those Beings still exist within the natural principle framework of the Lower Triad and thus are still evolving through the patterns of duality.

We wish you to understand that there are some such Volunteers here who are members of Lower Triad-based extraterrestrial groups, societies, communities, federations, and so on. These Beings do exist and some of their Volunteers are here on this planet.

These Volunteers are not Ascended Beings but are still evolving through the patterns of duality within the Lower Triad, just as are the extraterrestrial Beings with whom they are associated. These extraterrestrial-originating Volunteers will find themselves embracing some of the concepts and ways of life of the native Terran, which to them, the concepts and ways that they have accepted feels rather typical. They are not at odds with it within themselves.

Lower Triad-based extraterrestrial Volunteers may find themselves vibrationally relating to certain Terran concepts and ways of life and states of being. They often incarnate with what you call karmic issues, past life hang-ups, with attachments to certain things, substances, people and certain types of circumstances. This provides for them the format in mind, body and soul to be transvestites, to be homosexual, to be walk-ins, and so on, even as Volunteers for their extraterrestrial people. The consciousness and energy for those states of being is always relative to the natural principles in opposites governing the Lower Triad. And in that, there is nothing wrong.

The information that you hear, watch, read and so on, regarding ascension and life elsewhere, the people who claim to be Volunteers delivering that information are for the most part Terran incarnated members of extraterrestrial groups who are on various missions throughout the Lower Triad universe and its sub-dimensions therein. There are more extraterrestrial Volunteers on this planet than there are Ascended Being Volunteers.

If you feel very strongly that you are a Volunteer yet are also to any degree transvestite, homosexual, walk-in, and so on, then you are a soul who has not yet ascended, but one who is a highly valued Volunteer for their extraterrestrial group. If you feel an affinity to a particular extraterrestrial race and you closely identify with them, then you are an extraterrestrial Volunteer. And regardless of whether you are any of these things or not, being an extraterrestrial Volunteer is wonderful because you are here on important assignments particular to your people's mission objectives. They need you here doing your given assignment, and to fulfill it to the best of your ability. But in order to do that you need to recognize and accept who you are as such.

If you know that you are an Ascended Being who is here as a Volunteer from the Upper Triad, for the reasons already mentioned you will not be transvestite, or homosexual, or walk-ins, nor will you have any tendencies that you might be that way. These manners of being are not part of the soul memory of an Ascended Being, nor would the soul of an Ascended Being lead you into being or accepting those forms of being as part of your Volunteer life. If you know you are an Ascended Being Volunteer, but one who has presumed, through Terran-conditioned misidentification with these classifications defining who thought you were, and if you have no problem recognizing and accepting the fact that you are not those things after all, and if you feel no hesitancy whatsoever with letting go of those mistaken-identities, then the transition from your misidentity to your true identity will be immediate, easy and joyous.

So, we want you to understand the difference between Volunteers who are Ascended Beings, and volunteers who are extraterrestrials. With this information providing you the knowledge by which to know the difference between the two, you can then readily recognize which level of Volunteer you are actually part of.

And we want you to know that whichever level of Volunteer you are part of, it is all equally good for all of it is accomplishing things that need to play out here in the Lower Triad for the purpose of soul evolution. One is not better, superior, nor more divine than the other for they each exist in-and-of-themselves for evenly balanced purposeful good.

So do be honest with your assessment of which level of Volunteer you are part of, for once you do that then you can dedicate yourselves fully to the work you are here to do, in the way that you need to do it, and to associating yourself with the particular group of Beings that you are part of.

We hope this has clarified the matter for you. That is all for now.

I am An T'na of the Intergalactic Board of Council

IBOC COMMUNIQUÉ

Session 004

Shifting From Stage 1 to Stage 2, Then Stage 3 and 4
Disclosure Work Initiates Contact Event
Ascension of the Planet
Timing of Ascension
Death Process is Changing for Ascending Souls and Volunteers
Positive Effects of the Contact Event
Timing of Contact Event
Focus on Your Ascension Reality
Increased Releasing of Soul Memory
The Trick to Manifesting What You Want

(C/D = session facilitators   A = An T'na)

A: Good evening. It is good to be here with you again. We have something that we wish to address concerning our sessions. It is concerning the manner in which we are doing our communiqués.

We have set up these communications in stages. These sessions, up until this one, have been what we refer to as "Stage 1" of these communications. Stage 1 has been done using our oracle as the voice for vocalizing the information that we are presenting to you, to all Volunteers, and to all those who are ascending. This form of communication, which you call channeling, and the way that we have been going about it together as a group, has been for the purpose of, shall we say, getting the ball rolling for presenting these communications publicly.

From Contact to Ascension

We have reached a point now where we are satisfied that enough information has been imparted which can be put on your public sources. More information will be forthcoming over time.

As Stage 1 progressed in a channeled manner, we are now shifting the manner in which our communications are imparted. In other words, our oracle will begin to communicate the information by the use of what our oracle calls psychography. We will be conveying it through her in a setting where this information will come forth from us and flow through her as she enters it directly into her computer.

Now, our purpose for shifting away from the vocally channeled manner of these sessions, to doing it through psychography is because this will save time for our oracle from having to transcribe the channeled information that has been recorded, so that she can spend more time focusing on receiving additional information. This will save much time.

Beginning with Session 5 we are shifting from Stage 1 of facilitated vocally channeled information to Stage 2 of psychography. Gesanna is exceptionally experienced in this manner of interdimensional conveyance.

Stage 3 will consist of initial preparations being made for the start of the formation of core teams of Volunteers who will lead groups of people in the necessary endeavor of public education of all-things-extraterrestrial. This stage is the beginning of our work taking on physical form of action, circumstances and events that compose the educational work to be done, first locally then globally.

This work leads into the initializing of Stage 4. Stage 4 is dependent upon Stage 3 being accomplished successfully because Stage 3 is the point in time where the people of Terra show their desire and readiness for Stage 4 to occur because Stage 4 is connected with Ascended Beings making contact with all ascending souls and our Volunteers. At this stage, contact will be done through unconcealed, open affairs.

IBOC Communique Session 004

D: Is your descriptions of the stages related to the blueprint that you originally talked about, meaning all of this information, or is this different? We talked about the blueprint for the body, but I got the feeling that the blueprint was more than just the body; that there's more to it than that.

A: What you are asking about has many levels to it. There is a personal blueprint. There is a biological blueprint of your body. There is a blueprint of your life although that blueprint is very generalized because you have free will. There is a blueprint on a very large scale, on a universal scale of what is transpiring. If you would like to say that we have a blueprint for the ascension event that we are assisting with, then we could call that a "blueprint".

C: What about if we're choosing to create something…can we create a blueprint for that so that it comes in quickly?

A: Yes. You can create a blueprint for anything that you would like to bring forth into your life. The more clear you are on what the blueprint contains then the more specific are the things that you will receive relative to that blueprint.

So, we will be presenting our information in the manner we just described. If you want to call it a sort of blueprint, or a schematic, then that is fine.

We advise you, though, when receiving comments or questions from the readers, that there be no attention given to negative comments or questions that are aimed at being rude or destructive.

D: Are we going to be doing a sort of course for people in the future, like a weekend course, or something?

A: For the moment, precisely what all of this may lead to in the future is open-ended. That would depend upon those who are relating to what we are presenting for their benefit, and dependent as well as what they are wanting or requesting. So we will leave that as an open-ended potential.

C: Are you up for teaching, An T'na? You seem to be the one that's most qualified.

A: What you are asking has overlapping ideas to it. Let us be clear that there is a difference between our oracle conveying to you our information, and I myself teaching classes. Again, this matter depends upon how all of this work unfolds because much of that is dependent upon all of you to make it happen for you, or not, as you so choose to experience your lives. In other words, if you accomplish Stage 3 then we will set Stage 4 in motion.

During Stage 3, when our core teams have established teachers to educate the public about all-things-extraterrestrial-extradimensional, we could have our oracle be present for channelings during public gatherings.

Understand that this is not the same as classes being taught personally by me. This is not part of the plan of Stage 3 because Stage 4 involves many Ascended Beings coming in physically to your planet to assist your work, not take it over for you. You see?

Stage 4 will include more than just education, and this subject will be discussed at a later time.

But, it is our foreseen awareness that Stage 3 is going to develop very quickly on this planet into a particular circumstance where, shall we say, an education is going to be "asked for" or demanded by the public...not by your officialdom, but by your people. This education will be based in the subject matter of disclosure and contact.

We shall speak a bit more about Stage 3 now for this is where you are quickly heading.

IBOC Communique Session 004

We have previously discussed the fact that there are basically 2 types of Beings who will be making contact with the people of this planet.

To reiterate, first of all: There will be those Beings who we refer to as Lower Triad extraterrestrials. They are the ones who are making contact with Terran souls who are not evolving beyond the Lower Triad. They may be evolving within the Lower Triad to higher levels of understanding, and to higher levels of awareness within the Lower Triad, but they are not evolving yet beyond the Lower Triad.

Please understand the difference of that which we are speaking about here. Of these particular types of Beings, there are extraterrestrials who will provide beneficial educational information to those souls who are not ascending but who still have more information to gain through their experiences within the Lower Triad. Both parties will benefit mutually from this kind of contact event, as they will resonate eagerly with one another's exchange of information.

And then there is the group of Beings who have already ascended, who are of, and coming here from, the Upper Triad. These are the ones who will be making contact with our Volunteers and with all souls who are ascending beyond the Lower Triad. These Ascending Souls need educational information about the Upper Triad, which our Volunteers can also provide once they remember who they truly are, and once they remember what life is like in the Upper Triad. You must remember that Ascending Souls have never been there before so this souljourn is totally new for them.

As for the Intergalactic Board of Council, our contact with ascending souls is to help familiarize them with the many and various Beings of whom they will be coming in contact with prior to and once they are living in the Upper Triad. During the coming contact period, they will become increasingly more educated about what life is like in the Upper Triad. It will be sort of like a "prep school", if you will, for these ascending souls.

From Contact to Ascension

Now, our Volunteers could also use some prepping for remembering who they truly are as Ascended Being Volunteers.

Accordingly, our coming contact event with you will serve both groups – the ascending souls and our ascended Volunteers. For our Volunteers it will be a remembering; for ascending souls it will be an education, helping them to understand where it is that they are going. It is information that they will innately resonate with and be drawn to receiving.

Now, of the souls who are not ascending; when they make contact with the Lower Triad extraterrestrials, and they will be mutually drawn to one another as well, they will be doing so for reasons other than ascension, reasons that have to do with life that is relative to their continued evolution within the Lower Triad.

Because ascending souls are moving away from the Lower Triad, the information that will be coming forth from contact with Lower Triad extraterrestrials will be of no use to them because they are moving out of the ways of life as it is lived within the Lower Triad, meaning, in other words, of what use is such information when you have already gained all there is to gain from the understanding that such information offers?

While there is extraterrestrial contact occurring for non-ascending souls, the nature of that contact and the nature of the content of the information they receive, will be very different from the nature of contact and information that Ascending Souls and our Volunteers will be having.

Hence, there is a distinction with this matter that we wish you to become clear about. It is important that you remember that there is a difference so that when contact does occur, that you are be able to discern who is contacting which group of Terrans on this planet.

IBOC Communique Session 004

We impart this information within the context of your question because the information that will be coming forth through our communiqués has everything to do with educating ascending souls, regarding who they are and where they are going.

On the other hand, it will not benefit them to have information about what wars are or were going on in this galaxy with that other galaxy over there, or who the players are or were in those events, or other events of, say, space exploration that may be going on within the Lower Triad. Those events, historical and current, belong to the souls who are remaining in the Lower Triad because that information benefits their evolution until they are ready to move out of the Lower Triad. You see?

We want you to understand that there are two distinct groups of contact that will be made by two distinct types of Beings, which is relative to the two distinct groups of Terrans that each group will be contacting.

C: How many earth years do you think there are left before this planet ascends?

A: As we have said before, it is a matter of the timing of the natural processes themselves, and how quickly that transpires. As we said before, it will occur in your lifetime, and that's the best timing we can actually put on this because there's so much that interplays that has to fall into place to bring all of this about. And you are part of that interplay because, again, as we have said before, the process can be enhanced and accelerated by our Volunteers who are here on the planet, and by Ascending Souls, by having conscious, deliberate participation in infusing the light into the planet.

C: Like what we call "collective consciousness"?

A: Yes. Doing it collectively is good. Doing it consciously and deliberately on your own is still very helpful. When you're doing it as a group, it's more impactful, but this does not necessitate any formal gathering of minds or bodies. As more and more Volunteers remember who they are, and as more and more Ascending Souls understand who they are, you come together in a naturally induced common consciousness, a common awareness of what is going on, which intensifies the energy that is being anchored into the planet, causing it to accelerate the ascension processes of the planet.

Now we wish to point out that in your visions of the planet shifting into the Upper Triad, that you understand the planet is actually going nowhere in space-time. It's not moving up, it's not moving anywhere directionally.

This is very difficult to describe in your words. It is transcending itself into a higher frequency, vibrating at a higher frequency, yet it is going nowhere in space or time while it is doing this. It is transfiguring from one dimension and density into another.

As the planet is vibrating at a higher rate of speed, the 3rd density environment in which the planet has existed since its conception begins to shift beyond its 3rd dimensional environment within the Lower Triad, to being that of a 5th dimensional density within the Upper Triad, relative to the energies that exist there. Yet the planet has gone nowhere directionally in space or time.

Upon entering the 5th dimension, the planet remains in a state of physicality, albeit a 5th density one. For those who are ascending along with the planet, it is as if your ability to interact with the planet and all of nature remains the same as you currently experience it. You don't notice a difference in the tactility between you and the planet because both are ascending the frequencies synergistically.

Here is part of what is happening with this ascension process: When a Being is ascending, and if they pass away before the planet has completed its ascension, such as our oracles beloved cats, with the planet ascending into higher states of frequencies, life as you've known it has already shifted beyond the point of frequency where the process of death used to be experienced. As the planet is moving further away from that frequency of the death experience, all of nature and ascending souls have begun to shift so that you are no longer having the same processes once the body has died.

Now, please understand that this is not occurring for those souls who are not ascending. The reason for this has everything to do with meta-quantum physics, as we have previously explained in a very simplified manner.

Non-ascending souls are still connected to the same frequency wherein death has been experienced all along. Because they are not ascending, they will continue to experience death through the same processes that have existed all along for them, although we wish to clarify that what you have been told about death is not entirely true. You have made, and been given, false assumptions about it.

A lot of Terrans are beginning to realize that there is far more that lies beyond the typical death experience than they have been told about it. Advances in this area are serving their awakening, however slow and gradual it may be.

What we are getting at here is that once the person or creature has died, the soul then made its transition from its 3rd density state to a 2nd density state, which has a less complex scaffolding. As it does so, the soul goes through what you call the tunnel of light; in other words, it is seeing a more ethereal form and moves toward that light. The soul moves into what you call the zone of death, or the death zone, where deceased souls continue existing, so to speak, in a manner that is relative to that level or kind of existence. It is here where sentient souls prepare for future lifetimes.

In that zone there are meetings with mentors who help prepare the soul for its next lifetime. But you must understand that this does not apply to nature since nature does not reincarnate, regardless of how popular that idea is, because nature has no conscious self-will that creates karma or such concepts that impels it to require a step backward into a former state of existence.

Nature is constantly moving forward in its evolution. It does not stagnate. It does not repeat itself. Nature is on a path that innately conveys itself forward, possessing no opposing sense that it could, should, or would even want to do otherwise. That is how and why the planet itself is always ascending. The planet, which includes all of nature, has reached a point in its ascension process that is conveying it out of the Lower Triad and into the Upper Triad. You see?

Now, the death process that you have been familiar with even if in a limited sense, is what has been happening for everyone and everything that dies. But this no longer applies all across the board, as you would say.

What is happening for the planet, for nature, for ascending souls and, of course, all of you Volunteers, is that you've moved away from that process. Because the frequency that you are ascending into is higher and less dense, you are moving more away from the death zone and more into what we would call the "forever life zone".

Remember, this does not apply to non-ascending souls who possess self-will to resist ascension so that they can continue their evolution within the framework of the Lower Triad. This same option applied to all of us in every lifetime up until the one where we finally chose to ascend. So don't knock 'em for it, as you would say.

Therefore in-lieu of all of this, the new death experience for nature and ascending souls is no longer the same as it has been. They are no longer going through a tunnel of light. They are no longer ending up in the death zone. They have already entered into what we call the frequencies of the higher ascended realm. They are already entering it because the planet is already partially entered into that forever life zone. It has not completely ascended yet, but it is enough of the way there that it has moved beyond the frequency-clutches of the death zone. We hope you are understanding this.

This does not mean that the death zone itself no longer exists, for it still does but only for the non-ascending souls. It is an ethereal place that is being held intact by the non-ascending souls who are not ready to evolve beyond the concept of who they are.

Our oracle has been experiencing her cat who, as she likes to say, lost atomic density, so that he is still around her, not because he hasn't transitioned into the death zone but because he entered the forever life zone. Consequently, he hasn't gone anywhere because there is nowhere for nature and ascending souls to go now because the planet is ascending more and more into the forever life zone.

D: So where there used to be a sort of veil that separated us, that's becoming very thin, or non-existent?

A: Yes, but only for the planet, for nature and all who are ascending. The veil is still very much intact for non-ascending souls because they believe that this is part of who they are, how they are, what life is like for them. For them the death zone is still part of their experience where they will still go through the tunnel to the light, and so on.

For you, on the other hand, the more that the planet ascends in frequency, the thinner this veil becomes until you reach the point where there is no longer any sense of separation at all. Your physical body, then, has become its ideal blueprint to where it sees and interacts with all life that exists in the Upper Triad.

Even the plants, animals, and all of nature that has passed on in the past, because they do not reincarnate they themselves will become increasingly more interactable with you, such as your pets and your other creatures that have died. All of nature remains in the flow of ascension.

From Contact to Ascension

Souls who have already passed on, who are on the path of ascension, even if it they passed on in the past, these souls are ascending with the planet also. You will be rejoining them in the Upper Triad.

Now, if you're experiencing non-ascending souls who are not on the path of ascension, and you're experiencing their presence, then those are the ones who have not yet made their transition through the tunnel to the death zone. They may be stuck here, and need to be released and moved on.

But for Ascending Souls who pass on before the planet ascends, they are, shall we say, very busy going to school.

For instance, her mother visited our oracle soon after she passed away. Our oracle was surprised to see her mother, in her room at night. Our oracle asked her what she was doing there. Her mother said, "I am supposed to be in class, at the School For Masters, but I wanted to come and check in on you instead". Our oracle said, "Well, I'm glad to see you, but I think you better go back to school because it sounds important". And so, her mother, satisfied that her daughter was doing OK, left and went back to her class.

From this experience our oracle learned that even though her mother had passed on, she is on the path of ascension. She is taking classes, so to speak, that contain the same information that we are presenting to all ascending souls on this planet. She's simply in a school for Ascending Souls who "lost atomic density", so to speak, to have fun with you.

So yes, you will be coming across souls who have been on the path of ascension, who have been deceased. You will be coming across your former pets, and even plants that you may have had affections for, all of nature.

These communiqués of information that we are sharing is designed to help our Volunteers remember, and ascending souls to understand, the ascension process you are undergoing, to understand who you truly are, and to understand who it is that you will be encountering as the ascension progresses forward. It is to bring forth clarity. That is what we have been doing ever since we began giving these communiqués of information.

For now, do you have any questions that you would like to ask of us?

C: Could you tell us if the ascension process is being "synchronized" with or hinges upon on the complete breakdown of our government?

A: No. It doesn't hinge upon humanity at all, or what Terrans choose to do or not do. It hinges solely upon the fact the planet itself is an entity and it is ready to ascend, regardless of what its occupants decide to do.

C: Do you have a general idea, whether it's 10 earth years or 5 earth years, or when ascension will occur?

A: We have said before that it will occur within your lifetime. But to be more specific about the matter, we have to say that this is an overlapping question.

The fact is that there is the ascension of the universe that is occurring, there is the ascension of entities, and there is the ascension of stars, planets, nature and so on. Each of these ascension events has a different timing of the processes necessary for each to ascend.

If you are asking relative to your own ascension, then, speaking unto all our Volunteers regarding this matter, you each have 2 answers, both of which are determined by how you choose to experience your personal life. Neither choice is set in stone.

One choice you have is that upon the death of your Terran embodiments you will ascend back to your place and body of origin in the Upper Triad. While this choice of physical death is not what we have in mind for our Volunteers to experience, you do have free will in the matter. This ascension-upon-death will definitely occur within your lifetime on Terra.

As we have discussed previously, your other choice, and the one we prefer for you, is to ascend with this planet, but it is up to you to remain in your Terran embodiments long enough for the planet to make its ascension to the Upper Triad.

As for the timing of the planet's ascension, it depends upon natural factors of transformation that are beyond our control time-wise. We have said that the ascension of your planet is an experiment due to the fact that not only is the planet being ascended but it is being ascended along with its resident souls who themselves are ready to ascend. The timing of this co-ascension venture is an unknown, so a precise time for its completion cannot be given.

This is why we said that only a tentative time can be given of up to a 20-25 year period. And we say that with reserve because there are so many variables involved and, of course, since it is being done through natural processes, nature knows no time aside from its own innate timing. And, as we said, you are part of the variables.

But we're not saying for you to hold that figure as a definite future date because what we prefer you to focus on is the fact that it is done now. The now is the timing of nature and its natural processes so you must work with its timing, not your sense of it. It is accomplished now, because that is the only way that anything ever gets accomplished is in the "now".

As we have said, the ascension of the planet is being quickened by the presence of our Volunteers on Terra. That much we *can* do to quicken the process. Ascended Beings are endeavoring to assist the planet's ascension as quickly as possible while at the same time not doing it before the ascending souls on your planet are themselves ready to ascend. You see the complexity here?

By consciously sensing the planet already existing in the Upper Triad, seeing it already in its pure pristine state where there is no more 3rd dimensional manmade stuff and damage upon it, you deliberately accelerate the ascension itself. As we have said before, as you do this for the planet so you vicariously help quicken the pace of the ascending souls too. That much you can do.

So, the answer to the question, for all of our Volunteers, is that you have a choice and, per the choice of ascending with the planet, much of the timing hinges upon you remaining on the planet and seeing it Home now. This timing overflows to all ascending souls who are ready to go Home with you and the planet.

Thus, you see the complexity here as well?

Now, let us speak of how you can visualize your planet Home more quickly, to the Upper Triad.

In the Upper Triad, your planet is the "ideal garden", if you will, that you would like it to be. It is a wondrous playground. It is a place to enjoy, to relax at. It is a place to experience things that you have not had the opportunity to experience because of your limited state of density in the Lower Triad.

By that, what we are saying is that once you are in the Upper Triad, you can go swim with the whales if you want to. You can fly with the birds. You can communicate directly with your pets and all of nature. There is nothing that you cannot do there, which includes everything that you have not been able to experience in the Lower Triad. So there are a lot of things that you will be doing.

But all of our Volunteers were doing it before they came here to this planet because they were Ascended Beings prior to wearing 3D genes, and you still are Ascended Beings. You will do those things again once you return there.

From Contact to Ascension

You will resume your activities, as we call them, which you left behind when you came to this planet as a Volunteer. Those activities did not go away. They did not stop. They're on-hold, waiting for you to pick up where you left off, if that is what you want to do once you return Home, as we call it.

C: A question I have is, I have noticed that some Volunteers seem to be angry once they have incarnated here. Why is that?

A: What you are observing is not anger but is coming from confusion. They come here and have their memories blocked. They know or sense that something is not right, meaning that something is very different. They cannot understand what it is and so it becomes frustrating. We would not call it "anger". It is confusion in the mind generating frustration in the emotions.

D: We have also observed that when Volunteers are able to tap into their spiritual gifts, they would often be either punished or hushed, which also causes that confusion inside.

A: Yes. That kind of experience has been common amongst all our Volunteers after they came into their Terran family situations because your soul memory of those higher abilities are trying to come forward. Those who were around you, who were your family, friends, your teachers, did not understand it so, to them, what you were doing was fearful, frightening. They tried to silence you, but you simply learned to keep your abilities to yourselves.

None of our Volunteers have lost their abilities. They may have been repressed back down into the soul, but they are still there.

In-lieu of that, we want you to understand that our presentation of this information will help release soul memories to our Volunteers who need to remember, and impart essential knowledge to ascending souls who need to educate.

Part of what Stage 4 hinges upon Stage 3 of you helping educate the public about the forthcoming contact events. When contact with Ascended Beings happens for our Volunteers you will know who is contacting you because you will remember having already known them. Once that event occurs then your soul memories will come forth more and more quickly.

For ascending souls, contact with us will quicken their ascension process because they will be able to increasingly comprehend the information that they are being given. Their awareness will expand much more quickly.

So, there is a specific purpose for these communiqués and the information that is advancing forward to you in the form of preparing all of you for what is yet to come.

Now, we can confidently say the contact event will definitely occur well before the 20 years' time that we gave you earlier. Contact is on your doorstep and, in fact, it's a matter of little time before it knocks the door down, literally, even though those who are in charge on your planet do not want that to happen. But it's going to happen.

D: Do we have to be careful about having contact, because the government is coming down hard on such things? Do we have to be aware of what they're doing?

A: No. For our Volunteers and ascending souls we would like you to understand that the more you focus on them and what they're doing, the more worry and fear you generate within yourself. The stronger or greater is your fear of them, the quicker and more certainly you draw them to you. It's a relative universe, remember.

For another thing, what they are doing is for their own evolutionary purposes, which we shall go into another time.

From Contact to Ascension

D: As the ascension process gets stronger, we're pulling away from all that other stuff?

A: Exactly. But there's a catch here: the more attention you give to that other stuff, the more you hang on to it so that it's like creating an umbilical cord, or, if you will, hooking a bungee cord into it so that on the one hand you're trying to pull away from it as the planet ascends, but on the other hand you're being pulled right back to it by your focus upon what is being done those who aren't ascending. Your attention to it is anchoring you to the circumstances you say you want to leave behind.

D: So the information that we need to get out there to the public is for them to let go of all this fear and all of this political stuff, and to move on from it?

A: Only to ascending souls and you Volunteers, but not to those who are not ascending.

You see, we want you to understand and remember that for souls who are not ascending all of that other stuff is their reality, and it is your job to lovingly allow them to have it as their lessons in personal evolution because it what is assisting them to migrate to their next step of experience in the new universe. We shall speak more about this later.

Now regarding ascending souls, they are the ones who you need to help understand that the circumstances that non-ascending souls are going through is not a part of the world that you and ascending souls are going through.

You need to recognize the distinction between these two paths of evolution. You need to understand that at this time there are two very different realities superimposed upon one another.

Consequently, it is important that you identify which reality you belong to, and simply disregard the other one as being completely non-pertinent to you.

You see, non-ascending souls are already doing that for themselves. They are disregarding the reality wherein ascension is a occurring. To them ascension is non-existent. To them your personal ascension and that of the planet has no reality-base.

But you Volunteers and Ascending Souls are aware of both realities, and it is your job to recognize which one you belong to and dominantly focus upon it while allowing the other one to "just be".

Non-ascending souls are the ones who are all wrapped up in what's going on with politics, economics, what's going on in their neighbor's life, with sports, celebrity news, and all that other stuff. They are the ones who are innately vibrationally attracted to those things because that is their point in the evolution of their soul.

It is your job to lovingly allow them to be there. It's their right to be there, focusing on all that stuff because it is a vibrational frequency that they are attuned to, and it is all a part of path that they need to be on in order to gain a greater understanding from it.

So, we cannot rightfully expect them to leave that path simply because we don't belong on it or we don't like it.

It is your job to be aware that it's going on in that other reality, but being aware that it is going on for them. It is not your job to entertain its rightness or wrongness for them.

Instead, acknowledge that it's going on, and acknowledge who it's going on for. By doing that then you do not create an emotional attachment of fear within yourself for them.

From Contact to Ascension

Why would you do that to yourself and to them when it is their experience for personal evolution?

It is your job to create an allowing of them to have that experience, however nasty or unpleasant it may seem for them. By doing that, then, you are emotionally disconnecting yourself from that other reality that you've grown beyond, and when you are disconnected from that reality then it cannot affect you in any significant way. Only the ascension reality will affect you if that is the one that you claim as your one and only reality, despite the fact that both of them exist simultaneously.

Shift your attention to the ascension reality that is transpiring, and to all the wonderful and beautiful things that are happening with that experience, and you shall have them. There are wonderful things that are occurring in your ascension reality. And, if you need to refocus your attention back into the ascension reality, you can go out into nature, or look at some of those wonderful things on your computer, such as going to your plant and animal websites and admire what's going on there. Get creative with it.

For instance, our oracle made a wonderful slideshow on her computer of pictures of lovely, colorful tropical plants and creatures and scenery. She can let this slideshow run, staring at it until she feels better.

C: I have a question regarding the abilities of Volunteers to heal. Did we bring that in from soul knowledge, did we develop it after incarnating, or did we receive it from other Beings who have the same abilities?

A: Your healing abilities are all brought up from the soul level, as a memory, because all of you have already done those things before. And we're not talking about in this lifetime. You did them in a lifetime before you even had ever ascended. You did not learn them after you ascended because there is no need in the Upper Triad for such abilities. In the Upper Triad, there is nothing negative held within the soul. There is no psychosis or physical disorders of any kind. So, when you came to

Terra on this mission, that information was released from your soul, so you are remembering it. It isn't something you just invented, and it isn't something given you by other Beings. It was something you learned to do in your pre-ascension lifetimes and then remembered in this one.

All of our Volunteers need to get used to the fact that you will have these releasings of soul memory coming forth more and more as the ascension process moves into higher and higher frequencies.

As we have discussed before, you will notice changes going on within your body, such as diet changes. You will notice that you will not be requiring as many prescription drugs, if you take any. You will find yourself not needing as much of it. The same thing goes for vitamin supplements and such. Your body will have a feeling of "ugh" of consuming certain things or doing certain things. And it will fluctuate. Your body will let you know what it needs. Your body is part of nature and since all of nature is ascending your body is naturally trying to ascend as well; and when your consciousness is ascending along with nature, thus your body, then you're in harmony, and you're in harmony with your soul. And that's when you come into the ideal blueprint for your body.

We have stated before, contrary to what you have heard otherwise, ascension is a painless and pleasant process when you are in harmony with its flow.

Pain and discomfort arises when, for one reason or another, you have tweaked yourself out of harmony with its flow. Harmony does not generate pain or discomfort. Any pain or discomfort you experience is the body's way of letting you know that your mind is no longer harmonized with the flow of the ascension process, meaning that you have moved back into the non-ascending reality. Consequently, it means that you need to give attention to why or how you tweaked yourself, and then tweak yourself back into the flow where harmony generates comfort and rejuvenation once again.

The same goes for feeling pain or discomforts stemming from natural planetary activities. These activities are natural to the planet as it adjusts to its new 5th density scaffolding. If you are experiencing pain or discomfort relative to these natural planetary activities, then it is a sign that you need to relax into the flow of your new 5th density scaffolding as well. It's all about being in harmony with the flow of ascension.

So, these are topics that we are discussing contribute to helping you remember your Ascended Being Volunteer status. And they help Ascending Souls who need such prep school education because they haven't done this before consequently what they're experiencing can be confusing to them.

Therefore, it is our intention to bring forth clarity, as we have said from the beginning.

We wish to leave you with some wisdom that will help you manifest what you want more quickly.

You have been told by other spiritual educators on this matter to focus on what you want already being done, just as we discussed with seeing the ascension of the planet already done. Once you decide that there is no other reality but the one you want, that by so choosing that reality over all other possible or probable ones, all the other potentialities to the contrary simply vanish. Consequently, there is only one reality left – the one you want. That one is the reality for you to focus on; see it in your mind and feel it in your emotional state of being.

And, if necessary, dialog in a journal about it in order to somehow make it more real to yourself. There are many techniques and methods that you can use for creative visualization, as you call it. That will help.

But when you do these techniques the trick to success is to accept that the reality that you want as the only reality that exists. Once you do that, then you get rid of the opposites, the alternatives.

IBOC Communique Session 004

That kind of thinking, by the way, is what the Upper Triad is all about.

C & D: hmmm, that's right. That's a good thing to remember.

A: We have enjoyed our visit with you.

That is all for now.
I am An T'na, of the Intergalactic Board of Council

From Contact to Ascension

IBOC COMMUNIQUÉ

Session 005

Being and Living an Integrated Life

An T'na: Welcome! We are happy to continue imparting unto all Ascending Souls and our Volunteers information that clarifies the subject of immortality as you live your personal lives within the effects of that state of being.

In previous sessions, we brought forth clarity regarding the matter of ascension. To recap, this is a process that is occurring on a universal scale. It is an event that is happening to you because you are an aspect of the universe that is ascending. As such, you cannot separate yourself from that which the universe is transpiring because it is within you and all around you. In-lieu of that, you must be aware and understand what is transpiring in order to benefit from its flow to higher frequencies of existence. The more consciously in-tune you are with this flow, the grander will be your experience of it.

Now, that is what is occurring on the long-term scale of your lives. We shall now move more up-close and personal with information that clarifies how you can benefit from being consciously in the flow, thereby having a grander experience of it.

As a rule, your lives are lived in a manner that is highly artificial, meaning that most everything you do is for the purpose of keeping your bodies going long enough to "do your job", then be "retired" because your body has outlived its usefulness, and then dies. There is very little that you do that is not done for this singular purpose. That is why "time off", entertainment, vacations, are so welcomed by you.

From Contact to Ascension

Your leaders have created this manner of artificial life that keeps you focused upon the material side of existence because that is the aspect of life that most benefits them, not you. But it is not, in the least, a natural manner of existence. It is what we term "sophisticated enslavement".

You have been told that the 3rd dimension, which lies within the Lower Triad, is "the physical dimension", leading you to falsely assume that none of the other dimensions have physicality. We are here telling you that they do have physicality, as we have said in previous sessions.

In-lieu of that, you have been told that the spiritual realm exists apart from the physical realm, but we are here telling you that this notion is another deliberate spin on the reality of this dimension.

All dimensions have evolved to the point of having physicality and all are spiritual. The physical and the spiritual exist as an integrated whole on all dimensions. Before you became physical – which is initially accomplished upon the dimension you are currently dwelling in – you were spiritual, and upon becoming physical you added another component of frequencies to yourself which became integrated as a spiritually-physical and physically-spiritual Being. You cannot separate the 2 until the body has died and you revert back to being spiritual.

Death is a curse inculcated upon you by your enslavers because immortality is not good for their slave business. They cannot have their slaves living long enough to figure out what their game is because if they did then their sinister game would be up. No one would play anymore. Death is the greatest part of the artificial life you have been forced to accept as "reality". Your enslavers did not invent death but they use it against you to their own advantage.

So, if you were to figure out how to become immortal, and if enough of you engaged it for yourselves, then your enslavers' game would be up. But by far, not enough of you on your planet are ready for that in any great numbers that would have such a desirable outcome for you as a species.

This means, then, that you Ascending Souls and our Volunteers must engage it for yourselves, as part of how you experience your personal Way Home, and to do it not to "save the planet" from the gloom and doom that the non-ascending souls have chosen to engage for themselves, but to do it for your personal experience.

Now, immortality comes as a side effect of those who are ascending and our Volunteers who have previously already ascended, yet you can deliberately engage biological immortality by realizing that the dimension in which you are residing has its own integrated spiritual and physical frequencies. They are integrated within you right now, but you have been so busy focusing upon the material and physical frequencies that the spiritual ones have been, so to speak, "put on hold". They are there within you but they are dormant, latent energy waiting to be activated by you, by your integration of them.

And by this we mean not that you perceive your life in 2 distinct aspects, one aspect as spiritual and one aspect physical, but rather as an integrated whole. This is a new perception we are presenting to you with this clarification, but it is important that you "get it", to use your verbiage, if you are to integrate into your immortality.

Is integrating into your immortality something you must do in order to ascend? Absolutely not. But doing so beforehand will certainly improve, greatly, your quality of life, the condition of your experiences, which results in having joy during your time within your current dimension.

The fact is that this dimension you are in is no different from the other dimensions with regard to the basis of that which you can experience once you have shifted out of perceiving yourself as being a Terran-enslaved to being a Terran-immortal, for immortality exists on all dimensions, the dimensions of the Lower Triad being no exception. You simply have been led to believe "it isn't so". We are telling you "it is so". So, believe in this truth and this truth shall set you free from a life of enslavement, lifting you instead to a life lived in its frequencies that are natural to this dimension.

What we are asking you to do is to make a paradigm shift in your perception of life that this dimension has to offer you. You currently are not living that natural life, but are living the life that your enslavers have offered you, and we are telling you that there is a major, vast difference that you need to be aware of so you can "see clearly" how to set yourself free of the life you've been held captive to for eons.

The natural manner of existence upon each dimension is the same. Natural existence is based within the frequencies relative to each dimension, and when you are expressing yourself upon a particular dimension then you have direct access to those frequencies because you are those frequencies. You see?

You are the frequencies that compose the Lower Triad dimensions. You are all of them. This means, then, that you have absolute control over how to engage them for the design of your personal life. Yet you cannot access them until you come to realize this as a fact, and you perceive that your physical life is your spiritual life and your spiritual life is your physical life – each being the same thing composed of different yet interactable frequencies. It only seems like the frequencies are distinct from one another, therefore you believe that they reside in you as 2 distinct aspects of your life. But that is yet another lie you've been led to believe because it prevents you from being the integrated Being that you truly are. Integration is the key word here for you to comprehend.

Your enslavers have created and re-enforced the separation of spirit and flesh by giving you religion and your so-called new-age non-religious groups of "spirituality". All of these are designed to steer your perception of your spiritual aspect into being something distinct thus dissimilar from your physical aspect. They emphasize religion and spirituality as being an important part of your life, so that the concepts contained within religion and spirituality function as a corporate business that they are expanding larger every day; conversely they emphasize your physical life as being important so that they bombard you with an onslaught of material stuff to be required and desired by you without end. Thus they hold up before your eyes the idea that both aspects are so characteristically difference from one another, yet each important, all the while they keep creating the increasing dissimilarities of each aspect for the purpose of keeping you disintegrated, because they know, be it consciously or subconsciously, that your integration of both means immortality for you which puts them out of the slave business. You see how it works.

When you stop treating your life as if it has 2 distinct aspects to it, and treat it instead as it truly is – an integrated whole – then you will begin to experience many changes occurring within yourself and your life.

We share this clarification with you because it is, in-part, how you align your consciousness with your soul, your conscious identity of yourself with your soul's identity of you as an integrated Being. It is your conscious misidentity believing that your physical and spiritual frequencies are distinct thus dissimilar from one another which, among other things we've already discussed, keeps you disintegrated with your soul's awareness and beingness of full self-integration.

An analogy of this might be that of water and oil in the same bowl wherein although the 2 are always together they do not mix together – the one being distinct thus dissimilar from the other even though they exist together in the same bowl. This is what you have done to disintegrate your frequencies.

Now, we use the analogy of music to show you how you are actually all frequencies integrated harmoniously together wherein, although each note is a frequency of its own, they blend together at the same time. This is the way your soul knows you to truly be. Discordant cords sound harsh and feel unharmonious but they still mix together. There is nothing isolating one frequency from another.

From Contact to Ascension

To use another analogy, one of water and salt: Mix them together and they co-exist harmoniously as one entirely new state of being. Together the 2 substances have different attributes, behaviors, and qualities than they do separately. Together they can do things that cannot be done separately. This is how you are as a fully integrated Being.

As an integrated Being your life would be very different than it is currently. You would not be enslaved, so what do you think your life would be like then? You would no longer be enslaved to a job merely to keep the body going long enough to be of use to your enslavers, only to die in the end in spite of it all. What would your life be like if you no longer did that? What would you do if you didn't have to do the same things that you have to do every day just so that your body can be used as the means by which your enslavers acquire their plethora of enjoyment for themselves, as they benefit from your hard work and your advances and your inventions and your need to be a consumer of the material stuff that in-turn keeps you trapped as their slaves who are feasting off of the life that you falsely assume you are living for yourselves?

Can you even conceive of what you would do with yourselves if your lives didn't have to be lived as a slave engaged in providing a good life for your enslavers?

Strip it all away and what do you have left? Can you conceive of it? We ask you to give this some thought for until you can conceive of it you cannot achieve the immortality that comes along with it.

We shall end this communiqué here for we wish you to give this some earnest thought. We also wish you to take time to perceive yourselves into the new paradigm that "heals" what you erroneously distinguished as your spiritual life and your physical life back into being an integrated whole – that you integrate the 2 aspects back into the 1 beautiful symphony that they truly are. For when the 2 – physical and spirit – have become 1, then you shall enter into living that which has been termed "heaven on Earth" – in other words, you shall be and live life in its natural manner, as it is meant to be lived on this and all dimensions.

Thank you for your attention. That is all until next time.
I am An T'na of the Intergalactic Board of Council

IBOC COMMUNIQUÉ

Session 006

Take a Benign Approach

Greetings to All. Regarding our communiqués, we are aware that some of you are having difficulty with so-called "non-believers" of ascension, of immortality, of many matters that are positive and good, and these negative-focused people are expressing unkind, and even crude, rude and harsh thoughts toward you. This brief message is to bring forth clarity regarding what to do when you are encountered by reproachful comments regarding any of the matters that we have presented in our communiqués. We have addressed this subject to some degree in previous sessions, and herein we add a helpful suggestion for you.

When communicating with others, you can tell the difference from when someone attacks the truth and just wants to argue, and when someone sincerely desires to understand it further.

When the comments you come across present a case of attacking the truth, rather than having you defend the information that has become part of your own greater understanding as a truth that you are living, we prefer that you simply direct the attention of those unknowledgeable people to reading our communiqués for themselves, and then leave your response at that. They will either take you up on it, or they won't. That choice is up to them. If they read it, they will either comprehend it or they won't, and that is up to their soul. In response to them, you need not "push their shove" any further than gently nudging them to do this.

The reason for you taking this benign approach with such people is that it releases you from feeling like you should go to the arena, if you will, and truth-wrestle with such people. This compassionate approach will save you from expending your precious energy that is better used for more valuable purposes, such as assisting those who sincerely want to evolve their understanding to greater levels of truth, or perhaps for feeding the birds.

When conversing with people who simply want to argue rather than learn, you have a saying, "Save your breath to cool your broth".

Apply that bit of wisdom to what we are advising here, and you will engage the breath of your life much more productively.

That is all for now.
I am An T'na of the Intergalactic Board of Council

IBOC COMMUNIQUÉ

Session 007

Ascended Beings View of Disclosure,
And the Formation of the Forthcoming Core Teams Composing Organized Disclosure

Question: An T'na, the Intergalactic Board of Council has indicated that they have important and, I sense, urgent information to convey regarding Stage 3 of your work here. It is also my sense that you have more information to impart regarding the role that Michael will be playing in his work with you. If you would elaborate about how your work, as a group of Ascended Beings, fits into the coming disclosure and contact events that Michael is working toward, that information would be of use to us.

An T'na: We will address Michael's work with us and as we do we will weave into it other pertinent information, as it is all co-related.

First of all, we want to clarify our meaning of disclosure.

When we speak of disclosure, we use it in reference to the phase that you are currently in as an evolving species. Disclosure is about just that – meaning, the people of Terra will be made aware not only of the reality of extraterrestrial existence, but also of the reality of Ascended Being existence as well. We suggest that readers refer to our earlier communiqués for an explanation of our use of the term Ascended Being.

There are 2 types of disclosure – one that is brought on by your own efforts, by your own people doing the disclosing, so we will refer to this as public disclosure.

From Contact to Ascension

The other type is the one you perceive most frequently as that which you call official disclosure that is brought about by your government leaders. We do not recognize nor sanction official disclosure itself as an appropriate way to bring it about for they have already created covert plans to do it in a manner that is to their own benefit – a very old story for you by now we should think!

We do, however, recognize cooperative official support of public generated disclosure, which some of your countries are already doing – they are supporting, not overtaking the public's initiative of disclosure. Please understand the difference here in this regard. We highly commend these countries for their willingness to help your species take your next great leap toward becoming a member of the Galactic Society.

So, we wish you to be clear about the difference between these two types of disclosure. We sanction and encourage public disclosure, and we are here, along with many other non-terrestrial groups, to help you accomplish this immense goal.

Another clarification about our use of disclosure is, to disclose is to educate, and we refer to it in terms of the public educating the public – you are disclosing to your people the necessary information that your governments have kept from you, and you are doing so as close to the facts as you can. The information locked away in government files will not be of any further benefit to your people than the information you already have which is sufficient for the cause.

What you are wanting from your governments is their admittance to the truth of non-terrestrial existence – as intelligent Beings of the universe and not just as lowly pond scum on some lonely little planet or moon far, far away.

For some countries, this admittance will never occur because the stance of official denial, even in the face of all evidence to the contrary, legally shelters them from repercussions of lawsuits that some of your people would like to heap upon them. Your country [USA] is one of them. It is to your benefit that you cease spinning your wheels, as you say, in order to gain such admittances from your government, and instead sanction yourselves with the truth and go forward from there. No government is stopping you from educating your own people.

Now, we have chosen Michael for his role as one of our leading team members due to his experience engaged in circumstances of diplomacy, for his teaching skills, for the public work he has already pursued on this subject, for his willingness to donate time and energy toward furthering the issue of disclosure, for his personal initiative to delve into this subject, and his staunchness in the face of the controversy that has confronted him over the years.

Putting that into the context of his work with us, we are aware that he not only has extensive knowledge about the necessary topics, but that it is also grounded in reasonability and sensibility. It is the sound quality of his overall approach to bringing forth the information so needed by those on your planet that makes him a valuable team player with us. It is his ability to be diplomatic in breaching the gaps of understanding between peoples that have been inculcated upon your public by a very dishonest, secretive and, we must say, despicable group of planetary leaders.

He has created, and teaches, online courses in Galactic Diplomacy; he maintains a website with much information; he has written books about the matter and, more recently, he has published a lengthy and well-researched book which we consider to be worthy of use as a so-called primer for the masses that discloses much information that your governments have chosen not to disclose publicly. [See * note below.] Michael's disclosure primer, among others of such information, will help educate the masses for the coming contact event.

We call it a primer because it is basic essential, yet, straightforward information about this given subject matter, based upon your collected data of experiences and investigations that have occurred amongst the Terran peoples around the world. This collection of information is destined to become much more extensive, as well as corrected, as things shift into the contact event itself.

We wish you to understand that we do not claim that Michael and his work is what you say, the end-all of this matter. Please take note that he and his work is that of but one cooperative team player amongst many others who are also working around the nation and the world with the Beings whom they are in contact regularly. This is a very massive Plan for Terra that has been wisely created and orchestrated at levels beyond what is possible for you to do yourselves in such a short amount of time, which we will go into later.

For the disclosure effort, we have chosen Michael to work with our group, which is called the Intergalactic Board of Council, as one so-called leader amongst many other such leaders around your world who have been assessed as appropriate for this level of work. They serve as our feet-on-the-ground members who are capable of physically organizing local groups of Terrans to head-up the larger disclosure-educational networks in their regions, and then to help coordinate it with other regional networks on a much larger planetary network scale of accomplishment.

Now, because Terran knowledge regarding this matter has been deliberately limited with so much of it distorted by your negative factions, Michael's primer will serve as an appropriate introduction to many people, regarding all-things-extraterrestrial and extradimensional, and to some degree concerning what to expect, with regard to the contact event that is soon to occur.

Michael's book – and mind you, there are other books which are just as adequate but just to be clear, our group will be using his book amongst others – his book contains enough pertinent information to suffice public awareness, and to shed a reasonable enough degree of enlightenment on the matter.

So again, we say to you that you need not grasp for straws from government files until your governments agree to support the public initiative of disclosure and thus freely, and non-coercively, offer their files to you.

Upon contact, the expanded and corrected information itself will contribute to the greater understanding of all, for all; and it will be given freely to all Terrans by various extraterrestrial and extradimensional groups who are set to engage their contact events around the planet.

Prior to the contact event, it is very helpful for you to go through your disclosure phase, which we will focus upon more in-depth for now, since the event of disclosure is your next step. This current phase will include in-class educational programs – both in-person and through your Internet outlets; taught by Terran teachers who possess such knowledge. This will be done planetwide. It has already been occurring to a somewhat limited degree through various conference and retreat outlets, but the coming vaster educational network that we speak of and present to you now will be open and free to all people, for which there is very good reason, as you shall see.

We wish to see those Terrans who are engaged in various ways of bringing about assistance and education in this matter to begin to offer these freely to the masses, as much as possible, as often as possible. It is time for you to shift yourselves to your next step in how you do information sharing.

By making this shift you will be helping bring about, much more quickly and more broadly, the disclosure that you so greatly desire by perceiving it in a new and higher manner of sharing – that of being part of a globalized free-and-open-sourced effort of the people, by the people, for the people, as you say. Doing so demonstrates to us your determination that this is what you and your planet want to have as the next step in your life experience; you will initiate a show of your intent to live in a kind of non-monetary society that you say you want to have, and, by so doing, you will be helping your Global Society be accepted into the Galactic Society that you want to experience as your new way of life.

In other words: It is to your own benefit to show unto Those you want contact with at least the beginnings of being the life that you are wanting to have with us.

Shifting from required fees for attendances of services or lectures or ebooks or internet articles or video viewings, and so on – to receiving donations of money, or through work exchange, or other means of exchange for any portion of your efforts that works well for you and others equally, is an acceptable step toward initiating a show of a non-monetary society occurring on your planet.

We are aware that there are groups of people who have been moving certain aspects of life toward a non-monetary society on your planet, and we invite your so-called Spiritual and UFO Communities to do likewise by shifting away from charging money for information regarding disclosure and contact, to doing it for free or asking for donations of some sort for as many outlets as you can do – the more the better, of course.

We understand that you have developed monetary-specific patterns by which you orchestrate and execute your conferences, programs, seminars, retreats, books, and so forth, so that shifting gears to offer one or more of them free of charge means a change in how you perceive the situation and go about engaging them.

We are aware that you do have some alternative methods by which it can occur, and it is up to you to make use of these other options that are available to you.

Educational use of what you call your Internet is one of them. This is an instrument of far-reaching means that we have given you in order that, when the time arrives, you will use it as a disclosure-teaching tool, entirely free or on a donations only basis. Some of you are already doing this and we commend you for it. Now we are calling for an expansion of this willingness to share this particular information freely, as much as you can possibly accomplish, in order to expand the numbers of the populace that you have been trying to reach.

You need to understand that due to the limited time for disclosure, some of the ways and means by which you have been going about accomplishing the informing of the public on these matters are currently no longer effective nor pertinent as a practical process that must now become even more far-reaching than ever before in order to prepare the enormous populace on your planet for the coming global contact event. To use your term, it must become viral.

Think objectively about this matter and you will see that what we invite you to do has merit, credence, and truth. Living as a member of the Galactic Society is something new to you, which you need to get used to not only thinking-in-terms-of, but also living in the actions thereof.

And we cannot emphasize too much to you the importance for you to act quickly with engaging yourselves in public sanctioned, public endorsed, public created, public supported disclosure, for all and unto all Terrans equally; and to cease seeking after gaining official admittances and sanctions from those governments who show signs of resistance to joining, or signs of usurping, the public initiative disclosure cause.

Now, back to our prior comments. The education of the masses needs to occur as soon as possible, and we mention this due to the fact that your time-field is collapsing, or, shall we say, gaining momentum of speed into a higher dimensional state of existence where the time-flow is much higher or quicker than you are used to experiencing.

From Contact to Ascension

Your own sense of time speeding up is part of this enigmatic cosmic event that is transpiring, and this cosmic event is directly related to the reason for our presence here in your solar system.

As such, we have no control over that which is time itself. Throughout the entire universe we are all in its flow together, therefore we can only control our personal experiences within its much vaster actions exerted upon us.

Our presence here has everything to do with assisting your planet into its rightful place in the Upper Triad to where it, your planet, is flowing in-tandem with the universe as it folds up its Lower Triad.

The final fold-up is yet to occur some time in our future, near or far. We simply do not know for sure. But prior to that event it is our work here in the Lower Triad and, specifically, here in your solar system, to assist all planets that are ready for ascension, to metamorphose them, if you will, into the necessary higher or quickened state of existence well before the final fold-up of the Lower Triad.

The reason for this advanced assisted ascension of planets is because no one knows the exact timing of the cosmic forces being exerted upon the properties composing the Lower Triad itself. It is these natural forces that are increasingly in-play that determines when the final fold-up event will occur. Consequently, it could occur sooner than expected, and you have a saying, "Do not put off until tomorrow that which must be done today" for, we add in this vaster cosmic case, eventually "tomorrow will never come"…at least with regard to further tomorrows of this universe's Lower Triad. We strongly recommend that you do not confuse this event with any notion that the entire universe will cease to exist for, indeed, this is not the case at all.

This is also why you are being gradually induced into the knowledge and awareness of Advanced Being and extraterrestrial presences. It is why disclosure and contact with extraterrestrials and Ascended Beings are major events that are about to knock down your doors – starting a cascade of assistance of your awareness and knowledge of the particular entities who you each personally align with upon your current individual path of evolution for, indeed, you are not all aligned with the same species or groups of Beings and their particular paths of evolution.

Your assumption of how and why the disclosure and contact events are taking place at this time has been yet another matter distorted by your negative factions who are attempting to hijack your destiny into the Galactic Society by injecting distorted and falsified data into the information being presented to you through disinformants placed within some of your groups that focus on all-things-extraterrestrial and extradimensional. These falsified and distorted notions have made their way into many of the programs you view on your televisions and movies, read in your printed material, and coming from your computers.

Remember, confusion begets misunderstandings, and misunderstanding begets division, and division begets conflict. That is how the negative factions work, and it is your job to recognize these tactics when you see it and steer clear of the intended deceptions' intentions with you.

The actual reasons for disclosure and contact will not result into the presumed one-extraterrestrial-fits-all sort of scenario, where you all must interact with one or two groups of species. It will not result in an outcome where your planet's society is funneled into a situation that omits some Galactic Society members while accepting only certain others. That scenario is what your negative factions have planned for you.

While the portrayal of your Star Trek kind of society comes close to what you can expect so far as depicting how extensive will be your interactions with others of non-terrestrial origin, the real reason for the disclosure and contact occurring and, consequently, the real destiny-outcome, is far different than that which is portrayed by the writers and creators of your so-called fictional works. This is a detailed topic that we shall address more extensively during another session.

For now, let us clarify that your initial step in bringing about actual disclosure involves much of your own footwork on the matter, on you taking the bull by the horns, so to speak, and steering the matter in the way you want it to go as a Global Society.

The time has arrived for you to act now upon the destiny of your own Global Society. If you do not begin doing so at this time then your negative factions are prepared do it for you. We say this not as a threat to or demand upon you, but it is said as a fact of what awaits you through procrastination or inactivity upon the matter.

Understand, however, that it is not that your negative factions' version of disclosure will utterly prevent you from ever entering into the Galactic Society, for it is a certainty that you will, but taking that route will make it far more difficult for you by way of them generating discordant forms of physical and psychological confrontations between you and your negative factions regarding the entire matter. You will then have to make the long drawn-out and necessary course corrections, all of which can be wholly avoided now if you engage yourselves in the direction that we are endeavoring to guide you into, as we present suggestions for moving in that direction at this time.

Again, it is a direction that you claim you are wanting. It is now time for you to start walking your talk, as you put it, by doing all that is necessary to override and overrule all efforts of being hijacked into any direction other than the one that you want.

To do this we suggest, again, that you get beyond the negative faction's brainwashing that you "must" gain their blessings and sanctions in order to reach your goals of disclosure and contact. You are not forbidden to disclose to one another your knowledge about us and other Beings. You are not forbidden to ask us for, and engage in activities, that promote contact. You are not forbidden to educate one another, either one-on-one or in groups, using whatever public outlets will do the trick.

So, with this fact as your first line of defense, use your freedom of education for disclosure as a public initiative tool to steer yourselves into the direction you want to go, and by so doing you will demonstrate that you as a Global Society are ready to become a member of the Galactic Society.

We suggest that you begin your public disclosure initiative by setting up local grassroots educational networks, as you would refer to it. We suggest that it eventually becomes statewide, and expands from there to become national and international.

To begin with, you need not have a global one-program-fits-all curriculum, for that would be a monumental task to create right away. Eventually you can bring it into such a unified field situation, but it is of more importance for now that you focus on getting started with what you have, where you are, everywhere.

For those of you who are able to travel to other locations, statewide or nationwide, or even planetwide, you can be instrumental in helping to get the educational programs initiated locally, as well as eventually helping set up the regional networks into a much larger global scale.

It would be helpful for those of you who are knowledgeable in this matter, who have been or are presenters and teachers and educators of the subject, to initiate ongoing and regular educational meetings in your local areas, and then to coordinate with others amongst you in other regions, updating your information and your curriculum and your presentation endeavors so as to generate a larger scale of improved approach.

In order for this to work properly, it is time for all such people of this knowledge to put aside all personal differences of opinions about all-things-extraterrestrial and extradimensional, and to do so under the agreement that none of you know or have the complete and/or undistorted facts about any of it, but that you can generously pool the information that you do have, cross-referencing it for its commonalities that can be agreed upon if even only temporarily until you receive the greater facts from us and other members of the Galactic Society who will lovingly make any necessary corrections and expansions of that information.

Our point here is that you get beyond who's right or wrong about any of it, and get on with the needed task of actually educating the people of your planet with the necessary, and however basic, information.

Make this an enjoyable experience amongst yourselves, and uncritizingly unselfishly pool your knowledge, your information, and your efforts. As mature people who may be about to become members of the Galactic Society, sharing it freely and openly amongst yourselves in order to educate your people for your peoples' sake.

Books of information such as Michael has published are acceptable sources of knowledge for the masses. Based upon the information gathered from across your planet and across time, it is a historical overview of the related issues that you've dealt with on your planet; it is a moderate compendium of who's-who out there and, so far as known, what their presumed interactions with you have been and perhaps still are; and so far as known, it includes descriptions of Beings who have ascended to other realms in the Upper Triad, not merely of extraterrestrial or inter- or intraterrestrial or subdimensional beings.

While the information in his book, as all such books of yours have been, is not complete in every respect, and while it is based upon information that is not wholly accurate in its entirety, it is nonetheless sufficient for public education regarding disclosure to begin with.

As we stated, once contact has been made, you will be given the complete and accurate facts. We will continue to impart fundamental information regarding Ascended Beings and the nature of Their Higher

Dimensional realms of residence. It is our intention to allow other groups of extraterrestrials to impart unto you information that pertains to them, for who knows best about them than they do.

The key point is that you take the initiative to begin disclosure with what you have now, begin it with where you are, and your actions will demonstrate, to those not of your world, what you say you are wanting.

No one is here or is going to come here and judge you or test you on the accuracy or quantity of information that you have worked so hard to attain on this matter. You are being observed, not judged, regarding your ability and determination to shift gears and live, right now, what it is you say you are wanting as your new way of life, as a member of a Galactic Society.

Now, we have said that books like Michael's are acceptable sources of public education – they are primers that lead your public into eventually receiving the fuller version of information directly from those Beings who will be contacting you. In-lieu of that, we now further suggest that people like Michael, who have relative knowledge about these matters – and you know who you are – and those of you who are able to organize local and regional groups for educational meetings, that you begin to include this altruistic endeavor into your schedules of activities; that it be done openly and freely to all.

Let us point out that throughout the ages on your planet many benevolent Beings on, or visiting your planet, have freely given you vital information and essential assistance regarding all-things-extraterrestrial and about Ascended Beings, wholly without charge to you. It is time for you to be as selfless and pay-it-forward, as you would say, to your own people amongst you. As it has been lovingly done unto you, so do likewise to those around you. As you have so freely received it, so freely give it forward. Such is the consciousness of those Galactic and Ascended Beings with whom you wish to have contact.

From Contact to Ascension

Thank you for your attention. We shall continue again soon. That is all. I am An T'na of the Intergalactic Board of Council

(* Note: for Michael Salla's online courses in Galactic Diplomacy, articles and other information about this subject matter, please visit his website, http://exopolitics.org)

IBOC COMMUNIQUÉ

Session 008

The Grays Futile Attempts to Ascend, And Your New Cousins

Question: An T'na, in a previous communiqué you mentioned that the unevolved group of extraterrestrials who contacted our governments, back in the 1940's, did so because they wanted to take resources and DNA from us and from our planet. Would you clarify, please, the reasons why they would want to do this?

An T'na: Yes. The common view of a lot of people in your UFO and extraterrestrial community is limited in the extent of the purpose for this act, and the subject has also been the product of much speculation.

Let us enlighten you a bit more about this matter.

While you have assumed that the taking of your resources and DNA has been done for the purpose of gathering compatible genetic material in order to rescue, through genetic modification, their own species from physical extinction – who, in this case in particular, are those you call the Grays – and this endeavor is but half of the fact, half of the all-inclusive purpose for which it has been done. While not completely false in nature, this assumption for the undertaking is true, but it is also nonetheless only a portion of their overall, greater objective. There has been a real madness to their desperate motives, in a literal sense, and we shall elaborate upon this for your understanding.

The history of how these Beings came to find themselves on the precipice of biological extinction is a lengthy one that shall be revealed in-full once contact has been made. The information that you have thus far acquired regarding this history is but the tip of a much larger iceberg, as you would say; yet, its premise is fairly correct.

From Contact to Ascension

For now, suffice it to say that these Beings arrived on their path of near-extinction by their own choices and doings – in other words, they were not externally forced into this dire situation.

These Beings have been well aware, for a very long time, of the pending collapse of the Lower Triad. But they were already well on the path to extinction by the time they learned about this cosmic fact.

You must keep in mind that their lifetimes span a much greater portion of time than does that of the Terran species. So when we speak of time relative to them, we mean it in terms of many, many hundreds of thousands of years relative to you.

Searching endlessly and frantically throughout the Lower Triad portion of the universe for a species whose genetics were compatible with their own – and not just any species' genetics would do, but, they discovered, it had to be one that was capable of assisting them into making a very rapid recovery of their own genetics because they knew that they had a deadline to meet – and you can take that as a pun on your terms, but for them it is a serious one.

Eventually they came upon the Terran species native to your planet and found that there was genetic compatibility. But they knew they could not just barge in and invade your planet so as to herd all of you into cages for the purpose of acquiring your DNA, because their fragile bodies cannot withstand the repercussions of you fighting back; plus your planet's atmosphere is not compatible with the kind of gasses, air pressure, and so on that allows their bodies to thrive. So the genetic project would have to be an off-world task, done while in orbit around your planet, disguised, or cloaked, as you would say, from your view thus your awareness of their presence and intentions with you.

So, their council determined that they would do the next best thing to an all-out invasion – they would make a covert bargain with the major national leaders of the time. And the scheme worked beautifully for them. Without question, due to their own continuous need for greed your leaders bought into the duplicitous nature of the Grays. You can read about these historical events, so far as known, in Michael's book and other books on the subject.

But what is not commonly known within all of this is that through the course of this bargaining process, these duplicitous Beings had inadvertently pitted all your major nations against one another – they themselves consequently served a Machiavellian role in their interactions with you. At first, they were not aware that this increase of international distrust would be the outcome of their surreptitious dealings with your global governments, and when they discovered what had developed, they cared not about it one bit. The damage that they had instigated was already done and well on its way to further disrupting what little peace was left on your precious planet. They would get what they needed from you and then leave you to sort out the global impairment that they had set into motion.

Now, we have already stated that your own national government leaders sold out your opportunity for global peace in exchange for extraterrestrial technologies capable of creating ever more sophisticated thus lethal weapons of mass destruction, as you refer to it. Once the exchange had been made between your governments and their dubious extraterrestrial partners, distrust moved into each country like a wild winter blizzard wind freezing the hearts of your leaders into cold-hearted war mongers who could not get enough blood on their hands fast enough to procure absolute power of control unto themselves. They had dealt themselves in behind walls of fortified security and dealt you out into a whirlwind of increasing greed that by now has found its way into every aspect of your lives.

This has been the outcome of the self-aggrandizing Gray's interactions with your own self-aggrandizing leaders. Remember, this is the result of like-attracting-like in this relative-based universe. It's not that your leaders didn't have a choice in electing to accept the helpful offer of the benevolent Beings, for they certainly did – even they have a heart, but instead they willfully chose to go with the flow of suspicion and fear of their own species, intolerances which resided in their altered egos for such was the imbalance within them between heart and head. And so even today it remains this way within some of your current leaders.

And this is why you must do the job yourselves of bringing forth a public disclosure program without their sanction, without their help, without their blessing.

Now, what has developed with the Grays' attempts to genetically modify themselves is that of one failure occurring after another. It is not that they cannot get the genetic modification to work, but that it won't work fast enough in time for their own embodiments to reach the point of biological ascension for, indeed, genetics alone will not do the trick, and this much they have learned after all this time of trying to make it happen. They have discovered that no one can biologically ascend by taking a genetically modified shortcut to heaven, so to speak, for that which creates ascension of the embodiment is far beyond what can be done by DNA-tweaking processes.

It is the full-range of emotion that is the magic key to unlocking the strands of ascension in the body. And the Grays long ago bred out their ability to be fully emotional in the ways that matter the most. That is not to say that they are completely devoid of emotion, but by tweaking-out all genes that are directly affected by the specific emotions that unlock the strands of ascension in the body, they became their own genetic undoing, unknowingly ensuring in the process that they would eventually never be able to biologically ascend either.

You see, there is no shortcut to heaven, to the Ascended Realms in the Upper Triad, and these Beings have proven that very blatantly. You must earn your own way there through the evolution of your own consciousness and energy. And many souls on your planet are accomplishing this marvelous feat on their own efforts and merits, all done without the help of technology for the reasons discussed in a previous communiqué.

So, the Grays are not to be trusted for they are a duplicitous species by nature. Leave them alone. They are not to be pitied for what they have done to themselves for it all amounts to lessons someday learned within their souls. Bless them and leave them alone. Yet neither are they to be shunned for they have managed to save themselves in a roundabout manner by creating hybridized Beings by mixing your genetics and theirs, as Beings who we call Zeta-Terrans, for their former place of origin was in the Zeta Reticuli star system.

Although they have been unsuccessful with creating the ascension of their own embodiments, they did manage to create a viable hybridized species who would, through another manner, carry on some of the genetics of the Gray species suspended within the blood of this new Zeta-Terran.

The Zeta-Terran embodiment has been tweaked in its appearance so as to be indistinguishable from your full-blooded Terran embodiments, yet the truth can be discovered only through genetic testing that reveals the markers of the Zeta-Gray genes.

In that these Zeta-Terrans are a fairly new introduction onto your planet, few of you will come across them. They have been living for the most part in protected garrisons disguised as businesses, in underground facilities, and the like, watched over and monitored by their "creators", their "guardians" who orbit above the planet.

What gives away the Zeta-Terran more than appearance is behavior. In that the souls who inhabit these Zeta-Terran embodiments are those of the Gray species, once they are incarnated or transferred into their Zeta-Terran embodiments, they being new to the ways and conduct of Terran life, their strange and unusual behavior stands out as what you would consider awkward. Until they learn to become more Terran, they will remain secluded for the most part.

In the meantime, their off-world Gray protector-guardians are dying out as their inability to reproduce their own Zeta embodiments takes its toll on their very small and quickly dwindling population. The entire species will be extinct well before the Lower Triad folds up.

The Zeta-Gray souls who manage to survive, by inhabiting the hybridized Zeta-Terran embodiments, nonetheless will not be able to engage biological ascension into the Upper Triad after all. The Zeta-Terrans are aware of this fact so they are resigned to becoming part of the vast number of groups of souls who are migrating to the new universe, to become the creators of that new adventure.

Having seen the personal evolutionary benefits of this new adventure, the Zeta-Terrans are now willing and eager to participate in this divine destiny that they so long ago set-in-stone for themselves, for indeed, whether one ascends with this universe or one migrates to reside in the new universe, both options are equally divine and necessary unto the existence of those universes. We ask you to remember this so you do not egotistically turn this cosmic fact into some form of duality of good/bad, right/wrong, better/worse, heaven/hell for there is no such thing regarding it.

Although a few Zeta-Terrans have already oriented themselves to live amongst you, once contact has been made you will see the open emergence of all of your Zeta-Terran cousins, for that is truly what they are genetically. We ask you to welcome them just as lovingly as you would any other beloved family member for, indeed, they are but only one of many other extraterrestrial species who will be making their physical presences known to you, interacting directly with you, assisting you in the ways that are relative to the current point in personal evolution of each one of you.

We hope that this has enhanced and broadened your understanding, and has brought forth clarity of the matter.

IBOC Communique Session 008
That is all for now. Stay well and be happy.
I am An T'na of the Intergalactic Board of Council

From Contact to Ascension

IBOC COMMUNIQUÉ

Session 009

The Difference Between Disclosure and Contact
Initiated By the People, vs. By the Government

Question: Please give us further clarification regarding citizen-based disclosure and contact with members of the Galactic Society, as distinguished from the one that our government leaders have planned for us at an official level.

An T'na: With regard to what is occurring per official levels, you currently have a scenario that has developed over a long period of time - a program handed down and refined over time.

In a previous communiqué, we spoke of two groups of self-aggrandizing aliens who made contact and connections with some of the leaders of your planet. We are speaking of your more recent past, for the planet's past is replete with visiting and residing extraterrestrials from a number of places throughout and beyond your galaxy. The third group who made contact with your leaders was of a benevolent nature, and upon your leaders' orders, this group departed from your planet. We shall discuss them in this communiqué later on.

These two more self-centered groups of aliens are still very much involved with your leaders, and each group is busily engaged in the respective agendas that they came here to accomplish.

We ask you to remember that while these groups have, for decades, been doing their thing, so to speak, with your leaders, understand that there have also been other benevolent extraterrestrials and Ascended Beings making contact and interacting with some of your common people. A small portion of this interaction has been done through person-to-person modes of contact, but for the most part it has been done through non-physical modes of telepathy and other types of interface such as lucid dreams, out-of-body experiences and so on. These passive types of interaction are still transpiring except that it is with only a smaller number of common people compared to a much larger number that your government people are in contact with.

In-lieu of that, we shall confine our discussion to your question of how contact and the outcome thereof, as initiated by the people of your planet, differs from contact brought on by your governments.

It is immensely important that you understand the difference between them because you can expect two very different outcomes from each one. Once you understand the difference between them then you will be able to focus yourselves upon the contact path that results in the kind of future that you want to have as your next step in personal and global experience.

Previously we stated that your governments have fought as much as possible against you having any knowledge about the matter, going so far as to make it illegal for you to have such knowledge, and never having any degree of contact with non-terrestrial beings.

The controlling elite has infested every area of your academics, religion, and media with their subordinate moles who are ordered to create the twisted bunk that is to be fed to the public regarding all-things-extraterrestrial and extradimensional. It is their sworn oath, to their higher-ups, to keep the truth from you under all circumstances. Consciously aware of it or not, this extremely strict order comes to them from the highest of their echelons who, each in their own ways, participated in hijacking the favorable destiny of this planet from you-the-people. Clear evidence of this hijacking was observed with their assassination of a president named John Kennedy, whence they began a more overt yet craftly disguised takeover of your government leaders and policies.

It is to their advantage that you have no knowledge of the presence of these invaders who want nothing to do with you except to keep you enslaved in order to accomplish for them whatever their agendas might be from one stage to the next. They are the ones unto whom your governments sold out your opportunity for increasing personal freedom, global peace and species advancement.

Is it any wonder then why your leaders have been so adamant about helping their non-terrestrial cohorts keep the truth hidden from you?

But, you must understand that this situation came about as a result of these leaders originally making this sell-out numerous decades ago. Many of them have since died and many others are close to it today. Other influential cronies who are loyal to the same groups of entities have replaced some of the ones who have died. But others of them have been replaced, covertly by us, by worthy people who's intent it is to break down the walls of secrecy and laws of forbiddance that were constructed on the foundations of the lack that had, so very long ago, generated the extreme fear and thus greed of one of these two groups of aliens.

How did they come to be in a state of lack? We said that long ago when the last group of non-terrestrial Beings was on your planet, most of them left Terra in order to return to their own home planets...and some of them remained behind because they felt they had better opportunities right where they were, on Terra.

It was the departure of their fellow people, who took with them all of their ships, all of their technology, and all of the information for creating it, that the ones who remained behind were thrown into a situation of lack. It very much angered them to lose their space shuttles and all their technology so that they had become stranded on this planet...not at all what they had planned to be the case for themselves, for indeed they had anticipated being able to carry on their journeys for the conquest of space, your planet being but merely one of them. For eons of time, the ultimate takeover of your planet had been a private plot amongst themselves. And this is another discussion for another time.

So, why did their own people leave in the first place? They had done all that they came here to do, and then some, until it became wholly boring and, you might say, evolutionarily outmoded for them to remain here any longer. They had interacted with enough Terrans to know that the species of this planet had quite a bit of evolving yet to do for, in-fact, their own species, save for the few who remained behind, had evolved themselves to higher levels of understanding about what they had done, to the point where they no longer felt vibrationally aligned with the Terrans who they had helped, to some degree, refine as a resident species of this planet. They wanted to bring the Terran species, unto whom they felt a sense of responsibility as their creators, if you will, into their fold, make them equal with themselves as partners, no longer as slaves. But a small group of their own people felt otherwise and refused to allow this to occur. The more evolved of them chose to leave the planet rather than fight amongst themselves over the matter, which they no longer wanted to do.

We stated before that many species have come and gone on this planet, and this group is one of them. Their departure, at that time, was the largest one in your recent history pertaining to this matter.

We have already spoken to some degree about one of the two groups you call the Grays, who are still here but, as we said, are less interactive with you as a dying species. For this other group we have been referring to now, you have a couple of popular names for them, which are Anunnaki and Nefilim. These are but two names used by a couple of cultures in your history. Other cultures had their own names for these so-called "gods of yore". And the history about them that has been handed down to you is considered "folklore" and "myth" but more correctly can be said to be a combination of both fact and fiction for indeed over much time the facts have been interwoven with fiction into something that we could call "factictious".

IBOC Communique Session 009

The recognition and separation of fact from fiction will be revealed to you once contact has been made...meaning contact initiated by the people, for the people.

Now, contact as planned by your governments will certainly not result in you having any knowledge beyond what they deem you to need to know...which, in their eyes will not be any more truth than what you have now. Remember that we just mentioned the matter of legal issues that would confront them should they "tell all" to you.

Although some country's leaders are beginning to cooperate with their citizens' initiatives for disclosure, it is the intent of your U.S. government, and that of a few other allied governments, to present you with a plan of disclosure and contact that fills your confused minds with information that misrepresents the selfish aliens who they want you to believe you are having benevolent contact with. In other words, they will tell you that these aliens are good and caring when they have no intention of being thusly toward you-their-slaves. They are selectively good and caring only amongst themselves and their Terran minions.

Bear in mind that even if this kind of disclosure and contact occurs, you will probably never see the real aliens, those who are the controlling ones. They prefer to remain as "the hidden, unknown, unseen, unnamable Gods" for indeed how can you take revenge on someone you have never seen or know not where they dwell. You will most likely only see their minions, their chosen or ordained priests, just as it has been for a very long time. Even at this moment, they dwell on your planet and you know not who they are or where they are. And they want to keep it that way for reasons that serve their greater good, not yours.

So, your leaders will give you falsified data, a rewritten history of who they are with regard to their affairs with you as a species. They will give you information that has been spun toward the furthering of your loyalty unto them thereby getting you to accomplish their agendas, part of which is to keep you enslaved for their own aggrandizement.

Government-generated disclosure and contact will not occur in any sense that generates the kind of destiny you want to have which makes your planet a member of a Galactic Society. You will not be admitted into the Galactic Society that you desire admittance into, for it is a sure thing that it is their plan to never allow that event to occur for you. They will tell you that you will be joining one, but it will be a mock-up non-terrestrial society composed of their own people and another collaborating species.

Were they to actually allow you to be admitted into the real Galactic Society then they would have to begin cooperating with your citizen-based initiatives for disclosure, and then they would have to allow contact with us to occur unto all people at personal levels, interacting openly and freely with all benevolent extraterrestrials and Ascended Beings. Their agenda does not allow for this because they have other plans to the contrary for you. We know for certainty that there is absolutely no sign whatsoever that these aliens, or your leaders, are cooperating with benevolent Beings for disclosure and contact.

They have, instead, gone so far as to develop elaborate devices and systems and methods of deceiving you into believing that what you are witnessing and experiencing as "contact" is real, but in-fact it will be a holographic illusion. It would all be part of an elaborate ruse, but only the very beginning of an incredibly extensive one designed to keep you as blind about the truth as you ever have been; yet, the ruse itself would serve as a counter to the real disclosure and contact.

Should they succeed in pursuing such a plan then the outcome would be one of ongoing enslavement to an ever-burgeoning technological mode of life that is wholly intended to remove from you, at an increasing rate, your ability to access the innate powers that lie dormant in your souls.

They know that they themselves can never remove your power from your souls, but they do know that they can remove your access of your powers by displacing your natural innate line of access through getting you more and more hooked into the use of technological devices, replacing your awareness of the lines of access with an ignorance of its existence as part of who you truly are. Once the lines of access are replaced by ignorance of them, you subsequently no longer have the ability to activate and engage your natural powers as a sovereign soul unto yourself. You will never be able to know who you truly are, and advancing you to that condition of Self-ignorance is the whole point of their goal. In other words, you will ignorantly belong to them because you will have no way to know that you actually do not.

Now, to be more specific with the kind of disclosure and contact that they will provide you with, it will be done through the afore-mentioned show of intimidation put on by the use of holographic technology. They plan to stage a scenario depicting themselves in charge of battling away the so-called "evil aliens" that one of your presidents spoke of so long ago to another world leader. The objective of such a monstrous display would be to make you believe that they are saving your planet from the evil ones so that you will then perceive, and believe your absurd leaders are the true saviors of your day.

But what is not commonly known, even by most of your UFO/extraterrestrial investigators and researchers who have spoken publicly of such things, is that the reason why this so-called official plan has not yet been initiated by them into action is because your leaders have been awaiting not only the specific day when benevolent extraterrestrials arrive in your local skies but also when Ascended Beings arrive amongst you for open contact.

This plan is intended to intercept and destroy, and fight away from your planet, all extraterrestrial ships arriving in peace and goodwill and desiring to initiate open contact with each of you equally. Your leaders have known that this day is bound to come and, for decades, they have been getting ready for it.

From Contact to Ascension

If having peaceful contact with benevolent Beings were actually part of their plan, then long ago they would have prepared the people of your planet for it, and it would have already occurred by now. Hence, there would never have been any secrecy about it nor laws made against it. The fact that there still are these forbiddances in place testifies to the further fact that they are not cooperating with benevolent extraterrestrials and Ascended Beings for open disclosure and contact that uplifts everyone equally. It blatantly testifies to the fact that their agenda is one of ongoing disempowerment of your awareness of who you truly are and thus how powerful you truly are.

Having you know that fact scares them more than anything else. It is a truth above and beyond all of the highest top-secret extraterrestrial subjects. Who you truly are tops and trumps everything else! When you understand that, then all the seemingly dumb stuff that they do begins to add up, but it is a twisted, despicable, dishonorable logic.

They know that once you have contact with benevolent Beings...both extraterrestrial and Ascended...then their self-aggrandizing game is up because you will come to know who you truly are so that your innate power never allows yourselves to be enslaved ever, ever again.

So, the big deal with having a cover-up of all-things-extraterrestrial is actually a much bigger deal with them having securely in-place a cover-up against you knowing and being who you truly are.

This entire cover-up is being executed not only by means of secrecy and lawmaking, but also punishments for not obeying it. Consequently we could rightly say that these punishments, inherent in the cover-up's laws against you knowing about all-things-extraterrestrial, is really all about punishing you for coming to know who you truly are. Astounding, isn't it.

This is why we stipulate and emphasize that if you don't take action to create your own citizen-initiated disclosure program, and do it soon, then your ability to access your soul's awareness of who you truly are, and the power that lies dormant therein, remains threatened.

As we have said before, any delays and procrastination with engaging a citizen-initiated disclosure program is to your own unpleasant undoing.

We refuse to force you into taking your initial steps toward this accomplishment. You must show interest and make obvious your choice by living like you are ready to join the Galactic Society; you take the initial steps, and we will meet you there.

Now, what would be the outcome of a citizen-initiated disclosure and contact? As we have stated before, it will be different than the one portrayed by your fiction writers and as seen on your films, and by some research-futurists on the matter.

First of all, many species, not just one or two, will contact you. You will not be going into one of their ships right away and dashing off into space.

Each species will have many of their own teachers joining your disclosure educational network groups worldwide, and they will expand your understanding in all-things-extraterrestrial.

And for all Ascending Souls, they will receive from Ascended Beings their knowledge of all-things-extradimensional. In other words, for a period of time, you will all be in school stretching your minds, so to speak, so as to hold all the truths that have been withheld from you by a criminal group of people, and their menacing alien bosses who are being removed off your planet over time. More than that, we shall not divulge at this time. Even when they are removed you still have your own loyalist leaders to keep the ball rolling for their alien bosses.

Now, regarding this worldwide schooling of truth, you will not be tested on anything. This is neither an exam nor a trial. You will each be evaluated for your own personal readiness to participate in programs and activities that you individually resonate with.

These are programs that are designed for bringing all of your own people out of poverty; out of hunger; out of disease; out of homelessness; out of crime - for what is crime but a lack of any of the things of necessity or desire; out of unemployment and employment as the slaves that you have been, working endlessly to build and maintain the ostentatious hives for the royal echelons.

You will have no further need of those mega-buildings of commerce and business and marketing and so on that have been used to keep the slave business intact. You will turn them into housing for the needy and homeless. In rural areas, you will build or rebuild houses for those in need of home repairs and upgrades to decent living conditions.

You will be engaging in activities that disregard all the boundaries and borders and all barriers that have been designed to separate and divide you from one another. You will be able to freely move about, visit, and relocate anywhere on the planet that you so desire, for it is your planet and you should never be barred from accessing any portion of it.

You will have different kinds of vehicles for travel that are unlike what you use now, consequently you will turn all roadways into playgrounds and parks and gardens of beauty for all people to enjoy.

You will close and tear down all zoos, and return the animals to their wild habitats. All animals will be healed of all diseases, and your pets will be free to roam with you without restrictions.

You will clean up and restore your precious planet.

You will not perform these tasks alone. It will not take many decades to complete for we will assist you by showing you how to do the tasks using modes of action that you haven't been privy to know you possess, individually or in groups.

With our assistance you will heal and restore your entire planet in a year's time for there are certainly enough of you currently living on your planet to get the job done efficiently and effectively, very quickly. Teach 7 billion people how to do their specialized task and imagine what can get done, and how quickly it can occur! Imagine how rewarding it will be for all of you - children and adults alike.

In other words, you will all be very busy, we assure you! But it will all be so very fun and gratifying because you will be engaged in the creation of productivity that uplifts yourself and all alike. Everyone will benefit, equally, including your beloved planet and all its wondrous creatures.

Eventually many of you will choose to leave your planet in order to take assignments on starships, or on what you refer to as motherships, and at other planets, happily engaged in activities amongst species you resonate with an idea and experience.

So, what will be the outcome when you-the-people create your own citizen-based disclosure and contact programs, rather than relying on your government leaders to do it for you? ... We assure you that it will be a grand and wondrous education in truth, and an outrageous life of freedom, peace and renewal in fabulous ways you haven't yet dreamed of.

All Ascending Souls will receive an education from our Ascended Being Volunteers and visiting Ascended Beings, receiving knowledge that is relative to existing as an Ascended Being in the Upper Triad. And in time, they will ascend with the planet, to dwell amongst other Ascended Beings with whom they resonate harmoniously.

All our Ascended Being Volunteers will return Home to the lives that they put on-hold long ago in order to engage the volunteer assignments they agreed to do with us, on your behalf. After a period of reorientation, they will resume their former activities.

From Contact to Ascension

So, all-in-all, what will make our contact with you different from that which you can expect from your governments' contact plans for you?

If your leader's plans go through for you, the most noticeable thing will be that life, as you know it will not change much. It will change more in ways that provide you with more and more technological devices by which to further drown your soul with, but not free it. You will continue to be enslaved to many of the same old ways and means of living as you are now but which will become more sophisticated-appearing. It's all just another ploy of seeming "advances in life". Your technological landscape will be the biggest change and you will be told that that is "progress", and that your job is to keep it up and even make it better. Well, not better for you, but better for your enslavers.

Your planet will continue to suffer from ongoing disregard to its needs. Advances in genetics will bring about greater divisions of people into genetic caste systems. You will find a fair depiction of this in your film called, "Gattaca".

Advances in robotics and cyborg systems will create an army of warriors worthy of battling other star systems for dominance and control in outer space. Your planet will become a kind of star wars headquarters for the ruling elite who have, for ages, been here on your planet with this goal in mind.

Compare that scenario to the one that we just described to you as the outcome if you choose to create and implement your own citizen-based disclosure and contact programs.

We wish you to recognize something important underlying all of this: You are now standing in front of your own past whence your planet was offered two choices of destiny by two different groups of aliens visiting your planet.

You-the-people are now being offered the opportunity to choose the destiny that is best for you rather than for your governments. Where in

IBOC Communique Session 009

the past your governments made an inappropriate choice for your planet's destiny, you are now presented with another opportunity to make the appropriate choice for yourselves. You are being given an opportunity to right the wrong done by your leaders so long ago.

We are here to present you with information that is relevant to the two options confronting you once again. Once you've made the choice of creating a citizen-based destiny then we will make open contact with you for direct assistance and camaraderie.

The proverbial spaceball is in your court, to have fun with you. Choose wisely. Be happy. We shall commune with you again soon.

That is all.
I am An T'na of the Intergalactic Board of Council

IBOC COMMUNIQUÉ

Session 10

Understanding Truth-Controllers - Why They Do It, Recognizing Hidden Truth. An Announcement, and, A Special Message to a Special Group of Souls

An T'na: Greetings to All. We are happy to speak to you once again.

We of the Intergalactic Board of Council wish to convey information regarding the abuse of truth, as is performed by a certain group of your leaders and their chosen minions who are strategically installed in your government and political seats of power, in your religious, education, health, social and media services, and so on.

On your planet, the abuse of truth is aimed at anyone who releases truth through the various sources of printed media as well as through the spoken word. We know that this group's main objective is to keep truth from you at all costs, as we discussed in a prior communiqué, stating that they will go to whatever lengths are necessary in order to insure that this clandestine order is carried out upon you all.

In a previous communiqué, we discussed this matter briefly, regarding how to deal with it when it confronts you personally. Now, in order that you have a broader understanding of this behavior that is confronting you, we present in this communiqué clarification regarding why they think and behave this way, and the motive isn't as shallow in purpose as you might presume it to be.

We have observed that it is a religious practice of your planetary controllers to ridicule those who speak truth, who put it forth in spoken word and published formats. These honest upright people in your public forefront whom your controllers choose to focus on are systematically ridiculed in personality, as well as their helpful information being publicly debased by lies and bunk that is predetermined to steer the public's attention away from all truth.

Besides the truth regarding extraterrestrial life being highly controlled and censored, you're not even privy to fully disclosed truth in areas of science, history, biology, anthropology, archeology, medicine, religion, national and international politics, and so on. And you think you're no longer in the Dark Ages of your past era? Think again, people.

Our purpose for presenting you with these informative communiqués is to help you end your Dark Ages that has permeated all areas of your lives as what has been called a "truth embargo", by shining a big light of clarification into the murky abyss that your controllers are holding you in.

In a previous communiqué we stated that we gave you-the-people computers capable of providing you with a global connection through what you call the internet, and that this is to be used as an educational tool, so that you have a broad-sweeping means by which truth will be disseminated equally and quickly unto all of you. At this time we are announcing the creation of our own website, designed for the purpose of making our communiqués more widely available to the public through your Internet systems. We are, therefore, acknowledging that the information we are imparting through these communiqués is truth and, being truth, we are herein helping you quell any negative fires that any truth-censurers and their minions may try to generate as a backlash against truth.

We wish to say to you-the-people: should you find any of our information denigrated and twisted into bunk of any type, understand that this kind of "outburst" made by truth-controllers is actually a tell-tale testament that what is being presented by us through our oracle functioning on our behalf as but a messenger, can indeed be construed as truth.

The reality on your planet is that unevolved souls, such as your controllers, do not make a fuss over those who present information that is non-relevant to truth so long as it falls within the boundaries of the agendas that they are unfolding at the time. They do, however, make a clamorous noisy fuss over those who publicly step outside of their designated boundaries in order to present truth that is pertinent to your personal evolution and that of your species overall.

In-lieu of that as your so-called reality, we wish that you keep this fact in-mind when embracing our, and anyone else's information because it is important that you not only recognize truth when it is revealed to you but it is just as important to recognize when and why it is being hidden from you.

When you understand this, then through their fanatical behavior when heaped upon those who present truth, you can deduce from there what is truth, what information is bunk, or what information is merely mundane stuff, as you would say, that is deemed "safe" because it has no evolutionary effect upon your own Self-Realizing process.

Such safe information would amount to sports, celebrities, entertainment, censored news, censored academic education, religion, sharing recipes, home and garden improvement, benign chit-chat on your various electronic devices, and so on. These commonplace matters do not fall into the zone of endangering the status-quos of the agendas that your controllers endeavor to keep intact for you as their slaves. Therefore, they feel no need to make a fuss over such people presenting agenda-safe information.

We wish you to understand that in most cases aggressive, harsh, relentless harassing words and behavior is one way for you to recognize that the information you are investigating or embracing unto yourself is based upon truth, and through that external action you can receive a fair degree of validation and confirmation regarding the matter of truth that is being bunked. The other way to do so is through knowing how you personally feel about it. Your soul will let you know what is suitable with regard to the soul path that you are on.

Now, we wish to clarify something about those who have set themselves up as your truth-controllers.

When slandering and invalidating truth, these souls are doing what needs to be done in order to influence and guide their fellow migrating souls away from what has religiously been termed "going astray", which when interpreted correctly means redirecting their attention away from a particular path, such as the path of ascension, and we shall go into this matter later.

Information being specific to their respective paths of evolution, there is certain information that keeps the mind aligned with the soul's path of evolution, and there is information that does not. Your soul always resonates with information that endeavors to align your mind with your soul path. When the mind strays off-course then through whatever means will work your soul will make every effort to influence your mind to shift back on-course so that you are focused on information that is relevant to your soul path.

This fact applies to all souls regardless of which soul path one is on.

In other words, the mind may stray but the soul never does. Your soul is your constant guide if you but listen to it. This same guidance-modality applies to all migrating souls as well as all ascending souls. Do you assume that ascending souls are in some way more deserving or privy to guidance-modalities that are somehow superior or more holy than migrating souls? Of course you're not. Once you understand what is transpiring in this universe and the forces by which it operates, then you have no need to think or believe that way; then you can get beyond your personal Dark Age that inwardly harasses you into perpetually harboring such bunk which for eons your controllers have inculcated upon you as so-called truth.

You are all on this learning curve whether you souljourn upon your path to ascension or to the new universe. As ascending souls, understand that the more attuned you are to your soul the more truth you recognize when it confronts you, and the less you end up straying off-course and having to make course corrections as a result later. You do this only because truth has been withheld from you, replaced with bunk and superstition.

We wish you to know that you all have that which is what you refer to as seen and unseen guides and mentors who inspire you, when necessary, to hear and heed the influences of your soul as it guides you from moment to moment on the path that is yours to souljourn. Know that ultimately it is your soul that determines the particular soul path that you must tread, not your mind. Your mind is the information-processing function, a tool that the soul employs in order to generate the lessons that it requires for its own evolution. But your controllers have nearly severed the connection between mind and soul, so that you function too much out of the mind, relegating the soul to the back burner, so to speak, as something either to be feared or disregarded as unimportant.

But your mind-soul connection is your synergistic function that serves as a balanced internal environment. You should be living balanced in the internal environment of your mind-soul connection than the landscape of the mind that has come to be focused too much upon that which is external. When you live in the environment of your internal balance, then when an external environment threatens to lead you astray, your soul will immediately call you back on-course, and sometimes your guides and mentors will help. They do not help all the time because they refuse to enable you to use them as a crutch to regularly get you through your own life experiences.

Perhaps now you realize why "going astray" has nothing to do with religion of any kind but everything to do with the nature of who and how you are, innately.

Now that being said, whether you are on the path of ascension or the path of migration, although the destructive and intrusive behavior of your controllers appears to be unacceptable or even evil to you, their behavior is serving an unseen purpose that is generated at the deeper level of all souls who are migrating toward the new universe. What you as ascending souls are observing is but the superficial layer of what is transpiring at the soul level, where their inner guidance occurs with precise regard to the path that migrating souls have chosen to souljourn.

Now, please understand that we do not condone their unhelpful words and behavior; we understand it relative to the purpose that it plays with regard to matters on the cosmic scale.

It is our intent therefore to clarify this matter to you in hopes that you understand its evolutionary dynamics so that you can move beyond your issues with all of this, because all of this has been forced upon you as a conditioning that does not benefit your souljourn upon the path of ascension. Issues of this matter are of vibratory frequencies relative to the field of consciousness and energy within the Lower Triad. If you hold on to these issues and the frequencies that they generate within you, you will hinder your progress of ascension by anchoring yourself to the Lower Triad. In order to ascend it is essential that you have no attachments to this matter whatsoever. This is why we are endeavoring to get you beyond the programming that keeps you hooked into it.

We know that this information is a new perception, perspective, or paradigm for many of you, but if you will sit for a while and reason it through then you will receive greater understanding about it. So please do stay with us herein as we bring forth this clarity for your benefit.

IBOC Communique Session 010

Regarding your planetary controllers - who, remember, are migrating souls - although their internal mind-soul connection hangs by but a thin thread, they have physical and non-physical based guides and mentors who endeavor to keep them on-track to their soul's next evolutionary step in the new universe.

Likewise, as we said, for those of you who are ascending with this universe thus with your planet, you each have your physical and non-physical guides and mentors who provide you with inspirational assistance along your soul path to ascension. You are happy, and relieved to have this kind of assistance, are you not?

Just so, all migrating souls are just as happy and relieved about the assistance that they receive, although most of them have no conscious awareness about this assistance consequently their lives become much more confusing, difficult and unpleasant to experience due to a lot of going astray which compounds their own ignorance. Yet, this entire mess is doing the necessary job of keeping migrating souls on-track to the new universe.

Once you understand the consciousness and energy dynamics that must play out on your planet in-particular in order for each group of souls - migrating and ascending - to remain oriented upon their proper soul paths, then all the dizzying craziness begins to make sense. It is dizzyingly crazy because you have been kept in the Dark Ages with regard to how this transpires and why. It would not be at all confusing or difficult had you never been held back from truth.

Bearing that in-mind then, you who are ascending must not fault migrating souls for having the same kind of guidance-modalities that you have - albeit each of you having it steer you in two different directions.

You must not judge nor condemn truth-controllers as existing in any manner that is inappropriate for the needs of their fellow migrating souls because indeed they and their guides and mentors are all there on your planet just as appropriately as you and your guides and mentors are there on your planet with you, for your ascension needs.

You all are living in the time that you refer to as the Harvesting of Souls, meaning that it is the specific era in the evolution of the universe when each soul makes its final orientation upon its essential soul path, of which there are but two, remember: the path of soul-ascension within this universe, and the path of soul-migration to the new universe. Each path has its guidance-modalities with relevant assistance and guides.

And while the controllers and all souls who are migrating have their place and purpose on your planet, you who are ascending and all our Ascended Volunteers need not take any concern over them and their purpose as migrating souls. It is your job to understand and lovingly allow them, while responding benignly to their harassment behaviors as we stated previously.

The comprehension and acknowledgement of this wisdom is where you fall short in your understanding of how the evolutionary dynamics of the universal and planetary harvesting of souls, so to speak, actually works. You know it only in a religious context and much of your so-called new age contexts as well. But this truth is not a religious belief or act but is instead a very natural one in its genuine cosmic function; a fact that religious and a few new age teachings have twisted into psychological fanaticisms of right and wrong, good and evil, God and demon, heaven and hell. We wish to move you out of and beyond that Dark Age bunk.

Once you understand that there are two groups of souls on your planet moving not in opposite directions, to where one is good and the other is bad, but in different directions of equal value and cosmic necessity, then this understanding gets you off the hook of being hypocrites unto your fellow migrating sibling-souls who, in essence, require a similar evolutionary approach as do you but each toward a very different yet very essential direction, and each direction is an evolutionary imperative. Once you comprehend that truth, then you've ascended that much more.

In other words, you have your ascension guides and mentors per your ascension objective, and they have theirs per their migration objective, and it's all as it should be. Once you comprehend that truth, then you've ascended that much more.

Our purpose with this message is to dowse any fires of animosity you may have toward your controllers for their unevolved words and behavior, to help you understand that when they attack those who present truth that it is helpful for you to use their negative behavior as a tool for ascension, as indicators that the information being presented is in-probability truth for you to look at. For remember, we said that they do not make fusses over information they deem safe for their fellow migrating souls to be exposed to because that information will not contribute to leading them astray from their path of migration to the new universe. Again, once you comprehend that truth, then you've ascended that much more.

At each level of your evolution, you will incorporate more truth for it means that in the soul you are ready to live that particular truth. Accordingly, we are aware that not everyone will resonate with all the information we impart in our communiqués - some will, others will not - and that is perfectly fine, as it should be.

Because they have a different destiny to engage, for those who are migrating to the new universe the act of recognizing, embracing and living new and greater truth has, shall we say, been put on-hold as they evolutionarily coast their way toward the new universe. Now you know why these migrating souls seem so stuck and stubborn with regard to knowing, being and doing "better".

The reason for this apparent evolutionary stagnation is because these migrating souls must remain within, not leave, the Lower Triad's field of consciousness and energy, because it is this particular field of polarized thought and quantum-soup-stuff of energy that encompasses the vital information and building-blocks that are critical for jump-starting into existence a whole new universe, to give it a "live birth" shall we say. It is therefore indispensable to the new universe that migrating souls remain within the Lower Triad by way of focusing attention on and living within the framework of what they currently know, believe and do. The exception at this point would be in the increasingly uncommon case that a migrating soul awakens and joins the path of ascension. A few are, most are not, and there is good reason for it being this way. We shall discuss this matter in a later communiqué.

Once a soul has chosen to be a creator in the new universe, simply honor it and accept that your path of ascension is not their path of migration. Your expectations that they should do otherwise, that they should be more like you who knows, believes and behaves better, well-meaning though this desire for them may be, it is in-reality an unreal prospect for them.

So in contrast to what you may contrarily think and feel about your controllers and their guides and mentors, they are serving just as vital a purpose unto the creation processes that must occur within the forthcoming new universe, as do your guides and mentors for assisting the ascension of your planet along with the ascension of this universe itself.

We know that it is when your controllers cross over the lines of allowing and go into harassing those who speak forth truth that it bothers you because you see such acts as unjust and unfair treatment, which, from where you stand, it is. But when you remember what they are doing and why, then you can take it in diplomatically, impersonally, treating it as a sign rather than a sin unto migrating souls, influencing them to stay-the-course toward the new universe.

Conversely, when you who are ascending embrace the abrasive behavior of migrating souls as a sign that such-and-such information is based in truth as an indicator for you to stay-the-course of ascension;

understanding that the same behavioral-message applies to both groups in two different directions, then you have ascended that much more so that you see right through all that dizzying craziness without ever having your buttons pushed, as you like to say.

As we stated in a previous communiqué, it is not that such higher, greater truth is forbidden unto migrating souls for indeed if such a soul has suddenly made an about-face in their acceptance of a truth, then that soul will "go astray" from the migration path in order to souljourn the ascension path. But at this last minute of the evolutionary timeframe, most souls have already firmly oriented themselves on one path or the other. At this point, few will change course. And that is as it needs to be, for good reason.

The intention here is that your embracement of this understanding will help remove the heat of reproach off of your hearts and minds so that you can see the signs for what they are trying to tell you.

We feel as if we are talking in circles around this matter, but it is a new perception for most of you and we want to present this understanding in various terms as clearly as possible to the many of you who are reading our communiqués for it is important that you get it so that you are neither thrown off course by such unevolved behavior, and that you know how to recognize truth that personally resonates with you in spite of what your controllers want you to believe to the contrary.

Now we wish to address the migrating souls who have set themselves up as planetary controllers, and their minions - all of you who might be reading our communiqués and positioning yourselves to issue forth harassment upon this or any other source of information presenting truth.

To you we say that we are very much aware of who you are, of what you do and why you do it. We understand it far more clearly than you do so we convey to you the proceeding clarification.

From Contact to Ascension

We know that it is not that you must go about guiding yourselves and your fellow migrating souls to the new universe through the use of corrosive attitudes and abusive behavior, for there are certainly much better, far more productive, efficient and self-satisfying ways to go about accomplishing the same objective. But so far you have not been willing to "see" these better options. And it is not that you cannot see them, but rather that you have chosen to employ a negative tact in spite of such methods being very difficult on yourselves as well as on those who you are fearfully herding, so to speak, toward the new universe.

This need not be a difficult nor unpleasant task for indeed we are aware of other planets of souls who are migrating to the same new universe as you, and they are doing so by way of engaging methods that assist the souls who are going there along with their migrating vanguards.

The result of them taking this supportive path to the new universe is that the souls who are trekking there through methods that are encouraging to one another, are far more prepared to participate in the creation of all things in your forthcoming new universe than are those souls, such as you on your planet, who's creative abilities have been thwarted and stifled by an onslaught of fear within yourselves and instilling intimidation unto others around you, which in-turn represses creativity, for fear does repress the accessibility of your power of creativity within the soul. As we said earlier herein, your mind-soul connection hangs by a thin thread, and it need not be so in order to accomplish the same objective.

As it is though, you are not only debilitating the creative potentials within the souls of your future fellow residents, in the process you are to a much, much larger degree debilitating the creative potentials within your own souls. In other words, you are vibrationally setting yourselves to the very back of the class of creation, so to speak, by weakening the accessibility of your power to create within your new universe. Is this what could be perceived some sort of punishment in hell? Absolutely not. It is a natural vibrational response to what you are currently setting yourselves up for in the long run, and only you can change that for yourselves.

The thing for you to remember with regard to this fact is that all migrating souls within the Lower Triad whose creative abilities are acutely accessible therefore strong and operational will always, through natural vibrational processes, take the lead in creational developments occurring within new universes. This is simply how it is, how it works.

And the only way to end up on the leading edge of creation, instead of on the lesser edge in the back of the class of creation is to be in that supportive mode within yourselves wherein you understand what is occurring on the cosmic scale, so that fear is removed from yourselves thereby allowing you to cease intimidating everyone else. Then and only then are the lines of access to your personal powers of creativity fully restored unto your creative application as a cooperative Being on the leading edge within the new universe. Where you choose to place yourselves in your new universe is up to you, but know that you are predetermining that matter now.

We wish you to know that we judge you not. We criticize you not. We dishonor you not. We disrespect you not, for indeed we have a great love of you because we truly understand what is transpiring on the cosmic scale, on your planetary scale, on your personal scale; and it is the power of understanding that allows one to access from the soul the power of compassion for others so as to honor everyone, as we do you in spite of your fear-based controlling attitudes and behavior.

We love you as evolving souls, negatively pursued though your souljourn may be yet we fully respect your evolutionary right to engage the path of fear toward your new universe but which is not to your personal greater benefit now or later.

And although you may in knee-jerk fashion want to bunk the truth that we present in our communiqués, and slander those who embrace and share it with others, we know that it is our loving honorable words imparted herein that is the saving grace of its innate truth which, in-turn, if you understand this message regarding a better way for you to migrate with your fellow souls to your new universe, then it becomes your own saving grace as well. And by that truth you shall be set free, restored as an awesome creative soul who stands on the leading edge of creation within your future new universe. And you need no judgmental God or god or intermediate savior outside yourselves to make it happen for you. You have and need only you in order to get the job done.

If you embrace this truth, what have you got to lose? Your soul? Never! That's bunk! Let it go as the bunk that it is. But, as a creator in your impending new universe, you can lose your naturally self-endowed place on the leading edge of creation. Yet, through fear you have every right to resign yourself to the lesser edge of it if that is how you prefer to evolve yourselves. And if so, we still love and honor you for who you truly are.

Unto all who read this and all our other communiqués, whether you embrace all or some of it, we express much love to you, equally. We honor and respect each one of you because we understand you, and with understanding comes compassion, and with compassion comes allowing, and with allowing comes love, pure and unconditional. Did you expect Ascended Beings to be any other way?

We bless you all, equally, for a day is coming when we shall be interacting openly, peacefully and cooperatively with one another, if that is how you want it. We do hope you do.

We leave this information and its intrinsic wisdom with you to pontificate within yourselves for further clarity. Be honorable and respectful of one another. Until our next communiqué, we bid you well.

That is all for now.
I am An T'na of the Intergalactic Board of Council

IBOC Communique Session 010

(*Please refer to Session 6 for more on this matter. Mahalo, Gesanna)

From Contact to Ascension

POSTSCRIPT FROM GESANNA
Stardate 12.11.2013   Startime 12.04.06

This is my first entry that comments on a communiqué or two.

There have been a couple of communiqué messages from the Intergalactic Board of Council with which I have had mixed feelings regarding including them in these ongoing series. But despite my personal feelings, I know that the Council is addressing a very large audience of people who are all perceptually diverse, wired differently therefore requiring different instructional approaches to the same concepts and mindsets, so I agreed to put them "out there" for all who resonates with the information. After all, as Their oracle I am just the messenger of Their messages, not the arbiter of the messages.

After conveying ten sessions now, there is a subtle yet detectable underlying objective in the messages - that of getting ascending souls and Their Volunteers beyond Lower Triad programming, custom tailored as it is to each one of us, so that we can in-turn unhook ourselves from the Dark Ages that we are externally immersed in, as They put it.

My observations of the progression of the messages indicates that this is a rather tough job akin to the effort of peeling perceptual layers off of a translucent onion - where does one layer begin and end, how thick and dense is it, and how is the next layer wired differently than the one before it that was finally dissolved away? And when you're sitting before a basketful of these onions that need peeled a layer at a time, the task of peeling away Lower Triad programming would be a bit daunting to me.

I know that it's not that the Council can't do the job, being Ascended Beings, but it's that our programming is so deeply grooved into our brains' neural pathways that these stuck records [for those of us old enough to know what a record is, hence this analogy] keep bumping up against the same old grooves, cracks or glitches in the neural ruts so that we are thrown back again into the place we were endeavoring to get free of.

Hence, the Council's advice to us of becoming unhooked from these brainwashing grooves that keep us tied-in to the Lower Triad's field of thought and energy. This is why They have said that so long as we are "hooked-in" to it, ascension progress is hindered, sort of like doing the 2-step dance where you take three steps forward and then one back so that in essence you've only actually gone two steps forward in each advancement.

I recall that They once stated something to the effect that we cannot have it both ways - i.e., be hooked-in by these Lower Triad neural encodings and expect to be unhooked so we can ascend to the Upper Triad.

I am getting that it is the brain-mind that has us hooked-in and it is through the mind that we get unhooked by creating new neural pathways that bypass the old ruts. Once we deprogram ourselves of our indoctrinated perceptions, attitudes and behavior, all of which are of the dual nature of the Lower Triad, then we free up the mind from focusing on those Lower Triad matters to where it can now focus on the wisdom thus guidance that is contained within the soul.

I believe that if our external world were of a far more positive orientation, as is the case for the inhabitants of most other planets, then we would not have such a major discrepancy between the information held in the mind and the information held in the soul - a psychological condition that generates a great deal of confusion.

But that is not the kind of world we live in here. The Council has said that Terra is one of but a few planets where negativity occurs in amounts greatly disproportionate to positivity. It is this imbalance that

Postscript From Gesanna

has rutted our brains in ways that makes it difficult to deprogram ourselves from the brainwashing we've grown up with.

Difficult but not impossible, I believe.

My take from Session 10 in-particular, is that this is a very serious situation we're in that needs serious attention for resolving, and from personal experience, I would say the sooner the better.

I have been asking my soul how this can be done; what is the process by which the resolve for restoring the mind-soul connection is triggered and finally accomplished. I feel that there is something I'm not getting - perhaps due to some habitual programming that blocks out my ability to see it clearly, to reach through that encoded layer to the core truth of it all.

But I am determined to see it, to get at it, to find and engage that particular truth that will set me free enough to restore my mind-soul-body connection to its total functioning state.

I am aware that the Intergalactic Board of Council has more to say to us about all of this in forthcoming communiqués. This information will be posted as I receive it.

Till then everyone, remain vigilant about recognizing what your particular programmings are, and realizing that they are no longer important or necessary now for your souljourn of ascension. Be meek enough to resign yourselves to letting go of them in favor of engaging wisdom from your soul.

And before I end this entry for today: One way to begin consciously recognizing what your habitual Lower Triad programs are is to choose at least one person you regularly interact with each day. Make it a point to watch your beliefs and attitudes regarding that person; watch how you act, react, interact with him/her; watch how you speak with him/her, the tone of voice you use; watch your attitudes and behavior with yourself, and so on. Notice all of these things, write them down or journal about it if that helps, and identify the ones that are of negative charges. These are the ones that keep us hooked-in to the Lower Triad. Promise yourself to let them go as the hindrances that they are unto you. There are plenty of self-help books, groups to join, and people trained in clinical therapeutic assistance that can help get us deprogrammed.

My deepest Aloha goes out to every one of you.

In peace and joy, Gesanna

Index

1st Wave, 57, 58
1st Wave Volunteers, 57
2nd Wave, 55
2nd Wave of Volunteers, 57
3 Waves of Ascension, 23
3 Waves of Volunteers, 21, 23, 55, 60, 101
3rd dimension, xi, 27
3rd Wave, 55
4th dimension, 28, 29, 32, 67, 86, 112, 153
5th dimension, 29, 86, 87, 110, 112, 139, 140, 165, 198
7th heaven, 141
abuse of truth, 261
alien overlords, 179
altered egos, 40, 242
An T'na, xii, xiii, 13, 18, 21, 44, 45, 47, 49, 53, 55, 64, 65, 78, 79, 84, 85, 113, 115, 119, 121, 169, 181, 190, 191, 194, 213, 215, 221, 224, 225, 238, 239, 245, 247, 259, 261, 274, 290
anchor the light, 49, 52, 95, 135
ancient scripts, 36, 79, 113, 146
angelic, 92
Anunnaki, 250
Ascended Being, xii, xvi, 3, 11, 13, 16, 23, 25, 32, 33, 35, 42, 45, 46, 92, 100, 132, 137, 149, 156, 157, 159, 165, 166, 167, 171, 173, 174, 175, 177, 178, 180, 182, 183, 184, 185, 188, 190, 192, 194, 204, 205, 207, 225, 232, 236, 237, 247, 252, 253, 254, 255, 257, 274, 277, 289, 290, 295
Ascended Being Volunteers, 15, 16, 17, 18, 145, 189, 196, 252, 257
ascended bodies, 38, 164
Ascended Masters, 92
ascended realm, 200
ascended souls, xi, 15, 38, 46, 121, 139, 141, 142, 164
ascending, xv, 4, 14, 15, 17, 18, 21, 22, 26, 29, 30, 32, 33, 34, 35, 37, 38, 40, 41, 42, 43, 46, 49, 56, 58, 60, 61, 62, 63, 65, 66, 67, 68, 69, 70, 71, 72, 73, 74, 75, 76, 77, 79, 80, 81, 83, 92, 93, 94, 95, 101, 103, 104, 105, 106, 107, 108, 110, 111, 112, 113, 116, 117, 118, 121, 122, 126, 128, 130, 131, 132, 133, 136, 144, 145, 148, 149, 150, 151, 152, 153, 159, 161, 162, 163, 165, 167, 168, 169, 170, 171, 172, 174, 175, 176, 177, 178, 183, 184, 191, 192, 195, 196, 197, 198, 199, 200, 201, 202, 204, 205, 206, 207, 208, 209, 211, 215, 217, 264,

265, 266, 267, 268, 270, 277, 290
Ascending planet, 36
ascending soul, 17, 22, 32, 33, 41, 42, 43, 62, 66, 71, 79, 83, 101, 107, 118, 145, 150, 151, 152, 153, 176, 195, 196, 199, 201, 205, 208, 264
ascension, xi, xii, xv, xvi, 3, 4, 13, 14, 15, 16, 18, 21, 22, 23, 24, 25, 26, 29, 30, 32, 33, 35, 40, 41, 42, 43, 45, 46, 47, 52, 56, 59, 60, 62, 63, 65, 66, 68, 75, 81, 93, 94, 95, 98, 101, 105, 106, 110, 111, 122, 124, 126, 128, 129, 131, 132, 133, 145, 149, 150, 151, 156, 162, 163, 164, 167, 170, 171, 172, 173, 174, 176, 178, 179, 180, 181, 182, 185, 187, 189, 193, 196, 198, 200, 201, 202, 203, 204, 205, 207, 208, 209, 210, 211, 212, 215, 223, 232, 242, 243, 244, 264, 265, 266, 267, 268, 269, 270, 271, 278, 279
ascension of planets, 25
ascension resistance, 22
Atlantic Ocean, 109
attuned to the planet, 129
automatic-writing, 11
beingness, 219
benevolent Beings, 123, 124, 126, 130, 132, 237, 241, 252, 254
biological ascension, 65
black hole, 34, 62, 77

blueprint., 35, 112, 144, 145, 193
brain-mind control, 130
cabal, 116, 119
cell phone tower, 127
cell phones, 127
channeler, 290
chosen ones, 57
COMMUNIQUE, 191
compassionate souls, 46, 118
computers, 18, 233, 262
conscious mind, 135, 136, 138, 158, 159
consciousness, xi, xii, 4, 25, 29, 36, 37, 41, 42, 66, 67, 68, 80, 81, 82, 83, 97, 98, 105, 111, 128, 137, 141, 143, 144, 145, 146, 149, 150, 152, 156, 164, 165, 166, 189, 197, 198, 211, 219, 237, 242, 266, 267, 269
consumerism, 127, 128
Controllers, 261
corporate minds, 132
Council, iii, xii, 1, 5, 11, 13, 16, 17, 18, 21, 44, 48, 53, 55, 64, 78, 84, 105, 113, 119, 121, 133, 195, 214, 221, 224, 225, 228, 238, 245, 259, 261, 274, 277, 278, 279, 289, 291, 294, 295
Creator, 74, 78, 81, 83, 96, 97, 161, 162
crystal children, 93, 106
Dark Age, 264, 268
death experience, 199, 200
death process, 200

Index

death zone, 199, 200, 201, 202
degree of power, 44, 52
densification, 152
density, 25, 38, 66, 67, 68, 69, 70, 71, 72, 76, 112, 113, 148, 150, 151, 152, 153, 164, 165, 166, 180, 184, 198, 199, 201, 202, 205, 212, 290
descended, 69, 71, 72
descension, 63, 151, 152
dimension, 3, 25, 27, 28, 31, 37, 46, 57, 66, 67, 71, 72, 74, 75, 86, 87, 88, 92, 111, 112, 139, 140, 152, 165, 166, 198, 216, 217, 218, 289
Disclosure, 1, 180, 191, 225, 247
divine, xi, 4, 17, 18, 42, 51, 63, 118, 119, 168, 171, 172, 176, 183, 185, 190, 244
divinity, 118
DNA, 124, 125, 239, 240, 242
do-gooders, 115
donations, 230, 231
dual shifting, 71
duality, xi, 4, 36, 37, 77, 87, 88, 91, 134, 138, 139, 140, 141, 143, 150, 157, 160, 164, 185, 186, 187, 188, 244
earth, 39, 197, 203
earthquakes, 130
emotional, 38, 209, 212, 242, 294
emotional attachment, 209
empowered soul, 93
evil aliens, xvi, 253
evolutionary timeframe, 271
Exopolitics Institute, iv, xii, xvii
extradimensional, 18, 194, 228, 229, 233, 235, 248, 255
extraterrestrial, xi, xii, xv, xvi, xvii, 16, 18, 123, 125, 126, 147, 149, 183, 184, 188, 189, 192, 194, 196, 225, 228, 229, 232, 233, 235, 236, 237, 239, 241, 244, 248, 253, 254, 255, 262, 294
extraterrestrial overlords, 123
extraterrestrial Volunteers, 189
fallen Volunteers, 50
fight-or-flight, 117
first contact, 294
FIRST CONTACT, 291
first Wave. *See* 1st Wave
folding up, 27, 28, 29, 30, 31, 35, 62, 71, 77, 101, 112, 164
forever life zone, 200, 201
free will, 31, 45, 46, 51, 52, 56, 63, 66, 84, 96, 173, 193, 203
frequency jamming technologies, xv
Galactic Society, 4, 226, 230, 231, 233, 234, 235, 236, 237, 247, 252, 255
galaxies, xii, 13, 16, 123, 147
Gattaca, 258
Gesanna, iii, iv, xii, xiii, 11, 12, 13, 98, 100, 102, 181, 182, 192, 275, 280, 289, 296
God, 96, 97, 268, 274
going Home, 17, 49, 98
grand adventure, 4, 17

Grays, 239, 241, 242, 243, 250
great event, 32
guides, 50, 149, 265, 267, 268, 269, 270
HAARP, 127
Hawaii, xii, 11, 291
heaven, 37, 167, 221, 242, 244, 268
hell, 75, 167, 244, 268, 273
higher dimension, 165
higher dimensional energy, 23, 31
Higher Dimensional frequencies, 38, 39, 50
Higher Dimensional Realm, 25, 26, 37, 50, 51, 52
Higher Dimensional Volunteers, 55
higher dimensions, 13, 23, 26, 96, 132
higher frequencies, 80, 82, 126, 127, 130, 170, 179, 211, 215
higher frequency, 15, 91, 112, 173, 198
Higher Power, 96
higher Triad, 77
homosexuality, 86
homosexuals, 85, 90, 91, 93
immortality, 92, 99, 215, 216, 217, 219, 220, 223
impeccable blueprint, 35
incompassion, 89
indigo
    children, 93, 118
individual ascensions, 26
industrial age, 116

infiltration by incarnation, 55
instant manifestation, 146
intelligent design, 74
Intergalactic Board of Council. *See* IBOC
Internet, 229, 230, 262
John Kennedy. *See* Kennedy Assassination
Kennedy Assassination, 248
Kennedy, John F.
    Kennedy Assassination, 303
light anchorer, 101
light energy, 38, 43, 149, 164
lose your way, 45
Lower Triad, 13, 14, 15, 16, 21, 27, 28, 29, 30, 31, 34, 35, 36, 37, 38, 42, 45, 46, 49, 50, 51, 58, 60, 61, 62, 63, 65, 66, 67, 69, 71, 72, 73, 74, 75, 77, 79, 80, 81, 82, 83, 88, 89, 92, 96, 98, 101, 106, 111, 112, 121, 124, 131, 133, 134, 137, 138, 139, 140, 141, 147, 148, 149, 150, 153, 154, 156, 157, 161, 162, 164, 165, 166, 169, 171, 176, 183, 184, 185, 186, 187, 188, 189, 190, 195, 196, 197, 198, 200, 205, 216, 217, 218, 232, 240, 244, 266, 269, 273, 277, 278, 279
lucid dreams, 156, 248, 294
Machiavellian, 241
manifesting, 66
Mars, 125
materialistic agenda, 116
materiality, xv, 107, 116

Index

Mayan Calendar, 23
mentors, 199, 265, 267, 269, 270
meta-physics, 68, 171
Michael Salla, xvii, 225, 227, 228, 236, 237, 238, 241
military minds, 131
misidentification, 138, 141, 147, 169, 190
mission duty, 16, 58
mother universe, 73, 74, 161, 163
motherships, 257
nature is ascending, 65, 150
Nefilim, 250
negative faction, 41, 45, 50, 51, 61, 93, 98, 99, 104, 119, 125, 126, 130, 167, 178, 234
negative presence, 41
new Creators, 73
new skin, 42
new universe, xv, 29, 30, 31, 34, 37, 40, 43, 62, 65, 71, 73, 75, 77, 78, 95, 98, 106, 117, 118, 126, 131, 149, 161, 162, 163, 164, 168, 169, 171, 176, 177, 184, 208, 244, 265, 266, 267, 268, 269, 270, 272, 273, 274
non-ascending, xv, 17, 33, 42, 62, 66, 71, 75, 79, 83, 118, 145, 150, 151, 152, 153, 176, 184, 201, 208
occupied planet, 26
official disclosure, xvi, 4, 226
oracle, xiii, 13, 16, 21, 100, 101, 139, 151, 157, 158, 160, 181, 182, 191, 192, 194, 201, 202, 210, 262, 277, 289, 290, 295
original blueprint, xi, 35
oversoul, 87
paradigm shift, 81, 218
pathology, 118
personal evolution, 4, 17, 84, 166, 168, 185, 208, 210, 244, 263
phantom body, 34, 72
phantom planet, 42, 72, 76
physical ascension, 65
physicality, 25, 29, 37, 38, 68, 112, 113, 140, 152, 165, 198, 216
planet's ascension, 26, 59, 66
planet's core, 52, 56
planet's soul, 132, 133
possessions, 91, 93, 137
power to manifest, 146
priests, 123, 251
Prime Directive, 23, 63, 149, 175, 176, 179
psychic powers, 130
psychography, 11, 192, 291
public disclosure, xvi, xvii, 4, 225, 226, 235, 242
pulsing of time, 23
quantum, 112, 140, 149, 199, 270
reincarnations, 89
Rome, 142
Saturn, 109, 110, 181
scaffold, 66, 69, 70, 71, 72
self-aggrandizing, 91, 123, 124, 131, 241, 247, 254

Self-ignorance, 253
Self-Realizing, 263
singularity, xi, xii
soul, xv, 4, 16, 17, 23, 24, 29,
    31, 33, 34, 38, 40, 42, 43, 45,
    46, 47, 50, 51, 52, 55, 58, 59,
    60, 61, 62, 63, 66, 68, 72, 73,
    74, 78, 81, 84, 85, 86, 87, 88,
    89, 90, 91, 93, 95, 96, 97,
    104, 105, 107, 108, 111, 117,
    128, 129, 130, 131, 132, 133,
    134, 135, 136, 137, 138, 139,
    140, 141, 142, 143, 144, 145,
    146, 149, 152, 154, 155, 156,
    157, 158, 159, 168, 169, 171,
    172, 177, 178, 181, 182, 184,
    187, 188, 189, 190, 199, 206,
    207, 209, 210, 211, 219, 223,
    253, 255, 258, 264, 265, 266,
    267, 268, 269, 270, 271, 272,
    273, 274, 278, 279, 290, 294
soul control, 130
soul mate, 88
soul memory, 104, 144, 290
soul path, 264, 265, 268
soulmates, 88
source, xii, 50, 95, 163, 271
speeding up of time, 29
spiritual moles, 118
spirituality, 115, 116, 218
split apart, 154
spoiled generation, 107
Star Trek, 177, 233
star wars, 258
starseeds, 93, 106
starships, 257

strands of ascension, 242
sub-atomic, 152
subconsciously, 40, 116, 219
substitute planet, 151
Terra, 3, 14, 15, 16, 17, 24, 33,
    43, 51, 59, 86, 99, 100, 121,
    169, 180, 182, 192, 204, 211,
    225, 228, 249, 278, 289, 291,
    295
Terran, 13, 14, 16, 17, 23, 24,
    57, 58, 59, 61, 65, 89, 99,
    100, 102, 103, 104, 106, 107,
    111, 122, 123, 124, 125, 127,
    128, 130, 135, 136, 138, 139,
    141, 142, 143, 144, 145, 146,
    147, 148, 150, 157, 159, 168,
    169, 184, 187, 188, 189, 190,
    195, 203, 204, 206, 217, 228,
    229, 240, 243, 244, 250, 251,
    290, 294, 295
the call, 187
thought form, 165
Three Waves, 85, 104
time travel, 166
timeline, 30
transformation of matter, 66
Triad, 13, 14, 15, 16, 17, 21, 28,
    29, 30, 35, 37, 46, 47, 49, 50,
    58, 61, 62, 63, 65, 67, 68, 70,
    71, 72, 73, 75, 76, 77, 78, 79,
    81, 82, 83, 89, 92, 98, 99,
    100, 101, 104, 108, 110, 111,
    112, 121, 126, 129, 132, 133,
    134, 135, 136, 137, 139, 140,
    141, 142, 144, 145, 146, 147,
    148, 149, 152, 153, 156, 157,

162, 164, 165, 170, 171, 173, 176, 177, 180, 182, 183, 184, 185, 186, 187, 188, 189, 195, 196, 197, 198, 200, 201, 202, 203, 204, 205, 210, 213, 232, 236, 242, 244, 257, 266, 270, 278, 280
true identity, 97, 98, 135, 136, 139, 140, 142, 143, 145, 147, 190
truth embargo, 262
tunnel of light, 199, 200
UFO, xiii, 230, 239, 253
unascended, 58
universal shift, 27
universe, xi, xii, xiii, xiv, xv, xvi, 3, 4, 14, 23, 24, 26, 27, 28, 29, 30, 31, 34, 35, 37, 40, 51, 62, 71, 72, 73, 74, 75, 76, 77, 78, 95, 96, 101, 118, 126, 131, 139, 140, 161, 162, 163, 164, 168, 169, 171, 189, 203, 207, 215, 226, 232, 240, 241, 244, 264, 267, 268, 269, 270, 272, 273, 274, 289

Upper Triad, 15, 28, 37, 46, 61, 81, 82, 83, 100, 101, 110, 111, 121, 133, 139, 140, 146, 148, 149, 156, 173, 186, 187, 195, 210
vast intelligence, 74
vibrational, 25, 27, 29, 34, 38, 39, 43, 62, 66, 68, 69, 70, 71, 72, 110, 112, 121, 134, 150, 155, 165, 166, 184, 186, 209, 273, 289
void, 25
Volunteer, xi, 13, 32, 35, 40, 42, 47, 49, 50, 51, 56, 57, 58, 59, 63, 99, 102, 104, 110, 121, 133, 134, 135, 136, 137, 138, 139, 142, 145, 157, 182, 187, 188, 189, 190, 206, 212, 295
vortex, 109, 110
walk-ins, 91, 92, 93, 188, 189, 190
Wave interval, 56
weapons of mass destruction, 131, 241
Zeta-Terran, 243
zoos, 256

ABOUT GESANNA - ORACLE FOR THE INTERGALACTIC BOARD OF COUNCIL

(Name pronounced as jez-awnaw; meaning, "the light of grace")

Aloha to All! I am Gesanna, one oracle among others for the Intergalactic Board of Council. I came by this occupation by way of being an Ascended Being prior to my descent from a higher or quicker vibrational level of existence to that of this 3rd dimension, more specifically as one of many Volunteers on a particular mission for this loving group of Beings.

With regard to this Great Plan For Terra, there are many of us who as Ascended Beings volunteered to physically return to this level of existence in order to be of service to all of life and, vicariously, unto those souls who are ready to ascend along with this universe into a more evolved state of existence.

As you will learn from the IBOC's communiqués herein, the purpose for our presence here is multi-level, not merely singular in goal. Each of us Volunteers is actively engaged in the accomplishment of a common objective yet we each are employing our innate talents in many different ways - ways that are necessary so as to achieve the objective overall. Also, of all of those of us who are doing this great work, not everyone is incarnated into 3rd density, only those of us who are on this planet as well as Volunteers on other planets that are ascending.

One talent, which I brought with me into my Terran life on this planet, is that of an oracle - a transceiver of information capable of hearing (with Thy inner ear) then transmitting to others, that which has been received (into Thy inner knowing). Other terms for this activity are prophet/prophetess, seer/seeress, visionary and, more conventionally, psychic, channeler, and psychographer (what used to be called autowriting).

But, a psychic by any other name is still a psychic.

You will learn how, in a nutshell, my talents as an oracle resurfaced from soul memory, triggering my transceiver ability into action. I must say that at first, and through the ensuing decades, it was all very confusing as the remembrances of who I truly am that is beyond my Terran identity began to move from soul memory to conscious awareness.

What I now know about myself - as the bigger awareness of my identity - came to me not from other people telling me things like, "Such and such is who you are. Here is your real name. This is your life purpose...." and so on, but over time it came forth from within me as information from the depths of personal experience stored within my soul.

Such is the ability of Ascended Beings who volunteer to return to the lower realms - to remember some significant things about themselves.

I remember some of the members of the IBOC, which includes the Ascended Being named AnT'na (pronounced, awn teh-NAW), as the woman who conveys to me the messages of the IBOC members, and as a group of Ascended Beings, they refer to themselves in the collective sense of "we" and "us" rather than as a single entity, unless An T'na is speaking of Herself personally.

About Gesanna

During "Stage 1" of my transceivership of her conveyances from the IBOC, which began at the start of 2013, the chosen mode was done through 4 verbally channeled sessions, lasting about 1&1/2 hours per session.

The Council then shifted me into "Stage 2" mode - from verbal channeling to that of psychography. This shift was done in preparation of Them relocating me back to my former post in Hawaii where I would no longer have the channeling facilitators or the recording equipment for the verbal channeling mode.

Although my mode of conveying to you Their communiqués remains that of psychography, They are currently at "Stage 3" with Their Great Plan For Terra. Stage 3 is a call for attention to prepare to engage you to receive or participate in the public-generated disclosure programs that will be implemented around this planet.

The information which They have thus far imparted herein is designed to help prepare you for that next step, as well as to help you become more clear about who you truly are and how you fit into the bigger picture of the universal adventure that we are all caught up in, the essence of which boils down to...

How do you want to experience it for yourself?

... For you do have a choice in that aspect of the overall adventure.

So, let us begin this journey together with the story of my own FIRST CONTACT.

FIRST CONTACT

It was a very warm night in Colorado, that summer of 1958. My three young siblings and I slept soundly in a shared bedroom of our small house. Little did I know what was in store for me when my younger brother and I awoke, thirsty. The bedroom was extra-darkened because our mother put blankets over the window so her children would be more likely to go to sleep while outside the dusk light of summer lingered beyond our usual bedtime hour. Whispering to one another across the darkened bedroom, my brother and I agreed to venture together through the moonlit house toward the kitchen for a drink of water.

Because there was a bright light streaming through the kitchen entryway into the dining area it seemed to us that our father was still awake and painting on his picture, as his easel was set up in a corner of the kitchen. Bravely walking onward, assuming a typical reason for this light being on, we were confronted by something quite different, so mysterious that our 5 and 4 year old minds could not fathom its presence.

There, not more than 3 feet away from us hovered a soccer ball sized sphere of light - silent, motionless, radiating an icy silvery-blue-white hue. Standing together in awe, completely perplexed by what we were seeing, my frightened brother hid behind me, asking what it was and what we should do.

I vividly recall being baffled as to how this strange ball of light was able to hover above the floor. My young mind mused over how I could crawl right underneath it since there was nothing to hold it up. I wanted to reach out and touch it, but for some reason I dared not go any closer to it...or crawl under it.

Unable to explain what it was, I ordered my little brother to run and get our father. He refused to leave my side, insisting that I go with him. Not too eager to depart from this mystery that held me spellbound, I led the way to fetch our dad from his bedroom. But on the way there, he took an immediate detour to the bedroom to hide under the blankets of his bed.

About Gesanna

It was very difficult to awaken my father; he seemed very deeply asleep despite how I shook his shoulder. Excitedly I told him about the light in the kitchen. He was very insistent that he had turned off all the lights when he'd gone to bed, ordering me to go back to bed. But because this was not an ordinary light but one that simply had to be examined, I nearly yelled, "But Dad, there's a light in the kitchen!" That's the best way I could put it.

He finally decided that I sounded serious to warrant getting out of bed in the middle of the night to investigate his young daughter's unusual behavior.

With caution, my brother joined the trek to the kitchen. Even before we reached the kitchen entryway I could see that the stream of light we'd seen minutes ago as it flooded into the dining room was now gone. I began to feel perplexed that the ball of light itself had vanished without a trace. I was disappointed that it was nowhere to be seen.

Baffled by the odd behavior of his young children our father flipped on and off the light switch, just to be sure it was working properly, asking what it was that we had seen. I described it the best that my inexperienced mind would allow me. Then suddenly he wondered, "What are you doing up from bed so late at night anyway?" to which I replied, "We're thirsty. We want a drink of water". He gave us our drinks and then sent us back to bed, puzzled by his young children's strange story about a mysterious hovering ball of light.

Neither I nor my brother nor our father ever forgot the enigmatic experience of that summer night so long ago yet only the blink of a memory's recall away.

This childhood experience was the start of my conscious "remembrance" of not only the fact that there is much more to life than can be seen and explained by conventional knowledge, but the fact that I myself am an enigmatic part of that unconventional life - of an entirely "other life" that would make itself known to me over the decades to come. I have to say that actually this was my first contact on the conscious level. I was to learn several decades later that contact had been occurring even before the age of 5.

But, my life, and that of my brother was, for some time to come, pretty much "normal" until I was age 11 when our father quit his ministry profession, and he and my mother left religion behind forever, taking a totally new direction into metaphysics and an awareness of all-things-extraterrestrial, as the Council members say. That's when we, as a family, began to go out at night sky-watching for UFOs. That's when I began to observe balls of light from a much greater distance. But the one my brother and I saw in the kitchen was different. It would be decades later before an explanation for it came forth from soul memory.

Prior to that recall, though, my life was steered back into the garrison of religion, through my first marriage. Fourteen years and four children later I also withdrew from religion forever.

It was just prior to the divorce when the bulk of my awareness began to be restored to me through the releasing of soul memories in the form of lucid dreams, revelations, psychic phenomena, and during sleep the regular spontaneous OBEs with "those who knew me more than I could remember about myself". This information, regarding who I truly am, what my "other heritage" is, and why I am really here on this planet, was released to me slowly and gently over nearly 30 years.

Not only have I been able to piece together many pieces of information into a comprehensive overview of the "bigger picture" of myself, it took me that much time to come to emotional terms with this enigmatic "other" part of myself and the unusual way that it is intricately woven together with my conventional life as a Terran, an Earth-born person.

It is only beginning with the start of this year, 2013, that my true life-purpose on this planet revealed itself to me and thus, since the appropriate time has arrived globally, I am now able to engage myself

About Gesanna

in the "Higher Work" that I had preincarnationally agreed to do, as a Volunteer for the Intergalactic Board of Council's Great Plan for Terra.

This Work has been done by me with a certain degree of reluctance at times, as my channeling facilitator friends will testify to, as well as the IBOC members who referred to me as their "reluctant oracle". I am still endeavoring to overcome my bouts of reluctance as I continue to engage my most extraordinary Work with these loving and wise Ascended Beings, as is revealed herein throughout the pages of Their communiqués.

Thus I thank my facilitator friends and all others who encourage and inspire me to push through my own hesitancies in order to continue being an oracle of some much needed information being conveyed to the people of this planet at this time.

Prior to incarnating into wearing Terran genes, having taken on this monumental task as an Ascended Being, I vowed to myself and to others to see it through, even though there are times when I wonder why I am bothering, along with accepting the enormous responsibility that is connected with it. Someday the outcome of it all will be acutely clear - for myself and for everyone else involved in this Work. With that clarity, it will then be thoroughly understood why it was all-worthwhile.

It is to that end that I continue to push myself along despite all adversity - including my own even as I reluctantly began to create a website that, through a lucid dream, the IBOC instructed me to do for Them.

What you see herein is the outcome of my strength to push through my own reluctances, because the information herein is not for me, for my sake but for yours, as a service unto all Terrans.

May you be uplifted and edified by the contents of the information in this book that is the Work of the many members of the Intergalactic Board Council. I am merely Their oracle who is passing on to you Their wisdom and advice. Take of Their information what feels good to you to accept and bypass the rest, remaining open-minded for its eventual intake.

With the grandest of Aloha, blessings to all.

-Gesanna-

A Note From An T'na Regarding the Following Information

Greetings one and all! I am An T'na. I have been asked by members of the Intergalactic Board of Council to comment on various topics that you are or will be encountering in the communiqués that are being increasingly corroborated by sources of information such as those listed on the following pages of this book.

The following list of various sources of information, are given to you per your preference of furthering, or not, your own personal research and education into the matters of which we speak.

Most of you have been unaware that these scientific matters are being investigated not to mention that it has not been made widely known on *general* public levels. It has been kept more on levels of people who have an interest in such matters, who are more likely to learn about these important findings than those who have had no interest in it. In other words, the *general* public has not been *generally* exposed to this information.

While it may be of great surprise to you what is being discovered by your scientists regarding the potential collapsing of the universe, plus discoveries of new types of light-energy being emitted from black holes, and what the potential implications of these matters are for us personally, including ourselves as Ascended Beings, it is of importance that you realize the fact that you've been *generally* kept in the dark about it, and that fact in and of itself should be just as significant to your awareness as the discoveries themselves.

As we state in our communiqués, your planet is one of but a couple of others whose inhabitants have not been informed of this truth. It is ignorance that generates confusion, and confusion generates fear.

From Contact to Ascension

This information is not imparted to you to instill fear or to generate panic, but conversely to *prevent it* by helping you gain a greater understanding of what is occurring with regard to this universe that is home to us all.

We are here to help you dispel fear by imparting truth about these matters that you've be *generally* unaware of.

The inhabitants of several other planets, whose leaders are in *seats of guidance* of their people, have revealed this information to them openly and candidly. Consequently, they are all aware of the coming events and, amongst themselves, are cooperatively preparing for it. *This is the ideal situation.*

We are here to help bring your planet of inhabitants up-to-speed, as you would say, with regard to these coming events that we speak about in our communiqués, and which these sources of information speak of as well.

We want you to know that these events are completely natural, meaning that they are occurring through the innate processes of an evolving universe. Even the truth that the universe *evolves*, meaning that it continuously refines and becomes greater than it ever was, is knowledge that has been kept from your awareness.

We wish you to realize that the information which your scientists do make public is always "*softened*" with timings of the events that are so far into the future that it causes you to *react* by disregarding the information all together as inapplicable to your current life experience.

We are here to help you realize that it **is** applicable by shedding clarity on these matters for you so that you will not be thrown into fear and panic when the events themselves do occur. There is no need for that to happen because you are always presented with options of how you wish to experience every event in your life.

A Note from An T'na about following information

It is our desire that you have as wonderful an experience as possible, but you can only do that when you understand *how* to do that. In other words, *you shall know the truth and that truth shall set you free to have wonderful experiences.*

It is when you are unaware that a life-changing event is approaching, taking you by surprise before you have time to prepare for it, that you are suddenly thrown into fear and its consequential state of panic. This scenario has been mounting for you as your leaders continue to *generally* keep you in the Dark Ages about it, which would result in fear and panic on a mass scale.

We are here to bring you into the Age of Light and Awareness through knowledge, truth, and sound reasoning.

Which scenario do you prefer to experience? Whichever you choose, we love and respect each of you greatly for our love of you rests not in *how* you choose to experience your lives, but in *who* you truly are, and it is because of who you truly are that we wish the best of experiences for you.

We shall speak of these matters more in forthcoming communiqués, so please do stay tuned-in.

On behalf of the Intergalactic Board of Council, I am An T'na, wishing you all well.

Links and Resources
Articles

BLACK HOLES SPEW OUT SURPRISE
December 13, 2012; By Nola Taylor Redd, SPACE.com Contributor
http://www.space.com/18893-black-hole-jets-similarities.html
Black holes come in a variety of sizes, ranging from 10 times the mass of the sun to a billion times as massive. But new research shows that black holes of completely different masses, ages and locations can produce jets of ionized gas that behave similarly.

BLACK HOLE DISCOVERED WHICH EMITS BRILLIANT LIGHT
November 30, 2013; By Douglas Cobb
http://guardianlv.com/2013/11/black-hole-discovered-which-emits-brilliant-light/
When a recently-discovered black hole was discovered which emits brilliant light, scientists were baffled, and scrambled to explain how a black hole could shine with such brilliance. According to a new study, the black-hole system called ULX-1 in the nearby Pinwheel Galaxy is twice as bright as astronomers had believed one could ever be.

WHY THE HIGGS BOSON MAY SEAL FATE OF THE UNIVERSE
February 21, 2013; By Clara Moskowitz, LiveScience Senior Writer
http://www.livescience.com/27329-higgs-boson-universe-apocalypse.html
The apparent discovery of the Higgs boson particle last year has opened doors to new calculations that weren't previously possible, scientists say, including one that suggests the universe is in for a cataclysm billions of years from now.

CONFIRMED! NEWFOUND PARTICLE IS THE HIGGS
March 14 2013; By Jeanna Bryner, LiveScience Managing Editor; LiveScience.com
http://news.yahoo.com/confirmed-newfound-particle-higgs-130317830.html

From Contact to Ascension

A newfound particle discovered at the world's largest atom smasher last year is, indeed, the Higgs boson, the particle thought to explain how other particles get their mass, scientists reported today (March 14) at the annual Rencontres de Moriond conference in Italy.

COLLAPSE OF UNIVERSE 'MORE LIKELY THAN EVER AND MAY HAVE ALREADY STARTED'
December 12, 2013; By Hannah Osborne
http://www.ibtimes.co.uk/articles/529747/20131212/universe-will-collapse-calculations-higgs-field-different.htm
The collapse of the universe is more likely than previous calculations have estimated and may have already started, experts have said.

UNIVERSE IS GOING TO COLLAPSE SOONER THAN EXPECTED
Dec 14, 2013; By Kamal Nayan
http://www.counselheal.com/articles/7960/20131214/universe-is-going-to-collapse-sooner-than-expected.htm
The mortal universe, in due course of time is either going to expand to the point of heat death or it'll collapse. Till this study, it was going to take very, very long time but now scientists believe it will just take just one 'very' long time.

Websites

Center for Healing LLC is an alternative wellness center where we offer you alternative ways to heal your body. We have many techniques that can help you deal with your stress, anger, grief, and many different ailments in your body. Just to mention a few, we offer Reiki, Cell memory Release, Acupressure, Reflexology, Quantum Hypnosis Therapy, and much more. .... We have over 300 types of herbs in the store, and that is just a drop in the bucket, but we can "special order" at your request. Our herbs are organic or kosher, meaning they are pure, raised without pesticides and no fillers. We work with companies that certify herbs organic or kosher. Our herbs are available in Cut/Sifted, Powdered, Extracts, and Encapsulations.
http://www.centerforhealingllc.com/
http://www.caeranddeesplace.com/

Links and Resources

Exopolitics.org - This is the main website of Dr Michael Salla which contains books and information recommended by the IBOC that will prepare for the contact event. Galactic Diplomacy: Getting to Yes with ET (2013), was described as a primer for the different extraterrestrial civilizations visiting our planet. The IBOC also mentioned his Exposing US Government Policies (2009) as a means of learning what has been happening behind the scenes. His latest book, Kennedy's Last Stand, (2013) reveals why JFK desired to educate the American public about extraterrestrial life, and why this led to his demise .
http://exopolitics.org

ExoNews - For news that's out of this world! This website provides topical news stories related to extraterrestrial life
http://www.exonews.org/

The Exopolitics Institute supports the study and dissemination of information and technologies from 'whistleblowers' or 'private citizens' who claim to have physically interacted with extraterrestrials, or had access to covert military-corporate programs involving extraterrestrial technologies. The Institute promotes 'citizen diplomacy initiatives' for peaceful communications and interactions with extraterrestrial civilizations that evidence suggests are interacting with or monitoring humanity. The Institute seeks to prepare humanity for interacting with extraterrestrial civilizations whose existence is supported by credible evidence, and supports full public disclosure by government authorities of all evidence concerning the extraterrestrial presence. The Institute supports the vision of an interconnected global human society that interacts with extraterrestrial civilizations in a peaceful, harmonious and mutually respectful manner.   http://www.exopoliticsinstitute.org/

From Contact to Ascension

The Earth Transformation Project provides resources for those wishing to learn about new science paradigms, <u>alternative energy</u>, intentional healing, raising planetary consciousness, and extraterrestrial life. These collectively make up the Earth Transformation that humanity is undergoing during 2012 and beyond. This website provides information on the Earth Transformation series of conferences held on the Big Island of Hawaii. from 2006-2011. All conference videos will be available for free viewing through the Earth Transformation TV Channel. You can also learn more about upcoming events supported or recommended by the Earth Transformation Project. Please click the menu above or banners below to learn more.
http://www.earthtransformation.com/

Prepare4contact is a discussion forum dedicated to how individuals, communities and humanity can best prepare for open interaction with extraterrestrial races, and to the study of exopolitics. The forum seeks to disseminate accurate information about extraterrestrials, their agendas, activities and history, and assist members in making informed choices about how to prepare for the time when extraterrestrial life becomes widespread public knowledge. The forum promotes the idea that it is only through a self-empowered humanity, that open interaction with extraterrestrials can do justice to humanity's need for equality, freedom and sovereignty.
http://www.groups.yahoo.com/neo/groups/prepare4contact/info

Victoria's Light. Welcome to the World of Victoria's Light. A very special journey of "Seeing Beyond this Reality" through personal encounters with the Angelic Realm, Jesus, Mary, St. Germaine and Other Dimensions, Merkabah Light Ships and with our Star Family, captured on film and photography. Sharing my Visions and Special Messages received telepathically to expand the understanding that WE ARE NOT ALONE IN THE UNIVERSE.
http://victoriaslight.com/

Made in the USA
San Bernardino, CA
17 February 2015